PERIOD GARDENS

PERIOD GARDENS
PATRICK TAYLOR

FOREWORD BY
Penelope Hobhouse

PHOTOGRAPHS BY
Eric Crichton

PARKGATE
BOOKS

For Annabel
with much love and admiration

First published by Pavilion Books Limited, 1991
This edition published in 1998 by

Parkgate Books Ltd
Kiln House
210 New Kings Road
London SW6 4NZ
Great Britain

1 3 5 7 9 8 6 4 2

British Library Cataloguing in Publication Data:
A catalogue record for this book is available from
the British Library.

ISBN 1 85585 518 6

Designed by Andrew Barron & Collis Clements Associates

Printed and bound in China
by Sun Fung Offset Binding Company Limited.
Produced in association with the Hanway Press, London.

Frontispiece: The Laburnum Pergola, Newby Hall

CONTENTS

Foreword

'A GARDEN reflects, perhaps more accurately than any other art form, the character of its maker and the cultural climate of the time. But if it is to survive beyond the maker's lifetime, an understanding of the principles that formed it is fundamental in guiding its development and renewal.'

John Sales, Chief Gardens Adviser to the National Trust

Period Gardens is not simply a book about garden restoration, or even about conservation. It is far more than that; it is about breathing new life, based on historical principles, into old and worn-out gardens. It is about the revival of the spirit of a garden as well as the reinstatement of layouts and planting patterns. Patrick Taylor has chosen gardens which convey a sense of the horticultural excitement and progress of their time rather than seeming to be museum-like effigies. When originally laid out, each epitomized new fashions and made use of new opportunities in planting.

While recognizing from the outset that we can never 'see' any work of art through contemporary eyes, Patrick Taylor places each garden in its period context in just the way that John Sales, I think, would envisage. Without neglecting the 'how-to' aspects – indeed, he goes into the process of restoration in considerable practical detail – he establishes each garden's place in the broad sweep of history and illuminates its original *raison d'être*. Garden history is social history and reflects the tastes, politics, lifestyles, travel opportunities and reading matter of society as much as it reveals the specific details of gardening practice. The history of an individual garden reflects also the viewpoint of its owner or designer. It is interesting how often in the historical spectrum covered by this book the spirit of an individual strikes an impressive chord. Each seems to tower over his or her contemporaries in the field and it may be this individuality of design interpretation that separates their gardens from the run of the mill to make them worthy subjects for preservation or restoration.

In *Period Gardens* the author describes the 'restored' gardens chronologically in terms of changing fashions, which in turn were influenced by the availability of plants and the continuous improvement in horticultural opportunities. From Hatfield House, its terraces first laid out in the opening decade of the seventeenth century, to Lady Londonderry's twentieth-century triumph of eccentricity at Mount Stewart, we run through history to capture a bird's-eye view of both classical and naturalistic formulae. At Hestercombe, Mount Stewart and Newby Hall we see that perfect English synthesis in which both styles combine: a formal layout is planted with maximum informality. At Monticello in Virginia in the late 1700s, house and garden were designed by the genius of Thomas Jefferson. He blended the Palladian classicism of his house with an interpretation of the English eighteenth-century landscape, in which groves of trees provided shade for winding pathways flanked by beds of native flowers, although useful fruits and vegetables were still laid out in traditional grid patterns. Rather than considering Monticello in a European or American context, Patrick Taylor helps us to see Jefferson the man and interpret the garden through his words and ambitions. A description of the gardens at Gravetye Manor in Sussex, made a hundred years after Monticello, reminds us that William Robinson, who today still epitomizes the 'wild' garden, continued to use conventionally laid out terraces and flowerbeds to frame his Tudor mansion. Patrick Taylor's strength in describing these various gardens is that he takes the broad view. He is not bogged down by the sheer weight of available historical detail, nor is he a design practitioner or horticulturist with an axe to grind in support of one style or another. Without sacrificing accuracy and scholarship he interprets in order to inform and inspire the reader with essential and fascinating nuances, which illuminate the purpose and spirit of any garden. The result is that, without his labouring the point, we can grasp why a particular garden is worth restoring and perhaps grasp also some of the eternal truths of good garden-making.

Initially, perhaps, we restore gardens to preserve our heritage, but ultimately we use restorations as inspirational themes for modern garden-making. By choosing to include only gardens which combine historical importance with, more subjectively, considerable beauty and charm, this book not only provides instruction in the history of design, but also – perhaps as important for today's gardeners – emphasizes design integrity. The great American garden designer Thomas D. Church (author of *Gardens are for People*, 1955), in discussing both utility and beauty in the garden, pointed out that 'Style is a matter of taste, design a matter of principle.' In this book the criterion for inclusion is not only that a garden was trend-setting when first created; each one, encased in its period authenticity, must also be a garden to which we can return again and again for inspiration.

PENELOPE HOBHOUSE

Acknowledgements

I am extremely grateful to John Sales, Chief Gardens Adviser to the National Trust, who could not have been more helpful. Isabelle Van Groeningen, of his staff, took much trouble in ferreting out elusive documents and I am very grateful to her. Dr Brent Elliott, Librarian of the Lindley Library, without whom the writing of gardening books would be much harder, has produced books, journals and references with unfailing expedition and courtesy. The various owners of the privately owned gardens about which I have written could not have been kinder, accepting my intrusions cheerfully and being endlessly co-operative. Above all, the Head Gardeners and their staff have been very generous, giving me their time and priceless knowledge unstintingly. For information about the gardens indicated I should like especially to thank the following: Peter Mansfield (Claremont); Mike Snowden (Erddig); Peter Herbert, Helen Greenwood (Gravetye Manor); Tony Lord (Ham House); The Marchioness of Salisbury, Robin Harcourt Williams, David Beaumont (Hatfield House); Roy Cheek, Lorna McRobie, Andrew Paul, David Usher (Hestercombe House); Bill Beiswanger, John Fitzpatrick, Libby Fosso, Peter Hatch (Monticello); Nigel Marshall, Graham Stuart Thomas (Mount Stewart); Robin Compton (Newby Hall); Lord Dickinson, Paul Edwards, Tim Mowl (Painswick Rococo Garden); Eric Robson, Douglas Westland (Pitmedden). I am also grateful for the assistance of the Thomas Jefferson Memorial Foundation, Inc., which owns and operates Monticello.

In England Colin Webb and Helen Sudell of Pavilion Books smoothed paths with Jeevesian resource; in America John Barstow of Atlantic Monthly Press did the same. Various people commented very helpfully on my text, including Penny David, Tony Lord and Margaret Willes. I am grateful to them all. It was very agreeable to work with Eric Crichton, a sort of Scarlet Pimpernel of photographers, who was apparently able to be at Claremont at dawn and at Pitmedden at dusk on the same day. Andrew Barron has designed the book most beautifully.

PATRICK TAYLOR

Opposite: E. A. Rowe's watercolour, 'July, Hatfield', painted in the early 1900s, shows high Victorian garden taste in the setting of the Jacobean house and garden walls. This part of the garden has now been replanted by Lady Salisbury as a scented garden.

INTRODUCTION

THIS book is about breathing new life into old gardens. The restoration of a garden is a unique and enthralling challenge, because gardens are the only works of art which may be successfully resuscitated after they have apparently breathed their last gasp. A garden may become choked with undergrowth, walls crumble, the layout disappear in a sea of weeds but still, as I shall show, its ghostly essence may remain intact.

To be interested in old gardens is a new obsession. Celia Fiennes, the indefatigable traveller and observer, who rode about England between 1685 and 1712, described gardens in fascinating detail, but she was interested only in garden style 'as the mode now is'. It was not until much later, in the nineteenth century, that people became

Opposite: Pieter de Hoogh's painting, 'A Game of Ninepins', shows a characteristically Dutch type of garden pavilion of the sort seen in Kip's 1720 engraving of Westbury Court (above).

preoccupied with historical styles of gardening. Today, however, the intimate details of the past generally are of intense interest to us. Just as it has for long been the quest of history to discover how things really were, so we now want to know exactly how works of art were in the past. Musicians want to know how Mozart's music was played, what instruments were used and what were the acoustics of the rooms in which his music was performed in his lifetime. Such questions have also become of absorbing interest to gardeners who will no longer accept 'Tudor' gardens full of nineteenth-century Floribunda roses. We now want to know exactly what plants were used in the past, how gardens were ordered and the thinking that lay behind them. Accurate information about these things is now more abundant than ever before. The techniques of archaeology have been fruitfully applied to gardens and research in primary archives has immensely increased our knowledge of which plants were grown when. Garden historians have made gardeners more clearly aware of the horticultural practices and philosophy of the past and their bearing on the appearance of gardens.

Some of the gardens described in this book, such as Claremont, Westbury Court and Monticello, are meticulous restorations based on detailed archival research. Others, like Pitmedden or Hatfield, are twentieth-century versions of historic gardens which have capitalized on skeletal remains which included some fine bones. At Pitmedden there survived the original seventeenth-century garden walls, gate piers and decorative double staircase leading down into the garden. No details were known, however, of the original planting and the restoration is a free adaptation of seventeenth-century ideas interpreted in modern planting. At Hatfield the incomparable house and the lie of the land have provided the setting for Lady Salisbury's virtuoso twentieth-century visions of terraces, knots and richly formal planting, all of which are in keeping with the seventeenth-century atmosphere.

Much more recent gardens, even those of the twentieth century, may decay and lose their essential appearance with alarming speed. William Robinson's own garden at Gravetye Manor which he started making in 1885 fell quickly into neglect after his death in 1935. When the present owner bought it, only twenty-two years later, there was little of it left. In the case of a garden like Hestercombe (made between 1906 and 1910), with a strong formal framework of walls, terraces, paths and enclosures, almost all the planting had by the early 1970s decayed beyond redemption. But it was possible to replace it and bring back to life Gertrude Jekyll's and Edwin Lutyens's incomparable masterpiece. The garden at Newby Hall, although it has fascinating survivals from several periods, is essentially a twentieth-century garden where the present owner, Robin Compton, has restored the best of the past and added much of his own in the same spirit.

It is very rare indeed that any great garden dates from a single period. In the restoration of the gardens at Erddig or at Newby Hall there has been no attempt to revert to some 'correct' historic style but rather to enhance the character of the place, in which there are features of at least three hundred years of gardening, and to honour the survivals of the past. As John Sales has written, 'The essential quality of many older gardens lies in the sense of continuity that they convey, and this quality should be cherished where it exists.'

Besides, certain aspects of the true detail of the past can never be recaptured. It is impossible, for example, to look at plants with the same unjaundiced eye that looked upon a Tudor garden. Our visual environment today is such a jangle of vivid colours, full of visual 'noise', whereas in the sixteenth century all colour was natural. Today, vividly bright synthetic colours surround us and anything less colourful may seem insipid. At Westbury Court there is a rare opportunity to see beds filled with plants of which none is later than 1700. There can be few garden sights which convey so emphatically the nature of the visual past. It is not merely the colour of the flowers but the character of the whole plant that has been changed by the frenzied hybridizing of the nineteenth and twentieth centuries.

The exact *texture* of a garden in the remote past must remain almost impossible to know. Before the invention of mechanical mowers, lawns were cut with scythes and gardeners were skilful enough to cut the grass to a fine sward but, no doubt, the effect was different from that achieved today by motor-mowers. The flawlessly sharp parallel lines they give to a lawn have an inescapably twentieth-century air, yet who would regard their use in period gardens as inauthentic? There is a limit to what may be discovered by any amount of delving in the archives – the spirit of a garden, what may be seen and sensed on the ground, may be more informative about its essential nature.

Gardens are fragile things and change is an essential part of their being. Seasonal variations and the appearance of the garden at different times and in different weathers are vital dimensions of its appearance. Plants grow old, change and die. Within a border the rate of growth will vary from plant to plant, so that the relative scale of the planting scheme will alter. The larger woody plants in a garden, too, will change their surroundings as they grow, removing nourishment and moisture from the earth and crowding out less vigorous plants. All this is part of the unique appeal of a garden. It is not an exaggeration to say that any large and complex garden will *never* in its lifetime appear exactly the same at the same time on the same date in two consecutive years. Who would have guessed in 1906 when it was planted at Bodnant in Gwynedd that the wonderfully sprawling shape of *Arbutus × andrachnoides*, with its strikingly decorative mature bark, would be such a dominating presence today on the rose terrace?

Gardens change for other reasons. Owners become bored with old-fashioned schemes and introduce something new. In great estates like Hatfield, where the Cecil family took an intense interest in horticulture, there has been repeated experimentation for almost four hundred years of which many traces survive. But excessive veneration for the past alone can turn a garden into a lifeless mausoleum. At Gravetye Manor Peter Herbert gardens in

a Robinsonian manner but uses many plants unknown to Robinson, of which he would surely have approved. That is especially appropriate because Robinson's philosophy was more a way of gardening than a dictatorial aesthetic.

Gardens, unlike paintings, are very rarely the work of one artist and few gardens are designed and executed at one fell swoop. The formal gardens at Hestercombe are one very unusual example of gardens bearing virtually no trace of what was there before. But who is to say that the Lutyens/Jekyll garden was worthier of restoration than its predecessor, the great eighteenth-century landscape garden of Copleston Warre Bampfylde? Tantalizing features of that earlier garden survived and were carefully preserved by Edwin Lutyens. Other gardens, although the result of a concerted vision over a relatively short period, such as Sissinghurst in Kent and Hidcote in Gloucestershire, gradually changed with their makers' experiments and restless search for perfection.

The problem of historical diversity, and what importance to attach to different periods surviving in a garden, is sharply illustrated by Erddig. Here there are features of both the eighteenth and nineteenth centuries and some twentieth-century innovations. In restoring such a garden, what emphasis should be given to the work of different periods? The same problem is found in restoring houses and any restoration of houses or gardens will, in some measure, reflect the taste of the time in which the restoration takes place. Victorian restorations of Elizabethan gardens seem more strikingly Victorian than Elizabethan. In the restoration of houses and their interiors there is sometimes an attempt, in my view futile, to revert to some hypothetically 'authentic' moment when house and contents were all of the same period. But in the past such a state would scarcely ever have existed in a house, nor did it frequently happen in gardens, and a restoration on that basis can be entirely misleading.

The idea of attempting to restore a historic garden to its original appearance is a modern one. Some regard this obsession with the past as distinctly unhealthy, a self-indulgent reluctance to confront the present. Why, one may ask, bother to restore a garden at all? One reason is because enough of it survives, tantalizingly revealing signs of its true merit, like a fragment of virtuoso painting in an old master glimpsed through layers of discoloured varnish and hamfisted overpainting. Other works of art – paintings and sculptures, for example – once they are lost are gone for ever and will linger only in the form of descriptions, reproductions or prints; nothing can be done to bring them back to life. But a garden is different. With original plans and plant lists, possibly with the aid of detailed contemporary paintings (as at Painswick or Ham House), the garden may be brought back from the dead, as if by magic. Thomas Jefferson of Monticello kept a detailed journal for most of his gardening life, which has been an essential resource in the restoration of his garden.

The two overwhelming reasons for restoring a period garden are because it is known that an excellent garden existed on the site and enough is known of it to re-create it; and because an architecturally distinguished setting *needs* an appropriate garden – great houses should have great gardens. The garden of such a house may be a vital part of the house's relationship with its larger physical setting. A third category of restored garden is what one might call the museum garden. Here an attempt is made to re-create a hypothetical garden from a certain period to give something of the gardening flavour of that time. Although this sort of re-creation may vividly show the kinds of plant used at the time, and some of the features of garden layout, to me they too often smell of dusty archives.

Any garden, merely to survive, needs constant re-planting as the evidence of many twentieth-century gardens shows. As someone wisely said, a garden is not a thing but a process. In a certain sense everyday garden maintenance is a kind of constant restoration. There may be a tendency in restoring a garden to leave *any* plant simply because it is old. This respect for longevity, doubtless admirable among humans, can lead to preserving moribund, excessively large or inappropriate plants

simply because they are there. In some cases such plants have survived only because the garden has been neglected.

In restoring a garden it cannot be too strongly emphasized that no plant should be removed without identifying it and, if it seems very ancient, trying to make some estimate of its age. There are still countless unsolved problems about the history of garden design and especially of planting, so that *any* ancient evidence must be treated carefully. Furthermore, in garden history, tangible evidence on the ground is of much greater value than any amount of *post facto* theorizing. The National Trust has pioneered a procedure of meticulous surveying before any irrevocable changes are made. Information is gathered from a field survey, showing all surviving features, to which is added any relevant archival information. The survey in itself is not conclusive and its interpretation depends on subjective judgement. It is part of the garden restoration philosophy of the National Trust, for example, that a garden *should* reflect a diversity of styles if that is true to the spirit of the place. That can be a fairly nerve-racking business and it may be essential to take some unpleasant decisions. For example, at Claremont, splendid cedars of Lebanon, said to have been planted by 'Capability' Brown, had to be felled to make way for the restoration of something much rarer, Charles Bridgeman's amazing turf amphitheatre.

It is only quite recently that the techniques of archaeology have been applied to gardens. The results are of great interest to garden historians and anyone involved in restoring a garden. America was a pioneer in garden archaeology – one of the first uses of archaeology in discovering the detail of a period garden was at the Governor's Palace at Williamsburg in Virginia. The excavation, carried out in 1930/1, revealed foundations showing the exact shape of the garden walls and gate piers, and twigs, seeds and leaves were found in the excavation of an old well which gave unique information about what was originally planted. In England a pioneer excavation of a garden site was that done by George Chettle at Kirby Hall, Northamptonshire, starting in 1935. Here substantial parts of the layout of Sir Christopher Hatton's elaborate formal garden of the late seventeenth century were clearly revealed. The limestone edging of beds was uncovered showing their exact shape, and the facings of terrace walls were also found. Restoration of the garden is now under way to a very elaborate and interesting plan using original plant lists. Archaeological digs at Monticello in Virginia in 1958 and since 1979 have revealed all sorts of detail of Thomas Jefferson's original layout.

Correct restoration may be immensely helped by the findings of archaeology but information about plants will rarely be decisive. The technique of pollen analysis, which is laborious and expensive, yields little useful information about garden plants. At the fascinating excavation of a 1760 town garden in the Circus in Bath, Avon, the Bath Archaeological Trust carried out an analysis of pollen and was able to identify only one plant, fool's parsley (*Aethusa cynapium*), not, one might guess, a plant that would feature largely in an eighteenth-century pleasure garden.

It is for the layout and the hard features of a period garden that the findings of archaeology are especially precious. The excavation at the Circus was particularly valuable because very little is known about the design of town gardens in the eighteenth century – there are very few pictures or descriptions. The excavations at the Circus show vividly the values, and limitations, of the archaeological scrutiny of gardens. First, it is known that the garden was made at exactly the same date as the house, because it lies on top of soil that was removed when the foundations of the house were dug. Because of the curve of the Circus, the walled garden is rather wider at the far end, forming a slightly irregular rectangle. In the middle of the garden was a correspondingly irregular rectangle of gravel in which were set three oval beds on a central axis. Round the garden walls were paths of flags set on gravel. The excavation showed that the gravel here was completely unweathered, whereas that in the central area showed the effects of exposure to the elements. The beds were clearly revealed by the much darker colour of the soil that had been cultivated to grow plants. An intriguing detail was that the paths widened slightly towards the end of the garden to make it seem exactly rectangular. This fastidious optical illusion, and the formal arrangement of the beds, suggests that this was a garden to be viewed from the windows of the house. Planting holes were discovered, which give some idea of the size of plants used but no more than that. To know exactly what kinds of plants were used in such a garden we are dependent on separate, usually documentary, evidence.

The use of archaeological evidence in restoring gardens has immense potential. Often the evidence is only corroborative but that can be decisive. At Monticello, for example, a drawing by Jefferson survives showing the layout of an orchard, with exact details of the spacing of the trees and their varieties. A dig on the probable site revealed a pattern of planting holes exactly corresponding to the plan. But, as the excavation at the Circus in Bath showed, it sometimes reveals information about period garden design in great detail, which is unavailable from any other source. The application of archaeological techniques to the solution of specific problems is described in more detail in the chapter on the Rococo Garden at Painswick, where the Bath Archaeological Trust carried out some fascinating excavations which have been of great practical importance in the restoration of that garden.

Ghostly but informative traces of earlier features may sometimes be revealed by exceptional weather or by light shone at an oblique angle. The 'parchmarks' that emerge in areas of grass after long spells of drought have given much valuable information about early garden layouts. Seen from above, these often show the exact detail, for example, of elaborate parterres and of the overall shape of lost gardens. Beds that have been filled in are very rarely exactly the same level as the surrounding area. At Monticello the site of Jefferson's original flower beds were revealed by shining car headlamps across the lawn at night. So much of a garden's past may still remain, lurking on or near the surface, waiting to be interpreted or revealed.

PERIOD STYLES

THE MIDDLE AGES

 T is only from the late Middle Ages that we have any idea at all of the appearance of gardens in England, and even this is extremely fragmentary. To piece together some picture of medieval gardens is like trying to visualize an ancient Greek pot when all we have is one or two idealized pictures, a few scraps of pottery and a contemporary but not very detailed potter's manual. Very few pictures showing details of gardens in Britain survive from this time but, as John Harvey has argued, the scarcity of pictorial evidence, compared with that of European gardens, need not indicate that there were very few gardens. After all, there are few pictures of medieval buildings in Britain, but many examples of the actual buildings survive to challenge the implication of the absence of pictorial

Above: An anonymous early eighteenth-century painting of Newby Hall shows valuable detail of the garden. Opposite: The long canal and the pavilion at Westbury Court were painted in 1895 by E.B.S.Montefiore. The yew hedges on either side date from the original 1690s design.

evidence. On the other hand there are several detailed contemporary accounts of great medieval buildings in Britain, but none of gardens. Furthermore, there is such a richness of Northern European miniatures showing gardens, particularly in the later fifteenth century, that the lack of English pictures is puzzling. John Harvey argues that in the fourteenth century, for example, the kings of England were such central figures in European history that they certainly 'maintained a state – for instance in architecture – not inferior to any other in western Christendom. That their gardens matched their buildings should never have been doubted.'

Miles Hadfield, in his *A History of British Gardening*, argues robustly against the possibility of a high standard of garden art until the late medieval period: 'It seems not improbable that gardening as an art and the aesthetic appreciation of flowers scarcely existed until the late fifteenth or early sixteenth centuries. Before that, gardening was purposeful – to provide fruits, a few vegetables, herbs, and medicinal plants, a sheltered place for sitting.' Against this must be set the evidence of John Leland's accounts of ornamental gardening in the early sixteenth century – topiary on mounts at the Earl of Northumberland's castle at Wressle in Yorkshire, topiary at Little Haseley in Oxfordshire and other gardens

Thomas Robins's view of Painswick House and its garden dates from 1748. It records in elaborate detail the garden's features and served as an essential document in its restoration.

which were clearly for pleasure. It is inconceivable that this interest in pleasure gardens sprang up suddenly, as it were fully formed, at the beginning of the sixteenth century. There must already have been a tradition of similar gardening.

What can be said with certainty is that there were *some* pleasure gardens in medieval England and, thanks to the work of scholars such as John Harvey, we know something of the repertory of plants grown in them. By 1500 the typical garden was small, close to the castle, house or monastery walls, and more often than not partly enclosed by them. The famous plan of the monastery at Canterbury, dating from about 1150, shows a *herbarium* (i.e. a herb garden) which occupies a tiny plot, half the area enclosed by cloisters. In monasteries the chief purpose of such gardens would have been to provide plants for either medicinal or culinary use.

In ornamental gardens plants were grown either in pots or in square or rectangular beds, very often slightly raised and edged with planks. There were often fences of trellis, shaped palings or wattle. Turfed benches made of bricks and rose-covered arbours were frequently used. In these gardens there was grown an extremely limited range of plants. By the beginning of the sixteenth century something of the order of 250 different plants were grown in English gardens, including vegetables and fruit, and of the total, well over half were British natives. It is also possible, as John Harvey has argued, that there existed parkland that was cultivated for ornamental purposes.

There have been very few re-creations of medieval gardens but two fairly recent ones give something of their flavour. Both fall into the tradition of what I call 'museum' gardens – in both cases they are pure invention based on a general knowledge of the appearance of gardens of the period. Queen Eleanor's Garden at Winchester Castle is built in an authentic medieval setting, adjacent to the Great Hall of her husband Henry III (1207–72) who was born in the Castle. Designed by Dr Sylvia Landsberg it has a fountain from which water flows through lions' masks,

a flowery lawn and beds of flowers known to have been grown in Queen Eleanor's time. A reconstruction of a much later garden is Mavis Batey's cloister garden at Christ Church Cathedral, Oxford, which matches in date the rebuilding of the Cloister after 1499. There is no record of pleasure gardens being made within the cloisters in the Middle Ages but the Christ Church garden contains authentic plants in a fine medieval setting. It occupies one side of the area enclosed by cloisters. A flowery mead is scattered with cowslips (*Primula veris*) and violets (*Viola riviniana*) and narrow beds have rosemary (*Rosmarinus officinalis*), rue (*Ruta graveolens*) and Madonna lilies (*Lilium candidum*).

GARDENS SWEET – THE TUDOR AGE

In the early sixteenth century the reign of Henry VIII gave great impetus to gardening. Royal gardens were much influenced by new French ideas and Henry VIII extended his rivalry with François I into the realms of horticulture. Although there is a fair amount of information about ornamental gardening in the Tudor age, almost all of it refers to royal or aristocratic estates – Hampton Court itself is the best-documented garden of the period. There is a rare contemporary account of the Duke of Buckingham's garden at Thornbury Castle near Bristol. This was started in 1515 and contained 'knotts' which could be admired from a raised walk or from the windows of the castle surrounding an inner courtyard. The site of the garden, with its finely preserved walls, survives and one can still see the various interconnected compartments into which it is divided. This sounds quite revolutionary in comparison with Cardinal Wolsey's gardens at Hampton Court which were started in the same year. In a famous contemporary description they sound entirely medieval in spirit:

> My gardens sweet, enclosed with walles strong,
> Embanked with benches to sytt and take my rest.
> The Knotts so enknotted, it cannot be exprest,
> With arbors and alys so pleasaunt and so dulce,
> The pestylent ayers with flavors to repulse.

What little we can discover about more modest gardens in the Tudor age may be found in the increasingly widely read gardening books published in the period, which give invaluable detail about the practical aspects of horticulture. Thomas Hill's *The Profitable Art of Gardening*, which appeared in 1568, went through three further editions and appeared in a new version under the title *The Gardener's Labyrinth* in 1577. This in turn was a success and remained in print well into the seventeenth century. Hill's books are not amusing to read and are avowedly cobbled together, fairly indiscriminately, from various classical sources. It is not even certain that he himself was a gardener and the vivid descriptions of horticultural techniques may owe more to his journalist's skill than to his own practical experience. These books, among the very few sixteenth-century accounts of gardening, must be taken to reflect the real interests of gardeners of the period. They are concerned overwhelmingly with the cultivation of herbs and vegetables and husbandry in general rather than with ornamental gardening. Hill does give detailed accounts for making raised beds (600mm/2ft high in damp ground, 300mm/1ft high in dry), the appropriate width of paths, suitable materials for hedging and walls and the making of decorative 'herbers', by which he meant 'arbour'. There is very little indeed about aesthetic principles, the relative beauty of different plants or about garden layout, but the illustrations in his books do show valuable detail of the gardens of his time.

They are quite small with a formal pattern of often square beds which are sometimes raised. They are enclosed with stone walls, low hedges or fences (of palings or trellis) with decorative finials. Shady arbours or alleys are shown, often covered in vines. Hill mentions only a few decorative plants – rosemary, marigolds and roses – and even these are planted to be useful rather than attractive. All these are ingredients familiar from late medieval miniatures of northern Europe. What is less familiar is an illustration of an elaborately irrigated garden, with a geometric and very ornamental pattern of channels which resembles those found in the Moorish gardens of southern Spain in the early Middle Ages.

The characteristic feature of the Tudor garden, illustrated in Hill's books for the first time in England but only very briefly described by him, was the knot. This was a formal bed in which low hedges were worked into a regular pattern, sometimes appearing to be interlaced. They could be 'open', with a background of sand or gravel, or 'closed', with the spaces filled with other, contrasting, plants. The knot was designed to be admired from above, decoratively spread out below like an outdoor rug. Hill wrote in *The Profitable Art of Gardening* 'mazes and knots aptly made do much set forth a garden.' He describes the planting for a maze and recommends 'four sundry fruits to be placed in each corner of the maze, and in the middle of it, a proper herber [i.e. arbour] decked with roses, or else, some fair tree of rosemary'. He suggests that the walls of the maze 'may eyther be set with Hope and Lime [i.e. lime trees intertwined with hop], or with winter Savery and Thyme: for they do wel endure, all ye winter through greene'. Although Hill publishes several designs for knots the first detailed written accounts of them are not to be found until the appearance of Gervase Markham's *The Englishman's Husbandman*, published in 1613, by which time, he claims, they were distinctly out of fashion – 'at this day of most use amongst the vulgar though least respected with great ones, who for the most part are wholy given over to novelties'. Markham shows many illustrations of knots and explains how to achieve different background colours for the patterns – coal dust for black, chalk for white, brick for red, and so on. In fact Markham is misleading, for knots seem to have evolved with little discernible break into parterres. The knot designed at Ham House in 1672 for the Earl of Lauderdale and the knot designed by Peter Aram for Newby Hall in 1716 show the continuity of the tradition.

No knot survives from the Tudor period but there are several vivid restorations. At Little Moreton Hall in Cheshire there is a reconstructed open knot of box, yew and gravel based on an Elizabethan design. In the Tudor House Museum Garden in Southampton there is a late Tudor knot of clipped herbs and box forming a pattern based on a motif in the interior of the Tudor House. An open knot copied from a mid seventeenth-century design has been made at Moseley Old Hall in Staffordshire with box topiary and hedges and contrasting pebbles.

In the seventeenth century there is, for the first time, a wealth of plans and pictorial documentation giving much detail of garden styles of the period. Advanced garden taste of the late Elizabethan period is vividly shown in Robert Smythson's drawing for Lord Exeter's house at Wimbledon, then on the southern fringes of London. Although dated 1609 most of the planting had been done in the 1580s and 1590s. It shows an intricate series of garden rooms, enclosed by walls and hedges, each with a distinctive flavour. The drawing shows, immediately to the east of the house, four 'knotes' arranged in a square 'fitted for the growth of choice flowers, bordered with box', as a later description of 1649 puts it. These knots are not the intricate, small-scale arrangements of interlocking hedges of the earlier period; they more closely resemble, in a primitive form, the later parterre. The box mentioned may have been dwarf box (*Buxus sempervirens* 'Suffruticosa') which seems to have come into use in the very early years of the seventeenth century. There is rich documentation of Wimbledon showing, for example, the exact numbers and kinds of fruit trees, 'most rare and choice', planted in the orchard. There were ornamental orchards with roses planted among the fruit trees, a walk of lime trees 'both for shade and sweetness' and a 'Garden for Earbes' (i.e. herbs). Nothing, alas, survives of the garden today.

Another valuable source of information about gardening practice and the appearance of gardens in this period is William Lawson's *The Country Housewife's Garden* and *A New Orchard and Garden* (both published in 1618 and early editions are usually bound together). The first is also, incidentally, the very first gardening book aimed specifically at women. Lawson writes with great charm and

emphasizes the recreational and sensual delights of gardening. He describes an ornamental orchard, divided into squares, with a knot and mounts raised at each corner from which to view the tranquil scene. Here the owner may retreat 'from the troublesome affaires of their estate . . . to renue and refresh their sences and to call home their over-wearied spirits'. Every other pleasure, he says, except the garden 'filles some one of our sences, and that onely, with delight, [but the garden] makes all our sences swimme in pleasure, and that with infinite variety, joyned with no less commodity'. The attractive tradition of using fruit trees in the pleasure garden is a recurrent theme which is found at Hatfield, Westbury Court, Erddig and Painswick. John Parkinson's *Paradisi in Sole Paradisus Terrestris* (1629) is a book of the first importance. Parkinson's book describes 'the Ordering of the Garden of Pleasure' and is followed by a vivid account of over one thousand garden plants, untainted by the gullibility found in Gerard's *Herball* (1597).

THE SEVENTEENTH CENTURY – FORMALITY AND FLOWERS

The seventeenth century is the earliest period from which survive several gardens which still possess extensive original features. The great Stuart garden at Hatfield House (pages 33-47) still retains much of the atmosphere and the underlying layout of its period, some of it restored by Lady Salisbury. At Hatfield John Tradescant the Elder (*c*.1570-1638) was an early, pioneering example of what has become a familiar and important figure in English gardening, the profoundly knowledgeable plantsman, collecting plants from all over the world. In the seventeenth century arose the tradition of the 'florists', a word which until the nineteenth century meant anyone interested in plants for their beauty rather than for their uses. Tradescant regarded rare plants as fascinating curiosities of the natural world, a logical part of his Cabinet of Wonders. In Holland there was the extraordinary craze for tulips which reached its zenith in 1636-7. At first this was an interest of the elite, when a few rich and cultivated plantsmen began dealing in them. In the early days of tulipomania the bulbs were sold by weight and sometimes by the fieldful. New varieties were bred and they became the subject of frenzied speculation which resulted in a futures market in which prices doubled or trebled by the week and individual bulbs were bought and sold many times before they had flowered. Tulips became one of the flowers most admired by florists in England and by 1676 the second edition of John Rea's *Flora, seu de Florum cultura* listed two hundred named varieties. The other flowers collected by the early florists were carnations, anemones, ranunculus and auriculas. Many of these plants were painted by the florist and artist Alexander Marshall who was associated with Ham House (pages 49-59). In the garden these plants were arranged as specimens so that their individual virtues would be best displayed. A special part of the garden would be set aside, often near the house and secure against theft, because many of them were extremely valuable.

In the design of gardens in the Stuart period there was striking French influence. The brothers Isaac and Salomon de Caus, early examples of international garden designers, worked on several English royal and noble gardens. Salomon was especially interested in the use of water in gardens and designed extraordinary water parterres at Richmond Palace and at Hatfield House. Isaac was a masterly maker of grottoes and his grotto at Woburn Abbey in Bedfordshire, designed in 1627 for Lucy Harington, Countess of Bedford, survives. He also worked at Wilton House in Wiltshire where, alas, little survives.

The influence of French Renaissance garden fashion continued in the reign of Charles I whose wife Henrietta Maria, 'the rose and lily queen', was deeply interested in gardening. It was she who was responsible for introducing to England the French gardener André Mollet, who laid out gardens at St James's Palace (*c.* 1629-33) and at Wimbledon House (1642). A description of the first was written in 1637 by the Sieur de la Serre who described 'parterres of

different figures, bordered on every side by a hedge of box'. We know exactly the kinds of parterre that Mollet designed from his widely circulated book *Le Jardin de Plaisir* (1651). Here are lavish plans for *parterres de broderie*, 'parterres of embroidery', with elaborate swirling arabesques

of clipped plants. Mollet was a pioneer garden designer many of whose ideas, especially the principle of the relationship of parts to the whole, prefigure André Le Nôtre. The French influence was strongly felt, too, in Scotland. The great Scottish architect and garden designer

Sir William Bruce probably saw the latest French gardens on his visits to Europe in the 1660s and was possibly among the earliest foreigners to see André Le Nôtre's first major garden at Vaux-le-Vicomte. At all events Sir William made gardens at Kinross House in Kinrosshire and at Balcaskie in

A view of the south front of Ham House from the wilderness was painted by Henry Danckerts in about 1675 shortly after the new garden was made for the Duke and Duchess of Lauderdale. The restoration of the garden has copied many of the features shown.

Fife, with axial vistas centred on the house that are strongly reminiscent of the gardens of Le Nôtre. Sir William in turn influenced the maker of Pitmedden, Sir Alexander Seton (pages 61-71).

The Civil War (starting in 1642) followed by the Commonwealth (1649-60) together constitute an emphatic pause but not a break in garden history. Two especially precious gardening documents survive from this period. In the 1650s Sir Thomas Hanmer wrote an account of his own garden at Bettisfield in Flintshire (now Clwyd) and the *Musaeum Tradescantium* published in 1656 gives very valuable information about garden plants available up to that date. After the Restoration, Charles II, who had spent a large part of his exile in France, continued the French influence on English gardening. André Le Nôtre was commissioned to redesign the park at Greenwich (never executed) and a fashionable *patte d'oie* arrangement of avenues radiating from a semi-circle was made at Hampton Court. The French influence overlaid with the Dutch was magnified after 1688 in the reign of William and Mary who brought with them a new wave of French Huguenot artists and craftsmen. The Dutch tradition of botany and horticulture gave renewed impetus to plantsmanship which is seen vividly at Westbury Court (pages 73-83). The Dutch use of plants in pots as a kind of mobile horticultural décor is strikingly evident at this time as is shown in an inventory of *c.*1682 for the garden at Ham House. Here are listed many orange and lemon trees in pots but also myrtles, jasmines, pomegranates and oleanders.

The kinds of garden that were made at the end of the seventeenth century are shown in the irreplaceably valuable engravings by Jan Kip made from bird's-eye paintings by Leonard Knyff. These were gathered together and published in a book, *Britannia Illustrata* (1707). They show royal palaces and the seats of the 'Nobility and Gentry of Great Britain', paying great attention to the detail of the garden and the surrounding landscape. These illustrations are now thought to be extremely accurate views of what the artist saw rather than merely idealized interpretations.

It is frequently possible to corroborate this from quite independent sources. For example, the Kip engraving of Newby Hall (pages 173-87) accords precisely with the details seen in an early eighteenth-century painting that still hangs at the house. Furthermore, Celia Fiennes's description of Newby corroborates much of the detail.

Kip's engraving shows both the complete triumph of the formal style and the profound influence of André Le Nôtre. The garden typically has a walled forecourt to the main façade of the house with an axial path leading to the entrance. This axis may be continued on the other side of the house penetrating deep into the countryside with rides through woodland on either side. Avenues, sometimes in the shape of *pattes d'oie*, radiate out from the house linking it firmly to the landscape. Nearer the house there are parterres, frequently extremely elaborate in the style of Daniel Marot, the French Huguenot designer introduced by King William. There is often some water feature – ornate fountains, canals, or formal *bassins* with an island and a pavilion. The 'wilderness', a kind of giant maze of hedges (such as is replanted at Ham House, see page 57) is often seen. Formal orchards, with trees in neat rows or espaliered against walls, are common (as at Erddig, pages 85-99). Most of these features will be seen in some of the formal gardens I shall be discussing in detail such as Westbury Court, Newby Hall and Erddig. This was the period of the first great firm of professional garden designers, that of George London and Henry Wise, who codified ideas of formal gardening. These were the ideas that influenced early American gardens, too, such as the garden of the Governor's Palace at Williamsburg in Virginia, which dates from the early seventeenth century, and George Washington's garden at Mount Vernon in Virginia, started in 1758.

It was against this universal fashion for formality that early eighteenth-century garden taste in England firmly revolted. Alexander Pope, and other English writers of the time, ridiculed the symmetrical, formal garden where 'Grove nods at grove, each Alley has a brother'.

THE GENIUS OF THE PLACE – THE LANDSCAPE GARDEN

Nothing happens quickly in the evolution of gardening taste. The antecedents of the landscape garden, which reached its height in the second half of the eighteenth century, are found at least a hundred years before. Sir William Temple, writing in 1685, described part of the gardens at Moor Park in Hertfordshire as 'very Wild, Shady and adorned with rough Rock-work and Fountains'. In the past it has been usual to regard the landscape garden as an entirely English invention which appeared fairly suddenly at the beginning of the eighteenth century, promoted by Alexander Pope, Joseph Addison and other writers of the period. It now seems more likely, as John Dixon Hunt has persuasively argued, that its origins are much earlier, and derive from the much older English fascination with Italy. Paintings done in Italy in the seventeenth century certainly show landscapes remarkably similar to the eighteenth-century parks of Stourhead in Wiltshire and Stowe in Buckinghamshire. Claremont (pages 101-11), started in 1708, and Studley Royal in North Yorkshire, started in 1718, are both remarkable survivors from the early days of the English landscape garden. The latter, with its formal water garden reminiscent of Dutch and French seventeenth-century gardens, shows the transitional style between the formal and the informal. At Claremont the early formal layout designed by John Vanbrugh and Charles Bridgeman was de-formalized by William Kent from 1729 onwards. Painswick (pages 113-23), too, a rare and attractive example of provincial landscape design, shows a similar transitional mixture of ingredients. All these, though, are inward-looking gardens, whereas William Kent later showed that all nature could be seen as a garden. At his surviving masterpiece, Rousham in Oxfordshire (1737-41), the views of the curving river Cherwell and the surrounding rural landscape are carefully framed. Almost all the statues look outward, directing the visitor's gaze to the beauties of nature. At Erddig, too, there is an attractive mixture of formality and romantic landscape; the Big Wood was arranged with winding paths and a lofty terrace from which to view the countryside and the formal garden spread out below it (pages 87-8).

The culmination of the landscape movement was certainly the career of Lancelot 'Capability' Brown (1716-83). From the 1740s onwards, at an accelerating pace, he laid out parks for the old and new rich all over England. His style of undulating parkland punctuated by clumps of trees and with a serpentine lake, so familiar from countless surviving landscapes, was in his day immensely popular. Brown has been bitterly criticized by, among others, Russell Page: 'Lancelot Brown was encouraging his wealthy clients to tear out their splendid formal gardens and replace them with his facile compositions of grass, tree clumps and rather shapeless pools and lakes.' One of the curiosities of Brown's reputation is that, although his name is more or less synonymous with eighteenth-century landscape design, it is rare to hear any of his parks spoken of with much affection. Many other lesser known designers practised in his style which swept Britain and, in some degree, influenced garden design all over Europe. One of his distinguished followers was William Emes who laid out the park at Erddig.

It would be wrong to think of *all* gardening in the late eighteenth century as being landscape gardening. Although William Mason's famous flower garden made in 1775 within the park at Nuneham Courtenay was surely a rarity in a fashionable garden of the period, there was, no doubt, a continuity of flower gardening in the less fashionable gardens. Certainly, judging from the nursery trade lists of the period, there was a very wide range of plants and seeds commercially available. In any case, almost all great houses would have continued to grow flowers, sometimes in the kitchen garden but more usually in a walled flower garden where they would be arranged formally in beds. Mason's garden was exceptional not because he grew flowers but because he used them in a

landscaped setting. What Thomas Jefferson made at Monticello (pages 125-41) – a flowery walk leading towards a landscaped grove – was a sensitive response to the particular context of his garden setting.

The eighteenth century was a great period for garden ornaments and buildings. Landscape gardens made particular use of decorative garden buildings, many of which, following the seventeenth-century paintings of the Italian landscape, were temples in the classical style. There seemed to be no constraint, however, about mixing styles. Both Painswick and Stourhead, for example, have Gothick as well as classical garden buildings. Urns and ornamental benches were more or less mass-produced at this time. The invention of Coade stone – a composition

stone that could be moulded and fired – made the reproduction of classical urns, figures and architectural detail very easy. The Coade factory started in Lambeth in 1769 and continued well into the nineteenth century. There is a fine Coade stone plaque in the West Garden of Hatfield House and there are Coade stone pineapples and a magnificent figure of a River God at Ham House.

THE NINETEENTH CENTURY

Nineteenth-century garden styles have much in common with the architecture of the period. There was a vigorous eclecticism which restlessly sought examples to follow in different periods and from different cultures. The 2nd

Above and opposite: Two of a series of anonymous views of Claremont painted in the 1740s shortly after William Kent's work there. The island and Kent's pavilion (above) are seen across the new ha-ha. Charles Bridgeman's turf amphitheatre (opposite) was made before 1725.

Marquess of Salisbury's re-creation of the Jacobean terraces at Hatfield House in the 1840s is a typical piece of Victorian historicism. Perhaps for the first time in Britain the styles of the past became an important influence. There was also the influence of exotic gardening styles of which Sezincote is a precious example: here is an 'Indian' garden made to look entirely at home in the wilds of Gloucestershire. The garden at Biddulph Grange in Staffordshire made in the 1840s with its Chinese, Egyptian and Italian influences is typical of its day. A key figure in all this was the extraordinary Scottish writer and garden designer John Claudius Loudon. His *Encyclopaedia of Gardening*, published in 1822, is one of the very few gardening books which may justly be called great. Loudon had a restless

mind and astounding energy. His *Encyclopaedia*, among many other things, has a world history and survey of gardens, starting with the Garden of Eden, and describing in some detail major gardens in every country in the world. All this rich detail, from different cultures and periods, fed the Victorian horticultural imagination.

The nineteenth century was a period in which plant introductions flooded into Britain in unprecedented numbers. In the single period between 1789 and 1814, 7,000 new plants were listed at Kew Gardens. In America the Lewis and Clark expedition to the Pacific in 1804-6, sponsored by Thomas Jefferson, revealed astounding new plant riches. The most garden-worthy plants quickly made their way to Europe where, from the second half of

the eighteenth century, there started a fashion for 'American gardens' which displayed these new botanical discoveries.

Not only were plants being constantly introduced from the wild but the nursery trade was developing techniques of hybridization and the selection of cultivars which immensely increased the range of garden plants. Consider one favourite Victorian plant, the dahlia, the first species of which came from Central America in the late eighteenth century. By 1818, by a process of hybridization and selection, virtually every single colour known today had been produced and by 1841 the nurseryman Joseph Harrison had 1,200 different double-flowered cultivars. Many of the plant introductions were not hardy and the early Victorian period was the great age of the glasshouse and conservatory, which became standard features of many gardens after the repeal of the glass tax in 1845.

In the mid-Victorian period W. A. Nesfield (1793-81) became 'the master spirit of the age'. He designed vast parterres, inspired by those of seventeenth-century France, suitable for the gardens of plutocrats. In his planting he used bedding plants, the traditional box hedging and some of the fashionable newly introduced conifers of the day. In all this his training as an architect was revealed in a sensitive grasp of large-scale layouts and a subtle understanding of the site. He designed rather overwhelming gardens for a distinctly overwhelming age. He was only one of several architects who set up as garden designers and had a decisive influence on mid-Victorian taste.

In America the landscape designer Andrew Jackson Downing (1815-52) was a profound influence on middle-class garden style. His *Treatise on the Theory and Practice of Landscape Gardening Adapted to North America* (1841) was the first book devoted to the subject and his *Fruits and Fruit Trees of North America* (1845) went through seven printings in two years and had a wide readership through the Western world. The garden of Downing's own villa on the banks of the Hudson evolved from a rather mannered confection of curvaceous beds and winding walks to the

Hatfield House in an anonymous oil painting from the 1740s. The original seventeenth-century garden walls, here still intact, were swept away in the eighteenth century when the garden was landscaped up to the house.

full-blown picturesque of informal plantings of coniferous and deciduous trees, a rustic hermitage and a rockery.

The ideas of William Robinson (1838-1935) were formed by a reaction to the excessive artificiality of much of the gardening of the latter half of the nineteenth century. Containing much that was new, his ideas became a dominant influence in gardening in the late nineteenth and early twentieth centuries. He believed in a naturalistic style of planting, using hardy plants and, above all, giving them a site approximating to their natural habitat. He scorned what he called architectural gardens but he by no means excluded formality in his own garden at Gravetye

The flower garden at William Robinson's Gravetye Manor was painted by Beatrice Parsons in about 1912. The garden was in its heyday at that period and much of the detail shown has been used in its restoration.

Manor (pages 143-55). Robinson's books still make excellent reading and are richly informative about the plants he used – which he describes brilliantly – and the way he used them. *The English Flower Garden* was first published in 1883 and by 1926 had passed through fourteen editions which, as he revised his ideas, trace the evolution of one of the most enthralling garden philosophers who ever put pen to paper. He relished a good fight and particularly enjoyed an acrimonious tussle with the distinguished architect and garden designer Sir Reginald Blomfield, whose influential book *The Formal Garden in England* (1892) praised the great tradition of formal, enclosed gardens which were harmoniously related to the house within them. Much as Robinson would have disliked admitting it, Blomfield and he had many ideas in common. The triumphant resolution of their differences may be seen in the career of Gertrude Jekyll (1843-1932) whose finest gardens were made in collaboration with the architect Sir Edwin Lutyens (1869-1944): Hestercombe (pages 157-71) is certainly one of their masterpieces. Miss Jekyll trained as a painter and took a knowledgeable interest in the theories of colour perception which also inspired the Impressionist painters. She was probably the first gardener to use colour in the garden in a thoroughly painterly way, fully aware of how it was perceived by the human eye. In America, Louise Beebe Wilder wrote in the same tradition: her *Color in my Garden* (1918) shows a similar subtle understanding of colour.

Miss Jekyll was the fertile meeting point of the naturalistic and architectural styles of gardening. She shared with William Robinson an intense interest in vernacular architecture (about which they both wrote) and an interest in the garden use of native British flowers and in the traditional crafts of the countryside.

TWENTIETH CENTURY

Miss Jekyll was a vital influence on Lawrence Johnston who made Hidcote in Gloucestershire (from 1907) and on Vita Sackville-West who, with her husband Harold Nicolson, made the famous garden at Sissinghurst Castle (from 1930). Harold Nicolson's aim at Sissinghurst was to achieve 'a perfect proportion between the classic and the romantic, between the element of expectation and the element of surprise'. Lawrence Johnston himself had immense influence on advanced gardening taste between the wars when the new garden at Newby Hall was started. In all these gardens a discriminating and experimental plantsmanship is allied to a sensitive feeling for space and enclosure. The same could be said of Lady Londonderry's ambitious and idiosyncratic garden at Mount Stewart (pages 189-99), which was started in 1921 and which uses an immense range of plants, many very unfamiliar, with a sense of design disciplined by her first-hand knowledge of Italian Renaissance gardens.

The most influential twentieth-century British gardeners have been the brilliantly individual amateurs. The distinctive style of these gardeners has been to combine the classic and the romantic in the highest degree so that however extravagant the planting, a disciplined layout always provides structure and coherence.

In the twentieth century there has been the development of a sophisticated form of woodland gardening of which Bodnant in Gwynedd, the Savill Gardens in Berkshire and Knightshayes Court in Devon are outstanding examples. Trees and shrubs, often great rarities, are arranged in an idealized naturalistic setting. This may be seen as a development of Robinsonian ideas rather than any brave new departure. In the later twentieth century in England, other gardens such as Sissinghurst Castle in Kent, brilliant as they are, look to the past for their inspiration. In America, Thomas Jefferson's realization that he could not ape European styles under the burning sun of Virginia was an early foretaste of what has become a dominant theme in American gardening – the use of native or ecologically appropriate plants in a setting suitable to the climate. In Britain the climate is so blandly receptive that it imposes no bracing limitations of this sort.

HATFIELD HOUSE

EW great Jacobean houses today remain in the possession of the family that built them and fewer still have such a depth and interest of gardening history as well documented as does Hatfield in Hertfordshire. The origins of this remarkable garden are intimately bound up with the history of the house, and changes in the layout illustrate particularly vividly fluctuations in gardening styles over a period of more than 350 years.

Hatfield is associated both with the Cecils, who built the house and still live there, and with the royal family. Elizabeth I spent much of her childhood at Hatfield Palace before it passed into the ownership of the Cecils. Robert Cecil's father Lord Burghley became Elizabeth's most valued adviser and when Lord Burghley died in 1598 his son

Above: In the East Garden avenues of clipped holm oak (Quercus ilex) provide permanent decorative structure.
Opposite: In front of the surviving range of the Old Palace, built in 1480-90, a new Knot Garden contains plants of the sixteenth, seventeenth and eighteenth centuries.

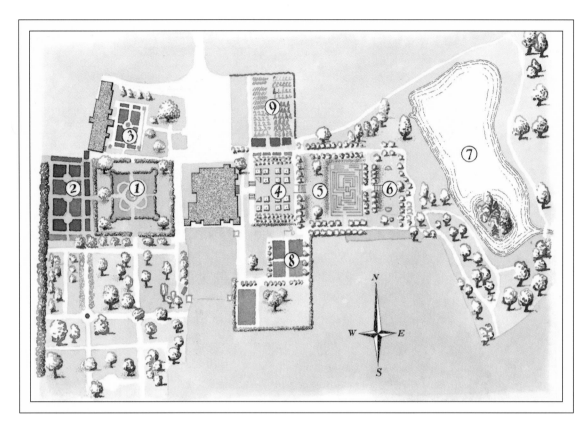

succeeded him to the privileged position he had held as the Queen's chief minister.

Hatfield House was built between 1607 and 1612 for Robert Cecil and the history of its building, and the making of the garden, is unusually well documented. Near the house, to the west, and forming an important building in the garden today are the remains of the Old Palace dating from the late fifteenth century. There survives in the archives at Hatfield a coloured plan of the Old Palace and its surroundings which dates from no later than 1608. It shows, immediately to the south of the Palace, intricate parterres, one elaborately scrolled, the other of straight lines. It is not certain whether this plan showed features existing at the time or was a proposal for alterations. At all events these parterres would have been occupying part of the same site as the formal West Garden that

exists today and they show the keen interest the Cecils took in the design of their garden from very early on.

As a young man Robert Cecil had designed a garden for his father's house, Theobalds, only twelve miles from Hatfield, in honour of the visit of Elizabeth I in 1591. The garden consisted of four knots, three of which were filled with emblematic plants: 'the Virtues were done in roses . . . the Graces of pansies partly-coloured . . . an arbour all of eglantine.' The eglantine or sweet briar (*Rosa eglanteria*, syn. *R. rubiginosa*) was a plant especially associated with the Queen, referred to in poetry about her and depicted in portraits in the kind of symbolism that was an essential ingredient of the gardens of great men in the Tudor age.

Robert Cecil brought with him to the new house at Hatfield Mountain Jennings, his gardener at Theobalds. In 1609 Jennings, Robert Bell, and 'Bartholomew the

1. Privy Garden and Lime Walk 2. Scented Garden 3. Palace Knot Garden 4. East Garden 5. Maze Garden 6. Pool Garden 7. New Pond 8. Orchard 9. Kitchen Garden

gardener' drew up plans for the new garden – 'wee did determine of a plott to bee drawne, shewed unto my lord, which I thinke will doe very well, & after may be chaunged or alltred at my lords pleasure.' Two things are clear from this: that the planning of the garden started while the house was being built and that it was expected that Robert Cecil himself would be intimately involved with it. Among these plans were details of the East Garden, separated from the house by a terrace, below which lay an upper garden followed by a lower one with the River Lea in the distance. Although there is no early drawing of this, Sir Roy Strong has pieced together its making from the Cecil papers.

A very important influence on the garden in its earliest days was John Tradescant the Elder who went to work for Robert Cecil in 1610. He subsequently worked for other aristocratic patrons and eventually became gardener to Charles I. He travelled widely in search of plants in Europe, North Africa and, through his membership of the Virginia Company, brought many North American plants to England – including the spiderwort, whose scientific name is *Tradescantia virginiana*, and the Virginia creeper (*Parthenocissus quinquefolia*). The archives at Hatfield give much detail of Tradescant's involvement with the garden. He was paid £50 per annum which was a very substantial sum and shows his importance in the household. From quite early on in his employment he was sent away on plant gathering trips to Europe. There survive, arguably from his day, a magnificent plane near the New Pond and an ancient sweet chestnut (*Castanea sativa*) in the Wilderness Garden. Tradescant was in touch with many other leading plantsmen of the day. In 1611 he records the acquisition of 'two fyg trees in an other basket called the whit fygs withe manye other Rare shrubs given me by Master Robyns'. This refers to Jean Robin, a pioneer plantsman, gardener to Henri III of France and founder of the Jardin des Plantes in Paris. Robin, too, had interests in America, and Tradescant and he grew the first acacias in Europe, grown from seed sent from Virginia and named

after him – *Robinia pseudoacacia*. Hatfield, in its day, must have had one of the greatest collections of plants in Europe. Many varieties of fruit were brought in – quinces, medlars, pears, apples, currants, apricots, peaches, nectarines, pomegranates, oranges and cherries. All kinds of ornamental plants – myrtles, oleanders, cypresses, many sorts of bulbs, anemones and gilliflowers (pinks) are also recorded. The quantities of plants acquired at this time were vast and give some idea of the scale of the garden. In 1611 the gardener to the French queen (that is Anne of Austria, wife of Louis XIII) sent 500 fruit trees – and three gardeners 'to see to the setting and bestowing of the trees'. In 1612, 453 cherry trees were bought and 1,200 lime trees sent from France, costing £140. It is rare that one is able to know exactly what kinds of plant were grown in a particular garden in the early seventeenth century and this

Seventeenth-century Italian statues look down on the East Garden from the terrace. Crisply edged with box, a series of square beds, here with lively spring planting, are filled in high summer with a profusion of herbaceous plants and shrubs.

information has given a special depth to the recent restoration. It has also enabled Lady Salisbury to emphasize one of the most precious qualities in an ancient garden, that of continuity. The spirit of Tradescant is still a powerful influence and the catalogue of his own garden at South Lambeth, published in 1634, is an exceptionally precious source showing the repertory of plants grown at that time.

Another major figure associated with the garden in its earliest days was the Frenchman Salomon de Caus (*c.*1576-1626), that early example of the international garden designer travelling widely in search of great patrons for his elaborate schemes. De Caus worked in several countries and came to England to advise Henry, Prince of Wales, James I's son, on the garden at Richmond Palace (where Mountain Jennings, Robert Cecil's gardener, had also worked). His legendary Hortus Palatinus in Heidelberg, the most famous garden of its day, was made for Frederick V, the Elector Palatine who had married James I's daughter Elizabeth. This garden, familiar from contemporary accounts and engravings, has now almost entirely disappeared. De Caus's speciality was symbolic set-pieces with mythological references, frequently on a gargantuan scale. He was a hydraulic engineer by training, and his ingenious and spectacular use of water is a common feature of gardens associated with him. At Richmond Palace, on the River Thames, he made elaborate ornamental islands. At Hatfield he made a formal diamond-shaped lake with an island and banqueting house. A very remarkable drawing of this survives in a letter dated 1611 from Lord Salisbury's secretary to his master. At two corners of the lake were a grotto (very fashionable in sixteenth-century aristocratic European gardens) and a pavilion. At a third corner was what seems to be a pumping house, possibly to provide water for pools and fountains on the terraces above. This is, presumably, what was described in the detailed account of the visit in 1663 by a Frenchman, Samuel Sorbière: 'a small River, which as it were forms the Compartiments of a large *Parterre*, and rises and secretly loses itself in an Hundred Places, and whose Banks are all Lined or Boarded'. Sorbière also described an elaborate

A framework of clipped holm oaks and box hedging provides a formal background for lavish planting in the East Garden. The seventeenth-century Italian figure was introduced by the present Lady Salisbury.

terraced garden which must surely have been on exactly the same site as the East Garden today: 'We Dined in a Hall that looked into a Greenplot with Two Fountains in it, and having Espaliers on the Sides . . . from this Terrass you have a Prospect of the great Water Parterre.' There is to this day a pool on this site, the New Pond, but it has been reshaped more in keeping with the eighteenth-century landscaping of that part of the garden. There also remains an island in the lake.

After the flurry of gardening activity in the early part of the seventeenth century little is known of the history of the garden until the mid eighteenth century. Preserved at Hatfield is a painting of the house and garden made in about 1740 showing the walled courts and terraces. But at the end of the eighteenth century all this was removed and in the characteristic fashion of the time, the garden was landscaped up to the very walls of the house except on the west. From about 1747–80, Lord Salisbury did not live at Hatfield and a desolate picture is given by Sir John Parnell writing *c.*1770: 'Excessive neglect . . . the whole being overrun with molehills . . . Lord Salisbury spends little or no time here.' J.C. Loudon, writing in 1825, was also unimpressed: 'The park is extensive, but not remarkably interesting; and the gardens afford little to gratify the amateur.' Loudon, not a man to lick even the grandest boots, adds: 'there is but little evidence of such a love of gardening in the proprietor, as would be sufficient to stimulate and encourage his gardener.' Loudon also mentions an eighteenth-century addition to the garden, the pleached lime walk, still surviving, that surrounds the Privy Garden – 'an antique flower-garden, with walks arched over with clipped lime trees'.

In the 1840s, however, the 2nd Marquess of Salisbury made many changes in preparation for Queen Victoria's visit in 1846, inspired by the current fashion for re-creating historic features, especially of the Elizabethan and Jacobean periods. Lord Salisbury wanted to restore something of the formal character of the original Jacobean garden and he rebuilt terraces about the house. These, unfortunately, did not follow the originals, being higher and wider and

therefore somewhat out of scale. In addition he made a new and elaborate maze of yew. It is not known if there ever had been a maze at Hatfield, but there certainly was in the Cecils' garden at Theobalds and it is possible that Lord Salisbury, with his interest in his family's history, was making reference to that.

The present Marchioness of Salisbury came to Hatfield in 1972 on the death of her father-in-law. She was already thoroughly experienced in the problems of restoring and managing a historic garden, since she had for many years been looking after the garden at another Cecil house, Cranborne Manor in Dorset. When she came to Hatfield she found a garden that was certainly not neglected but had, over a long period of time, increasingly lost touch with the spirit of the great Jacobean house. The essential character of the garden was by that time Victorian, with a few changes in the twentieth century. Lady Salisbury had two chief aims. The first was to bring the garden back into sympathy with the character of the house and the second was to reduce the burden of maintenance. Many of the later additions could be retained in this restoration if given a tighter focus on the Jacobean character of the setting. For example, Lady Gwendolen Cecil, in about 1900, had introduced a new scheme in the Privy Garden to the west of the house. A series of shaped beds of clipped box was surrounded by a yew hedge with very slightly undulating walls – an attractive idea that gives seductive charm to what might have been a severe line. This new layout was very much in tune with the revival of interest in formal designs in that period. It is illustrated in H. Inigo Triggs's influential book *Formal Gardens in England and Scotland* (1902). Lady Salisbury has kept these hedges and embellished them with a bench in each corner, half-concealed in a circular pavilion of yew, from which one may admire the beds from a leafy and secret seclusion. Throughout the garden, features have been retained which, although arguably not 'authentic', are good of their kind and in keeping with the atmosphere of the place. This gives the gardens at Hatfield much greater richness and character than striving for historical correctness might have done. And what can one say is 'correct' in a garden that has such a complicated history as this?

One of the oldest sites in the garden is the area immediately to the east of the remaining range of the Old Palace; in what was once an internal courtyard there is now a dazzling knot garden, made since 1981. There is no documentation to suggest that there had originally been a knot here but, overlooked as it was by the surrounding windows of the palace, a knot would have been a likely possibility. In the well-documented Thornbury Castle near Bristol, only slightly later than the Old Palace, there is a vivid contemporary account of the garden made by the Duke of Buckingham who employed a 'gardener diligent in making knots' in an enclosed yard overlooked by the windows of the principal rooms. At Hatfield this site had become a rose garden in the nineteenth century and when Lady Salisbury came it was a simple cruciform arrangement of four lawns with an ornamental crab apple in the centre of each. On three sides the area is surrounded by a raised walk built, no doubt, on the foundations of the Old Palace walls. The central fountain and the York stone paths were kept, but new paths were made surrounding the sunken area, from old bricks salvaged from buildings on the estate. The pattern of the knot is made of common box (*Buxus sempervirens*) 225mm/9in high; for this 7,500 plants were needed, which were propagated from other plants in the garden. Three of the knots are of the 'closed' sort, that is with the segments filled with plants. The fourth is an 'open' knot in the form of a maze with gravel paths. All these patterns were devised by Lady Salisbury, not copied from any particular design but influenced by much reading of contemporary accounts of old knots. The patterns were traced by the old method of tying a sand-filled bottle to a piece of string, the other end of which is fastened to a peg. Circles and segments may then be traced by allowing a trickle of sand to fall on to the earth. Incidentally, the old quadripartite division of this part of the garden seemed perfectly square, but when work started

the parts were found to be out of true which meant that the knots had to be laid out by eye. On old sites this is often the case, which emphasizes the need for measured plans.

The planting of the three closed knots is restricted to plants of the sixteenth, seventeenth and eighteenth centuries. Here are forms of the common primrose (*Primula vulgaris*) which were much loved by early gardeners. Both Gerard in his *Herball* (1597) and Parkinson in *Paradisi in Sole Paradisus Terrestris* (1629) describe these with relish. Gerard wrote that the double form, planted here, 'of all the rest is of the greatest beautie' and double forms appear also in the plant list of the Tradescants' garden at Lambeth. Also planted in the knot are the curious forms Jack-in-the-Green (in which the calyx of the flower has assumed the

A maze of clipped box forms one quadrant of the Knot Garden. Early mazes of this sort, with a single tortuous path, symbolized the soul's journey towards perfection. The surrounding paths are laid with old bricks salvaged from the Hatfield estate.

form of a leaf, forming a decorative ruff to the flower) and hose-in-hose (in which the calyx takes the form of extra flower petals). Among the many other plants used in the Knot Garden that are known to have been grown by the Tradescants are some of their own introductions – including the goat's beard spiraea (*Aruncus dioicus*) and the white-flowered Michaelmas daisy (*Aster tradescantii*). Another early feature is the use of variegated holly, much loved by the Elizabethans, in the form of a row of topiary 'dumb-waiters' on a paved terrace between the knots and the Old Palace. Also giving permanent decorative structure are plants of two different species of phillyrea, *P. angustifolia* and *P. latifolia*, planted round the knots. These decorative evergreens from the Mediterranean clip well and have been known in English gardens at least from the sixteenth century.

Three sides of the Knot Garden are edged with a hedge of hawthorn (*Crataegus monogyna*) which replaced an earlier, and unsympathetic, brick wall. On either side of each entrance to the steps which lead down to the Knot Garden, hawthorn plants have been allowed to rise above the hedge and have been clipped into decorative lollipops. From the hedges grassy slopes rise to a low fence of Tudor character, 750mm/2½ft high with a criss-cross pattern and finials regularly punctuating the uprights. The finials, incidentally, were made of wooden coconut-shy balls – a flagrantly inauthentic detail. They, and the fencing material, are made of softwood which is painted with a preservative every three or four years. The successful character of this Knot Garden is the result of Lady Salisbury's judgement of what is appropriate, together with various specific historic references, rather than any plodding interpretation of authenticity.

To the south of the Knot Garden is the Privy Garden. This is enclosed on all four sides with the eighteenth-century pleached lime walk described by Loudon. This had been covered in asphalt by the 3rd Marquess, who rode on his tricycle here, but that unsympathetic surface has been replaced with fine pale Breedon gravel. The limes

are pruned in February and March every year with three-quarters of the new growth being removed and the remaining shoots tied in. Leafy walks of this kind are familiar from engravings of Italian Renaissance gardens. In the north-west corner of the Privy Garden is the sole remaining mulberry said to have been planted by James I. Originally these marked the four corners and three new trees have been planted to replace the missing ones.

When Lady Gwendolen Cecil remade the Privy Garden she laid out a pattern of parterres within her new hedges of yew. In the design for these beds it is thought that she was influenced by a plan dated 1785 in the archives at Hatfield which shows the beds within this area apparently planted with blocks of clipped box in geometric patterns. By 1972 when Lady Salisbury came the beds had been planted up with labour-intensive, chiefly herbaceous, planting and some violently coloured modern roses. Here Lady Salisbury kept the form of the beds, which are set in grass, but edged them with brick in order to reduce edge-trimming. The planting is now in the style of a mixed border with many more permanent shrubs, including many roses. There is a rich mixture of herbaceous plants – pinks, geraniums, peonies, lilies, irises, delphiniums and pansies. There are forms of the common lawn daisy, *Bellis perennis*, including the ancient hen-and-chicken daisy in which a ring of miniature flowers surrounds the main flower-head. This is depicted in Gerard's *Herball* and has been known at least since the sixteenth century. Although use is made of ancient garden plants of this sort, Lady Salisbury uses with relish the very latest forms, including David Austin's 'English' roses. These hybrids of modern Floribunda and Hybrid Tea roses with old shrub roses combine the fine flower-shape, delicate colour and fragrant scent of the old roses with the perpetual flowering of the modern varieties. They make particularly valuable border plants because they are not excessively tall.

To the west of the Privy Garden is the Scented Garden which has been completely replanted by Lady Salisbury. It

*T*op: *Beyond the East Garden lies a yew puzzle maze made in the 1840s. Bottom: The Privy Garden is hedged in yew and surrounded by an eighteenth-century pleached lime walk. Following pages: The New Pond to the east of the house was the site of an exotic formal water garden in the early seventeenth century.*

is a walled garden, surrounded by fine old Tudor brick. At the entrances are placed intensely fragrant plants – lemon-scented verbena (*Aloysia triphylla*), protected in winter with straw, may be brushed in passing and another entrance is flanked by low hedges of the spicily perfumed Guernsey stock (*Matthiola incana*). A formal arrangement of paved paths cutting across lawns provides a firm grid for the varied planting. Topiary adds to the structural formality. Obelisks of clipped box spaced at regular intervals on the lawns give elegant vertical emphases. At the west end of each of the paths there is a seat set in a retaining wall with arms and pedimented back of clipped box.

The paths are dotted with camomile (*Chamaemelum nobile*) and where they intersect at the centre there is a formal herb garden with a sundial surrounded by a ring of standard honeysuckles (*Lonicera periclymenum* 'Belgica'). A series of curved beds extends outwards filled with fragrant herbs – artemisias, mints and rue – and hedges of lavender. The whole is enclosed by low hedges of two hybrid sweet briars – 'Meg Merrilees' and 'Amy Robsart', both of which have the deliciously scented leaves of the eglantine from which they are derived. The entrances to this formal arrangement are flanked with different varieties of rosemary – both *Rosmarinus officinalis* and *R. o.* 'Benenden Blue', which comes from Corsica and has more intensely blue flowers than the type.

Above: A formal walk of apple trees separates the maze from the Pool Garden. Right: A nineteenth-century Coade stone plaque in the Privy Garden shows a meeting between Robert Cecil and Elizabeth I.

On three sides of the Scented Garden the walls are lined with deep borders containing many shrubs with scented flowers. *Elaeagnus commutata* has intensely silver leaves and rather insignificant yellow trumpet-like flowers in June – but these have a piercing honeyed scent. There are winter-scented shrubs, too, including *Mahonia japonica*, winter-sweet (*Chimonanthus praecox*) and the box-like *Sarcococca humilis*. In the spring and early summer there are the scents of daphne (*D. odora* 'Aureo-marginata'), philadelphus, many different kinds of pinks, tobacco plants and the Moroccan broom (*Cytisus battandieri*). The Scented Garden is an instructive exercise in a potentially limiting theme.

An especially interesting aspect of Lady Salisbury's time at Hatfield has been her enthusiasm for organic gardening. At Cranborne, quite early on, she had been sickened by the intensive regime of rose spraying, which she abandoned. At Hatfield no inorganic materials are used in any of the plant-growing parts of the garden, although weed-killing chemicals are used on large expanses of gravel. She believes that a vigorously growing plant is less likely to succumb to diseases or pests and between 40 and 60 tons of compost are made and spread every year and even greater quantities of farmyard manure (which comes from the estate farm) are used. Also, a very large garden will provide the habitats and the nourishment for a very wide range of insects. Ladybirds, for example, hibernate in the crevices of the old brick walls and emerge in May to feast on aphids. Aphids are also consumed by the abundance of lacewing flies. In the kitchen garden

Roses are an essential part of the Privy Garden. The shrub rose 'Fritz Nobis' rises above pinks and geraniums, and beyond the yew hedge the top of the eighteenth-century lime walk is visible.

cabbages are protected from moths and pigeons with covers of Agromesh which is not pretty but is completely effective and, being porous, allows rain to penetrate it. Some plants, however well fed and cared for, will inevitably succumb to viruses. When this happens either the plant will be destroyed or, occasionally, it will be cut right back and fed lavishly. Lady Salisbury's Head Gardener, David Beaumont, shares this interest in organic gardening. For example, he has found that pruning rambler roses in the autumn after flowering makes them much more resistant to mildew. To return to the chemical-free gardening of the past is perhaps the most subtle form of authentic period gardening.

THE ESSENCE OF HATFIELD

The gardens at Hatfield are large and intricate and yet there is a harmony in them, and in their relationship to the great house, that is extremely rare. In a historic garden of this complexity there are plainly constraints on what can be done but in many ways Hatfield is an object lesson in contemporary restoration. In it the best surviving ingredients – plants and layout – have not only been preserved but their value has been enhanced. The whole garden has been brought closer in spirit to the house but, like the house itself, which has been much altered since the early seventeenth century, the garden reflects changing taste. There is no attempt to revert to some hypothetically 'correct' garden style.

The East Garden exemplifies the matter. Here the elaborate designs made at the time of Robert Cecil had already decayed when the landscape park was made in the 1780s. The 2nd Marquess of Salisbury reinstated a formal garden here in the 1840s in what he supposed was correct Jacobean style. In fact, it was a fussy parterre with elaborately patterned beds of intricate shapes, strikingly Victorian in feeling and unsympathetic to its setting.

Lady Salisbury's new scheme, with mixed planting in the beds and the eclectic use of ornament, is distinctly twentieth century, firmly of its time. But in its formal vivacity, and above all in its references to foreign garden styles, it seems much more in keeping with the cosmopolitan gardens made here in the early seventeenth century. There is a strong Italian flavour in the new East Garden that comes partly from the panache of the seventeenth-century Italian statues imported by Lady Salisbury, but also from the sprightly formality of the flanking alleys of clipped holm oaks (*Quercus ilex*), an essential ingredient of formal Italian gardens, where it is used for hedges and topiary. The beds in the East Garden, sixteen of them, each a generous 8m/27ft square, trimly hedged in box, are richly planted with shrubs and herbaceous perennials but they are given structure by a substantial pyramid of clipped box at the centre of each. Within that firm and decorative framework the many shrub roses, several species of cistus, and the Chinese *Ribes laurifolium* are underplanted with a prodigality of herbaceous plants – columbines, pinks, cranesbills, delphiniums and peonies. It is, in fact, a cottage garden rumpus with aristocratic control.

Below the East Garden the Tradescant influence continues with a very large collection of fruit trees woven naturally into the decorative scheme of the garden. Against the retaining wall are pleached apples and fan-trained pears interspersed with climbing roses. On either side, leading east, are two fine avenues of paired varieties of apples. One avenue consists entirely of varieties dating from before 1750, the other chiefly of nineteenth-century varieties. In old gardens bees were considered an essential presence to ensure the pollination of the flowers of fruit trees and several hives are kept in a formal orchard to the south.

In all this the spirit of the past is interpreted by the judgement of a single gardener. There is no blind conservatism here, but a sensitive striving to show the best of the old in a new setting. The most remarkable single aspect of Hatfield is that, in this very large and complicated garden, the lasting taste and judgement of one person can be felt in every detail.

HAM HOUSE

*A*FTER dinner I walk'd to Ham, to see the house and garden of the Duke of Lauderdale, which is indede inferior to few of the best villas in Italy itselfe; the house furnish'd like a greate Prince's; the parterres, flower gardens, orangeries, groves, avenues, courts, statues, perspectives, fountains, aviaries, and all this at the banks of the sweetest river in the world, must needes be admirable.' John Evelyn, the great diarist and connoisseur of trees and gardens, wrote that description of Ham House in August 1678, when it was in its heyday. There are two outstanding features about Ham today: first, the house itself is a remarkably complete and almost unchanged architectural ensemble of its period, containing most of its original furnishings; second, the site of

Above: The Parterre of box, santolina and lavender based on a 1671 plan of the garden. Opposite: The south front of the house seen from the restored Wilderness. In the foreground, Versailles boxes and seventeenth-century Venetian chairs have been copied from the painting by Henry Danckerts (see page 23).

49

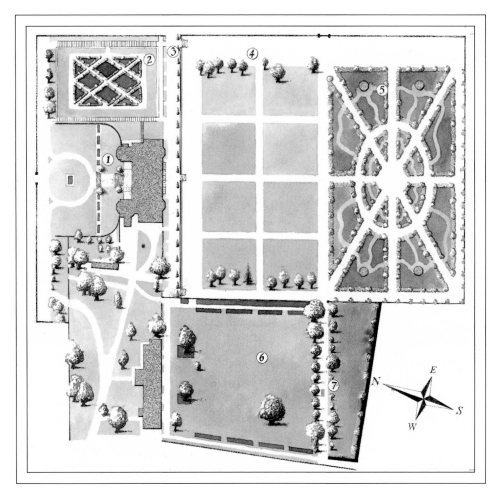

the garden has survived and its history is exceptionally well documented. The visitor to Ham House today may see a lordly house from one of the best periods of English architecture – with a garden to match.

Ham House lies in a loop of the Thames near Richmond in Surrey on the fringe of Greater London – a riverside site so attractive that many great houses and gardens were built here. On the other side of the river Orleans House and Marble Hill survive and they were formerly visible from the north windows of Ham. Daniel Defoe wrote in 1724, 'the whole country here shines with a lustre not to be described . . . the fine seats shine among the trees as jewels shine in a rich coronet.' The original house at Ham was almost exactly contemporary with Hatfield House and was built in 1610 for Sir Thomas Vavasour, Knight Marshal to James I. A drawing by the architect Robert Smythson from this time shows elaborate geometric parterres. That scheme was much altered later in the century but the broad terrace on the south side of the house in Smythson's drawing is still there and the garden is still disposed about the same axis as the house. This last feature is of interest because, as Sir Roy Strong has pointed out, Smythson's plan is the first example in England of a house and garden sharing the same axis.

1. Front Court 2. East Court 3. South Terrace
4. Parterre 5. Wilderness 6. Rose Garden
7. Ilex Avenue

The history of the present house and garden starts in earnest with Elizabeth, Countess of Dysart. Her father, William Murray, Earl of Dysart had acquired the estate in 1637 and she inherited it, and his title, on his death in about 1654. At Ham House there is a charming miniature of her made in 1649, the earliest known painting by the intriguing Alexander Marshall, an artist and one of the greatest florists of his day. Little is known of Marshall's life; his date of birth is unknown but he died in London in 1682 and his name keeps cropping up in the best plantsman's circles of his day. He knew the younger John Tradescant who commissioned flower paintings from him – a 'Booke . . . of choicest Flowers and Plants, exquisitely limned in vellum'. Marshall was also known to Evelyn who described a visit in 1682 to Fulham Palace to see the 'curious book of flowers' that Marshall was painting for the great plantsman Henry Compton, Bishop of London (in whose Palace at Fulham Marshall died). Most important of all for our purposes, Marshall lived for some time at Ham and must have influenced the collections of plants there.

Elizabeth, Countess of Dysart married as her second husband in 1672 John Maitland, Earl (later Duke) of Lauderdale, and they immediately set about enlarging and embellishing their house. Bishop Burnet wrote of them, 'they lived at a vast rate, but she set everything to sale to raise money, carrying herself with a haughtiness that would have been shocking in a queen.' The garden they made was entirely in keeping with their house. A rare detailed scale plan drawing of it, attributed to John Slezer, survives from about 1671. Additional detail is provided by other paintings and drawings made shortly after this time. Slezer also did a plan of one of Lauderdale's Scottish seats, Thirlestane, which has a lattice-patterned parterre remarkably similar to that at Ham. Slezer was a German surveyor, long resident in Scotland, and it may be that he designed both these parterres. However, although most of the details shown in his plan of Ham are corroborated from other sources, this design for a parterre is found only in the Slezer drawing.

After the Duchess's death in 1698 the estate passed to her son by her first marriage, Lyonel Tollemache, 3rd Earl of Dysart. His mother's extravagances had left the estate in perilous condition but he seems to have revelled in the enforced economies. At first the garden was kept up but subsequently both house and garden were neglected. The 4th Earl of Dysart married Charlotte Walpole, a niece of Horace Walpole who reported in 1770: 'I went yesterday to see my niece in her new principality of Ham. It delighted me and made me peevish. Close to the Thames, in the centre of all rich and verdant beauty, it is so blocked up and barricaded with walls, vast trees, and gates that you think yourself an hundred miles off and an hundred years back . . . Every minute I expected to see ghosts sweeping by.' Later still it was visited by Augustus Hare in 1879: 'In the afternoon we went to Ham House – a most curious visit. No half-inhabited chateau of a ruined family in Normandy was ever so dilapidated as this home of the enormously rich Tollemaches.' Shortly afterwards some restoration of the house was carried out and the Tollemaches continued to live at Ham until they gave it to the National Trust in 1948. James Lees-Milne inspected Ham for the National Trust in 1944 and wrote, 'The grounds are indescribably overgrown and unkempt . . . The garden is pitted with bomb craters around the house, from which a few windows have been blown out and the busts from the niches torn away.' After World War II the garden was tidied up, and underneath the dereliction and damage, the house and the essential layout of the gardens had remained remarkably unchanged. Thus, in 1975 when the National Trust was able to start on the restoration owing to some lucky benefactions, it had the unique opportunity of restoring a magnificent garden of the 1670s in an architectural setting to match.

The site of the lattice-work Parterre in the 1671 Slezer plan immediately to the east of the house was in the past known as the cherry garden. The plant list of 1693 refers to twenty-seven 'winter cherryes' which were planted out in pots in July, and these could be the dots shown in Slezer's plan. This was the half-hardy *Solanum pseudocapsicum* from Madeira, known in England since 1596, and still today widely used as a house plant with glossy cherry-red fruit that are much valued in winter. This part of the garden is marked on Robert Smythson's drawing as the 'Principall garden' and, remembering the Countess of Dysart's patronage of Alexander Marshall, it is tempting to suggest that this might have been the site of a great collection of flowering plants. Such things were always kept very secure at this time because rare plants were exceedingly valuable and in Smythson's drawing the garden is shown walled on three sides and open only on the side of the main garden which was itself enclosed.

When the ground was being cleared in 1981, traces were found of a circular path in the centre of the cherry garden and in the middle of it, brick foundations which were probably for a statue – the 1679 inventory decribes 'one marble statua'. However, in the absence of any other firm evidence the design from the Slezer drawing was followed. The Parterre was reconstructed in 1976 with dwarf box (*Buxus sempervirens* 'Suffruticosa') hedges 225mm/9in high to outline the triangular and diamond-shaped beds. These are punctuated at each corner and in the centre of each hedge with cones of common box (*Buxus sempervirens*) 900mm/3ft high. This design is a distinctly old-fashioned one, much closer to the geometric knot gardens of the Renaissance shown in Robert Smythson's 1610 plan for Ham. By the 1670s the arabesques of French-style *parterres de broderie*, introduced to England before the Civil War when Charles I bought André Mollet to England, would have been much more fashionable. In the reconstruction the beds have been filled with blocks of a single plant – Dutch lavender alternating with dwarf cotton lavender (*Santolina chamaecyparissus nana*) – kept clipped to the level of the surrounding hedges. At the centre, exactly on the old foundations where the 'marble statua' might have been, a mid-eighteenth-century sundial has been moved from a site near the orangery. The planting here has been criticized for being rather plain and seasonal

bedding schemes have been proposed. Such a scheme would certainly be jollier but it would also very greatly increase the burden of labour. Had that not been a consideration it would, perhaps, have been best of all to have made a collection of florists' plants of the sort painted by Alexander Marshall in his exquisite *Florilegium*, his only surviving substantial botanical work, in the royal collection at Windsor Castle. In a plant inventory of 1682 from the muniments at Ham House many of the plants that would have interested a florist of the day are listed – cyclamen, hollyhocks, hellebores, double sweet rocket, auriculas and polyanthus. The plants used in the reconstruction, however, are certainly historically possible – none is more recent than the end of the sixteenth century.

The east Parterre is surrounded with a yew hedge 1.2m/4ft high on three sides and 2.4m/8ft on the north side. On the east and west sides hornbeam (*Carpinus betulus*) has been interplanted with the yew, allowed to rise above the top of the hedge, and trained over iron hoops to form a pleached tunnel. This, too, seems to come from an earlier period, resembling the tunnelled arbours of the Renaissance – at all events, there is no sign of it on the Slezer drawing.

To the south of the house along the broad gravelled terrace a new border has been planted containing many plants of grey and silver foliage – sage, phlomis, cistus and rosemary interspersed at regular intervals with the strawberry tree (*Arbutus unedo*). Recesses made in this long bed contain high-backed oak benches. These, of late seventeenth-century design, were adapted from originals that survive in the forecourt arcade and are referred to in an inventory of 1689 as 'wainescot benches'. None of the contemporary records gives any information about planting here; indeed there is no evidence that there was any permanent planting and it is perfectly possible that some of the many plants in pots or tubs listed in the inventories were placed here in the summer. In the 1682 inventory many decorative flowering plants in pots are listed – lemons, oranges, myrtles, pomegranates and oleanders. Some of

*The Parterre is flanked by shady tunnels of yew and pleached hornbeam (*Carpinus betulus*). Such tunnels, more characteristic of the Renaissance, would have seemed rather old-fashioned for a grand garden of the 1670s.*

the plants used in the new borders are recorded in the seventeenth-century inventories, but the conception is an entirely modern one.

The southern edge of the terrace is edged with a stone parapet which has terracotta vases planted with cones of clipped box. A drawing of the south front of about 1671 (by John Slezer and Jan Wyck) shows urns of this sort in that position planted with tall plants – Italian cypresses (*Cupressus sempervirens*) would have been likely at that date. It is impossible to know whether this drawing represented the actual arrangement as it has many peculiarities about it (including a startling grove of larch-like trees in the foreground, which would have looked more than odd in a formal garden). The coping stones of the retaining wall, however, have flattened areas at regular intervals which suggest that some ornament was placed there. Wooden pineapples are mentioned in a joiner's bill of 1674 found among the Ham papers 'ffor 2 doosen & ½ of pinaples Carving', and it is possible that these were winter ornaments put out when terracotta pots were brought in to protect them from frost. The National Trust has had made handsome terracotta urns based on the carved stone urns that cap the piers of the north gates, which were made in about 1671 to designs of Sir William Bruce – a cousin of Lady Dysart and also, incidentally, another patron of John Slezer. I shall have more to say about Bruce in the following chapter on Pitmedden. Three sets of stone steps lead from the terrace down to the formal garden and in each case these are flanked by moulded pineapples, this time made of Coade stone and inscribed 'Coade & Sealey Lambeth 1800'.

The eight square grass lawns, or plats, spread out before the south terrace, were replanted according to the wealth of evidence about them that exists. In a bird's-eye engraving of the garden from *Vitruvius Britannicus* (1739) there are unexplained lumps in the middle of each of these lawns. It has been conjectured that they were plinths for either sculptures or beehives. The vast number of statues and plants in pots or tubs mentioned in inventories and

*T*he south terrace overlooks 'grand and beautiful plats or parterres of grass', as Batty Langley wrote in 1728. Terracotta urns, copied from seventeenth-century stone vases, are planted with clipped box.

seen in a painting of *c.*1675 by Henry Danckerts may have been used to ornament the lawns. The inventories list so many of them (for example a total of 327 different trees, shrubs and flowers in pots in the 1682 inventory) that they were clearly an important part of the movable décor of the garden. On the other hand, Kip's engravings show many gardens with large unadorned expanses of lawn in front of houses and Batty Langley writing in his *New Principles of Gardening* (1728) recommends that there should be no ornament on lawns – 'for the Grandeur of those beautiful Carpets consists in their native Plainness'. In the same book Langley goes on to specifically praise 'those grand

and beautiful plots or parterres of grass in the garden belonging to Ham House'.

Beyond the plats is the Wilderness, reconstructed exactly according to the Slezer plan, which is confirmed in detail in *Vitruvius Britannicus* and in Danckerts's painting. When the National Trust started work this area of the garden was a dense planting containing some fine old trees. Everything was removed and the whole area was ploughed and levelled. A wilderness – a formal, symmetrical arrangement of clipped hedges which enclosed 'rooms' – was a very common feature in late seventeenth- and early eighteenth-century gardens and may be seen in

*The north front of the house is flanked by sweeping brick walls decorated with stone busts of Roman emperors. The curves of the niches are echoed in the outlines of the drums of clipped bay laurel (*Laurus nobilis*).*

countless engravings in Kip's *Britannia Illustrata* (1707). One of the most famous was at nearby Hampton Court, possibly designed by Sir Christopher Wren, of which a part of the original design (the maze) still survives. Here at Ham the pattern is of a central oval from which alleys radiate. These alleys in turn run across a concentric oval path and the various segments enclosed form *bosquets* or green rooms (*cabinets de verdure*) which have 'doors' leading into them. Within these rooms there is grass with close-mown paths meandering across, linking the 'doors' on either side. Danckerts's painting shows trees rising above the level of the hedges at regular intervals and this scheme has been followed in the restoration. The bird's-eye view from *Vitruvius Britannicus* shows the exact spacing of the trees in relation to the hedges and these distances have been followed. The hedges are of hornbeam and the trees that rise above them are field maple (*Acer campestre*). Though it is probable that the original hedges were of holm oak (*Quercus ilex*), the effect is very close to the mood of the Danckerts painting in which the bushy crowns of the trees billow above the close-clipped hedge. However, the vivid account of the Wilderness written by Celia Fiennes in 1698 makes it sound much wilder – 'a very fine wilderness with many large walks of great length, full of all sorts of trees sycamores willows hazel chestnutts set very thick and so shorn smooth on the top which is left as a tuff or crown'.

Within four of the enclosed areas of the Wilderness are round pavilions which are copies from those clearly shown in the *Vitruvius Britannicus* print. They are made of wood painted white on the outside and blue within, containing a wooden bench, and the conical roofs are surfaced with unpainted wooden shingles, surmounted by glittering ball finials of gilded lead. In the long grass many wild plants are naturalized – ragged robin, cowslips, ox-eye daisies, primroses, jonquils, wood anemones and narcissi.

At the centre of the Wilderness Danckerts's painting shows a lively scene – figures walk among statues, seats and plants in Versailles boxes. The only statue surviving from that period in the garden today is the white marble figure of Bacchus, known to be no later than 1672, which is now in the centre of the ilex walk to the west of the wilderness. A surviving bill from 1672 is 'ffor 1 Pedestall for ye figure Bacchus 6'. An inventory dated 4 August 1679 headed 'The Garden and the Wildernesse' lists 'Six Carv'd wainescot benches, painted; ffourteen wooden sttooles with backs painted; Tenn statuas of lead whereof two upon Stone pedestalls; and eight upon wooden pedestalls.' Danckerts's painting shows eight lead statues on pedestals and several elegant white-painted garden chairs. These, with backs in the form of carved shells, are of a Venetian type known as *sgabello* (Italian for bench or seat).

The National Trust had new ones made, adapted from similar chairs at Petworth House in Sussex, and some Versailles boxes, and these are placed outside in the summer months. It is hoped one day to replace the statues with faithful reproductions. Most garden statues of that time were copies from classical or Renaissance models rather than original works of art; for example Danckerts's painting shows a figure of Mercury after Giambologna and the Medici Venus.

Beyond the southern gate of the formal garden the vista is continued in an avenue of limes stretching out across the flat land. This idea of continuing an axis beyond

A giant Coade stone figure of a river god reclines in the entrance court to the north front of the house. It dates from the late eighteenth century when other Coade stone ornaments were ordered for the garden.

a walled garden was a common seventeenth-century feature. A formal arrangement of trees (probably limes) is clearly shown in the background to Alexander Marshall's portrait of Lady Dysart. At that time the river frontage of the house was the more important and the avenue made a visual link between the landing stage and the entrance court on the north side of the house with its imposing and lively façade. Although some of the formal rows of limes on the north side of the house have been replanted, the visitor today is scarcely aware of the presence of the river and the axis of interest of house and garden has been shifted to the south, where the façade is much simpler.

THE ESSENCE OF HAM HOUSE

The essential key to the garden at Ham House is the painting made in about 1675 by Henry Danckerts. It is late on a summer afternoon and the south front of the house is a warm gold in the low sunshine. The sky is blue, flecked with clouds and in the centre of the wilderness are seen two figures who very possibly may be the Duke and Duchess of Lauderdale. Wearing a full frock-coat and a plumed hat the Duke is pointing something out to his wife – perhaps the two dogs playing in the middle ground. Ornate shell-backed seats, lead statues on plinths and

Left: An iron gate pierces the south wall of the formal garden, and beyond it a lime avenue continues the vista. Right: A marble figure of Bacchus in an avenue of holm oaks (Quercus ilex) is the only statue surviving from the many that were at Ham in the seventeenth century.

ornamental fruit trees in Versailles boxes encircle the lawn where grandees chat in the shade and finely dressed ladies saunter. This, then, is a garden to be seen in and, on a fine day, would fulfil exactly the same function as the grand rooms of the house, an appropriately lordly background that proclaims the importance of its owner and against which the Duke and his guests may be seen almost as garden ornaments themselves. But it also has an atmosphere of privacy, away from the public, river side of the house which was open to the view of boats passing on the water.

The visitor today can stand at the top of the double staircase that leads down from a French window in the middle of the south front to the gravel terrace. The garden is spread out before him, visually very much part of the house, echoing its mood. A firm vista carries the eye to the iron gates on the southern edge of the garden, and beyond its limit an avenue extends the view. About this vista the decorative features are disposed. Immediately below the terrace are eight giant square lawns separated by gravel paths and beyond the lawns is the Wilderness. Above the hornbeam hedges there is the festive glint of the golden balls at the top of each of the garden pavilions. If the visitor then walks to the far end of the central vista and turns round he will see the view shown in Danckerts's painting and realize that the main ornament of the garden is the house itself boldly set forth by the simplicity of its immediate surroundings.

There are two marvellous views of the Parterre on the east side. Inside the house the main staircase, a swagger affair of chocolate and gold, lies on this side giving wonderful angled glimpses of the Parterre through the old glass of the leaded lights. Outside, in the garden itself, the Parterre may be viewed while sauntering down the tunnels on its east and west sides. On a hot summer's day the tunnels are cool and views of the Parterre are neatly framed by the eye-level gap between the yew and hornbeam of which it is made. In winter, the deciduous hornbeam overhead does not block the sun but the evergreen yew preserves the formal lines. The Parterre itself is crisply formal but visually lively because it is laid out at an angle to the axis of the enclosing hedges, and the diamond shapes of its beds change with the shifting viewpoint. Also seen from these tunnels is a stately procession of hollies, alternately plain and variegated, clipped into large lollipops, planted in the beds that run along the tunnels on either side of the Parterre.

The entrance court on the north front of the house sets the scene. All the planting is formal, symmetrical and architectural. On either side are monumental drums of clipped sweet bay (*Laurus nobilis*), echoing the shape of the niches containing busts of Roman emperors in the curving

walls behind them. In the centre of all this is a great Coade stone figure of a reclining river god of the late eighteenth century which is probably of the same date as the pineapples on the south terrace. Two pairs of standard Portugal laurels clipped into mop-heads guard the entrance to the house and immediately below the entrance terrace cones of yew sit firmly in rectangles of clipped box. All this, like the overture of an opera, whets the appetite, sets the scene and gives a thematic foretaste of the splendours to follow.

*The golden finial of a rebuilt summer house is glimpsed over the curved walls of hornbeam in the Wilderness. Field maples (*Acer campestre*) rise above the crest of the hedge.*

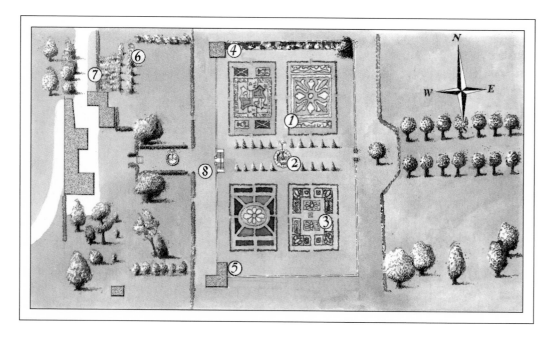

ancient and distinguished family long prominent in the political life of the country. His grandson, Sir Alexander Seton, made the original Great Garden, as it is called, whose walls carry an inscription showing that it was started on 2 May, 1675. It is very rare indeed that any garden as early as this may be dated so precisely. Moreover, it is something of a puzzle, since this very precise detail, and the garden walls, ornamental staircase, pavilions and gatepiers, are virtually all we know about its early history. The garden archives were presumably lost in the nineteenth-century fire that destroyed the original house. There is a persistent rumour that connects the architect Sir William Bruce with the Setons of Pitmedden but no documentary evidence supports it. But there is no doubt that the garden at Pitmedden belongs to the same tradition as the gardens that Bruce is known to have designed at Balcaskie in Fife and Kinross in Kinrosshire. All these gardens have a pronounced central axis, shared by the house, and extending beyond the confines of the garden.

To judge from the undeveloped state of gardening described by the first Scottish book on horticulture, John Reid's *The Scots Gard'ner* published in 1683, the new ideas about layout from the Continent must have made a profound impact on the aristocratic circles in which Bruce moved. Described by Daniel Defoe as the 'Kit Wren of Scotland', Bruce is a shadowy but attractive figure who lived from about 1630 to 1710. After the death of Cromwell in 1658 he involved himself in the Restoration of Charles II and eventually became Surveyor-General of the King's Works in Scotland and architect for the rebuilding of the royal palace of Holyroodhouse at Edinburgh. Bruce certainly travelled in Europe in 1659 and in 1663 but the only places mentioned in the Bruce archives are Holland and Brussels. It is thought on circumstantial grounds that Bruce also visited France in 1663. Certainly it seems likely that he received at first hand the striking French influence that permeates his work. Le Nôtre's first great garden, at Vaux-le-Vicomte, had been completed in 1661 and its bold and original axial composition is an obvious possible source for Bruce's gardening ideas. It is tempting to suppose that Bruce was one of its earliest foreign visitors. Furthermore, there are stylistic similarities between Bruce's

1. The Great Garden 2. Fountain 3. Sundial
4 and 5. Pavilions 6. Fruit Tunnel 7. Herb Garden
8. Entrance Steps

buildings and seventeenth-century French architecture, especially the work of François Mansart whose design of the Château de Balleroy in Normandy incorporated the main village street as part of a central axis. From 1665 onwards, Bruce had created a similar axial scheme for his own garden at Balcaskie on the coast of Fife where the house is pierced by an axis which links the peak of Kellie Law to the north and the island of Bass Rock ten miles away to the south on the other side of the Firth of Forth. In the layout of the garden for Kinross House, which he started in 1685, Bruce also constructed a great central axis linked, on one side of the house, by an avenue to the town of Kinross, and on the other side, focused on Loch Leven Castle which sits on an island in the loch. It was famous in its day and remains a spectacular sight. Sir Charles Lyttelton wrote to Bruce in 1688, 'Lady Lauderdale's gardens at Ham are but a wilderness compared to yours at Kinross.'

Nothing is known about the original house at Pitmedden which was virtually entirely destroyed by fire, with all its archives, in 1818. The last of the Setons to live on the estate was Sir William Coote Seton who was born in the same year as the great fire. The remains of the old house were eventually demolished and the present, more modest, house was built in 1860; at the end of the nineteenth century the estate was acquired by the Keith family. Photographs of the garden at this time show no trace of a formal garden except, of course, the walls and architectural ornaments of the Great Garden. These were well known to garden writers at the time and are illustrated in two important books of the day, Reginald Blomfield's *The Formal Garden in England* (1892) and H. Inigo Triggs's *Formal Gardens in England and Scotland* (1902). The Keith family transformed the Great Garden into an ornamental kitchen garden in which exuberant herbaceous borders consorted with cabbages. In 1951 Major James Keith gave the estate to the National Trust for Scotland.

Planning the restoration of the Great Garden started in 1954. The restoration of *any* historic garden was, at this time, a rare event. There were no instructive precedents

on which to draw. It was established early on by Dr James Richardson, the architect in charge of the restoration, that the restored garden should be formal, in keeping with the architectural features that had survived. The survival of this framework and its various embellishments, dated so precisely, provided a very rare opportunity to recreate in an authentic setting a formal garden inspired by the period. In the absence of any design for the original garden, or any picture of it in its heyday, some other source for inspiration was sought. An extraordinary bird's-eye view of Edinburgh made in 1647 by James Gordon of Rothiemay was chosen. This picture shows in very great detail the houses and gardens of the period. The royal palace of Holyroodhouse is shown with many ornate parterres and it was decided to use motifs from some of these for the designs of the restored parterres at Pitmedden. The purist will say that they are too early and may criticize the use of thirty-year-old decorative themes in a later axial arrangement. Indeed, the haphazard arrangement of the parterres at Holyroodhouse, unrelated to the house or to any unifying axis, vividly illustrates the old style which Le Nôtre's revolution was to sweep away. Furthermore, as

*T*he entrance to the Great Garden bears the initials of Sir Alexander Seton and his wife Dame Margaret Lauder. Below them – a very rare feature indeed – is recorded the exact date of the starting of the garden.

Dr Richardson was perfectly familiar with Bruce's work, he would have been well aware that the 1647 plan was well before Bruce's involvement with Holyroodhouse.

In 1955 work started on the restoration. The old fruit and vegetable garden was cleared and the whole area was grassed over. As soon as the new turf was established, four large rectangles were marked out for the parterres and their patterns planted in box. The variety of box used for the immense quantity of hedging and edging (three miles of it) is of an unnamed type distinct to Pitmedden. It is used with great subtlety, variety and attention to detail. The hedges that form the frames of each parterre are 900mm/3ft high and have been given a slight batter, sloping gently inward. An opening to the parterre in the middle of each side of the frame is flanked with square pillars of box, slightly higher and wider than the hedge itself, transforming what would have been a mere gap into an emphatic entrance. The hedging forming the divisions within the parterres is lower than the surrounding frame, 400mm/15in high. These frames are identical for each of the four parterres and have the effect of keeping in harmony the widely differing designs.

One of the parterres has scrolled geometric designs in the tradition of French *parterres de broderie*; a second

Above: A staircase of granite, with an ornamental fountain, leads into the Great Garden. Left: Looking down on the parterres from one of the viewing terraces – a characteristic feature of seventeenth-century gardens.

*T*he parterres are edged with a form of box unique to Pitmedden. Compartments are filled with modern annuals –
orange and yellow marigolds (top) and silver-leaved Senecio bicolor cineraria (bottom).
These are historically inauthentic but vividly evoke the seventeenth-century spirit.

provides the setting for an elaborate sundial (and has the words *Tempus fugit* worked in box); a third, a round bed surrounded by segments and rectangles; and the fourth depicts the Seton arms and motto picked out in shaped box, coloured chippings and bedding plants. In the *parterre de broderie* the box that forms the 'embroidery' is clipped square across at exactly the same height as the surrounding hedge. This gives the impression, when seen at an oblique angle, of a bed made of some exotic, deeply woven green damask and brings out vividly the essential idea of the *broderie*. Every three years, incidentally, the level is kept uniform by clipping against horizontal guidelines. The illusion of rich material is emphasized by using, as far as possible, bedding plants that will grow to the same height as the box compartments. In the first three parterres the spaces between the box patterns are filled with gravel or with summer annuals which are bedded out on a prodigal scale. The use of annuals in quite this way, in solid blocks of a single colour, is certainly not a seventeenth-century practice and, in any case, the plants used are without exception relatively modern cultivars.

The principle of using essentially nineteenth-century bedding in an ostensibly seventeenth-century scheme has been much criticized. Because of lack of detailed information about the original planting of the garden, and indeed about the general practices of the period, an authentic restoration was in any case impossible. It was a bold decision to use bedding plants in the parterres and, in my view, a much more satisfactory idea than some polite and insipid compromise. The coloured sand, brick dust or glass chippings used in parterres in their heyday created lively colour schemes. Indeed it is the contrast of these brilliant colours with the sober formality of box and yew that could be seen as the very essence of the parterre. Seen from afar, as was intended, there is no reason why the same effect should not be achieved with modern summer bedding. It is not so successful in the north-west parterre which traces the arms of the Seton family and the Scottish symbols of the thistle and St Andrews cross (or saltire as it

is called in Scotland), giving a distinctly Victorian flavour. Arms and monograms, worked in elaborate carpet bedding, were a common nineteenth-century feature. This is beautifully done but seems to me to strike entirely the wrong note, giving an atmosphere of municipal vulgarity.

A broad path was made down the centre of the Great Garden, with two parterres on either side. This axis was emphasized by planting an avenue of English yews (*Taxus baccata*) flanking the path, which have been gradually shaped into obelisks resembling those at Vaux-le-Vicomte. The Great Garden lies at some distance from the site of the house and is approached across a wide grassy terrace. From a distance the garden is completely invisible, but it is suddenly seen beyond a stone balustrade, spread below, like an intricate and richly patterned oriental rug. Stone piers, capped with carved pineapples, flank the entrance which leads down a double staircase. The eye is drawn by the yew avenue across the garden to an ornamental wrought-iron gate on the far side which pierces the high stone walls that entirely surround the garden. In the old orchard beyond the gate there is some suggestion that the axis was continued far outside the walled garden, but with no known focal point. The Ordnance Survey 6-inch-to-the-mile map of 1854 shows the remains of this axis quite clearly extending beyond the walls of the Great Garden. Incidentally, the position of the old orchard between the formal garden and the countryside beyond is found elsewhere in Scottish gardens of the seventeenth century. At Aberdour an orchard was the culmination of a series of formal terraces.

The idea of aligning the main axis with the rising and setting sun, that is to say running east and west, as it is at Pitmedden, is found at Versailles and other Le Nôtre gardens. In the case of Versailles where the garden was made for the *Roi Soleil* the arrangement is specifically symbolic.

In the centre of the south-east parterre is a 24-faced sun and moon dial which has always been in the garden. The angle of the gnomon of a sundial, incidentally, must be calculated precisely according to the latitude of its site.

Too frequently today sundials are brought into gardens and treated merely as ornaments and, because they were made for a different latitude, will not tell the time correctly. Very elaborate multi-faceted sundials are a distinctive feature of Scottish gardens in the seventeenth century. There are many surviving ones at Holyroodhouse, Newbattle Abbey, Drummond Castle and elsewhere. The purpose of the many facets is partly to allow the dial to be read from different angles and partly to provide for moon readings. Furthermore, because of the very long summer days in this northern part of Scotland, a dial on a single plane could not display the time throughout the hours of sunlight. There are two other sundials in the garden, mounted on the walls of the pavilion in the north-western corner. One is on the east-facing wall, and thus tells the time only in the morning, and the other is on the south-facing wall, for afternoon time.

At the centre of the Great Garden there is a fountain in a hexagonal pool, which was made in 1956, partly of fragments of a seventeenth-century Market Cross fountain erected in Linlithgow to celebrate the restoration of Charles II, and partly of fragments of the same period found at Pitmedden. The curious thing is that they seem to be by the same stone-carver. The fountain is surrounded

Sundials were a common feature of seventeenth-century gardens. In the north of Scotland long hours of summer daylight meant that dials could give the time for very long periods. Left: An afternoon dial giving the time up to 9 o'clock. Right: A multi-faceted dial that also registers moonlight.

by an inlay of split river pebbles from the Dee – a traditional local paving material – and worked into the pebbles are the hearts and crescents of the Seton arms.

Against the entrance wall, running the full width of the garden, are giant buttresses of clipped yew 3.6m/12ft high and the same in width, which were added in 1957. Where they meet the walls they flare outwards as though they form part of the very architecture of the garden. The tops of the buttresses are clipped into ogee curves and the outer corner is surmounted by a dashing egg-shaped finial. Similar buttresses are found in the garden at Balcaskie, where they are made of stone and, instead of topiary finials, have busts of Roman emperors. In the sheltered spaces between the buttresses are climbing roses, summer jasmine, the evergreen *Crinodendron hookerianum* with shiny dark-green leaves and hanging crimson flowers and the rare honeysuckle *Lonicera chaetocarpa* with primrose yellow flowers. At each end of the western wall are charming two-storey granite pavilions with ogee-shaped roofs echoing the lines of the yew buttresses.

These two pavilions needed much restoration. When the National Trust for Scotland took over, they had conventional straight-sloped roofs which needed urgent attention and were rebuilt with sweeping ogee lines. These curves do not conform to any regular geometric shape. Dr James Richardson practised drawing them freehand on the sandy beach near his home at North Berwick until he had the perfect curve. At Kinross House there are pavilions with exactly the same ogee roofs as those at Pitmedden. These were certainly designed by Bruce and are to be seen in his original drawings for the house.

Apart from their ornamental function, the pavilions provided shelter for viewers of the garden. They were comfortable, finely furnished miniature houses with quite elaborate interiors. The northern pavilion only has been restored to its original state. The lower room, at garden level, is finely vaulted and the upper room with panelling and fireplace is an elegant seventeenth-century parlour. The National Trust for Scotland was able to restore it with

seventeenth-century panelling from a mansion in Midlothian. This pavilion is entered at the upper level from a broad terrace which runs along the northern boundary of the Great Garden. There was another terrace to the south but that has gone.

Against the south- and east-facing walls of the Great Garden are herbaceous borders 4.5m/15ft deep and planted on a substantial scale. Advice was taken on the design of these borders from Lady Burnett of Leys who, with her husband, made the remarkable Arts and Crafts influenced garden at Crathes near by. These borders, very good in themselves, have nothing to do with the overall design of the

restored Great Garden and add a disharmonious note.

There are later developments, outside the Great Garden itself, which seem a little perfunctory. To the northeast of the house there is a small formal herb garden surrounded with yew hedges. Square beds are edged with box and separated with gravel paths. It is very hard indeed to imagine a Seton, or any other Scottish grandee, having anything to do with such a thing. Another recent addition is a tunnel, running alongside the herb garden, on which are trained espaliered apples. This is something of a mixed bag. Some are very early varieties which could have been

In the centre of the Great Garden a fountain has been pieced together from fragments of seventeenth-century carved stone. The paving is of local split river pebbles – a traditional material.

grown at Pitmedden in the seventeenth century such as 'Golden Reinette' (mid 1600s), 'Calville Rouge d'Hiver' (1600) and 'Catshead' (mid 1600s). Others are later introductions such as 'Pitmaston Pine Apple' (1785) and 'Cox's Orange Pippin' (1850). Of particular interest are specifically Scottish varieties such as 'Threave Castle' and 'Lady of the Wemyss'. Apples grow especially well in this part of Scotland and the previous owner of Pitmedden, Major James Keith, took a keen interest in them. Several of his original plantings survive on the walls of the Great Garden that back the herbaceous borders.

THE ESSENCE OF PITMEDDEN

Pitmedden is a riddle and its successful restoration is based on a mass of unwarranted assumptions. We just do not know in any detail what kind of planting was originally used at Pitmedden or in any other Scottish garden in the seventeenth century. We do not know anything at all about the original layout of the garden. There is no picture and no description of it before the nineteenth century. The restoration has been carried out with the thoroughly dubious and unhistorical intent 'to surprise and delight'. Yet the Great Garden itself is a triumphant success; it makes the best use of the beautiful setting in a spirit that does justice to it.

It must be said, however, that the approaches to the Great Garden, coming to it at an awkward angle, and the relationship with the rebuilt remains of the house, are thoroughly unsatisfactory. The strong axial symmetry of such a garden, in its prime, would undoubtedly have been approached from some point central to the house. Furthermore, some of the more recent additions – the apple walk and the double screen of hornbeams – in themselves attractive, seem capriciously placed. Having said that, the Great Garden, however inauthentic, is enchanting.

The surviving seventeenth-century pavilions, walls, double stairs and gate piers are full of character and the restoration has enriched this. For example, the arms of the

Seton family have three crescents and a bleeding heart (in memory of Sir Alexander's father, who was shot through the heart defending the king's standard at the battle of the Brig o' Dee in 1639). Crescents and hearts are worked into the pebbles at the foot of the entrance steps and surrounding the central fountain.

In the great tradition of Renaissance knots and later parterres the design of the restored Great Garden is one to be seen from above – from the terraces or from the windows of the pavilion. As one walks along the terraces the patterns of the parterres shift, as though seen through a kaleidoscope. There are also the variations caused by the angle of the sun (and this is a very sunny part of Scotland) at different times of day. Especially in late summer and autumn, early in the morning or late in the afternoon, drama is added to decoration as the long shadows of the yew obelisks steal across the gardens and the low angle of light emphasizes the detail of the parterres.

The south-west parterre was copied from a 1647 bird's-eye view of the gardens of the royal palace of Holyroodhouse. Summer bedding schemes – never the same two years running – contrast with granite chippings, clipped box and mown turf.

WESTBURY COURT

*I*T is very rare indeed that a garden should survive despite the dis-appearance of the house and the estate to which it once belonged. West-bury Court in Gloucestershire is an almost unique example of this, a garden distinguished enough to survive, by the skin of its teeth, the demolition of *three* houses on the site. Furthermore, the Colchester family, who owned the estate for almost 300 years, absented themselves for 90 years during the nineteenth century, although the garden was maintained during this time. Lastly, and possibly most perilous of all, the estate was bought from the Colchester family by a developer in 1960. Its life hung by a thread until, at last, it passed into the hands of the National Trust in 1967.

Above: A walled garden contains a collection of plants none of which is later than 1700. Opposite: The tall Dutch-style pavilion at the head of the Long Canal was built in 1702–3.

It is rare in other ways, too, for the formal water garden is of a type that was all but extinguished in the fashion
for landscape parks which swept Britain in the later
eighteenth century. It dates from the heyday of Dutch influence on English gardens, which began in the early years
of the reign of William and Mary, and is the only garden of
the sort which survives from that period virtually intact.
In Holland itself no formal garden of this date survives. It
is the earliest formal garden extant, in something closely
resembling its original state, anywhere in Britain. The
meticulous restoration carried out by the National Trust
makes it all the more valuable. It must also be said that,
apart from its undoubted historic importance, it is a place
of irresistibly seductive charm.

Maynard Colchester started the garden in 1696. The
formal arrangement he chose was perfectly appropriate to
the site, flat water-meadows less than a mile from the right
bank of the River Severn. Colchester was not a grandee
with money to squander on lavish display, although he
had married a rich wife, Elizabeth Clarke, the daughter of
a Lord Mayor of London. But the passion for gardening at
this time was not confined to great estates: many humbler
houses had distinguished formal gardens and it is significant that Colchester chose to spend his money making a
new garden rather than on modernizing his old-fashioned
Elizabethan manor house. In this low-lying flat landscape
the formal water garden was very much a local form – of
the fifty-eight gardens illustrated by Kip in Atkyns's
Ancient and Present State of Glostershire (1712), twenty have
some kind of water garden – but where did the Dutch influence come from? One of Maynard Colchester's great
friends was a neighbour, Catherine Boevey, at Flaxted
Abbey, a few miles from Westbury. The Boeveys had
Dutch connections and Catherine's father was an Amster-
dam merchant. Furthermore, it is known that the Boeveys
had made a garden with a formal canal before 1692 and
this, too, is illustrated in Atkyns's *Glostershire*. This could
easily have provided the inspiration for Maynard Colchester. The influences on any garden design are very often of a
local kind and research into other gardens of the locality,
and histories of the area, may yield valuable information.

An engraving by Kip of about 1707 shows the garden

1. *Parterre* 2. *Quincunx* 3. *T Canal*
4. *Long Canal* 5. *Pavilion* 6. *Neptune*
7. *Gazebo* 8. *Walled Garden*

very shortly after the first stage was completed but it also shows Colchester's proposals for the east part of the garden that were never made as shown. To the south of the gabled Elizabethan house lies an intricate parterre from which the water garden is separated by a wall. Running north-east and south-west, virtually the entire length of the garden, is a long, narrow canal with, at one end, a jaunty two-storeyed pavilion with a pillared loggia and, at the other, a *clairvoyée* piercing the enclosing brick walls. Not visible in Kip's engraving, but known to have existed, was an avenue outside the garden exactly aligned with the *clairvoyée*. On the east side of the canal there is an elaborate formal arrangement of trees, columnar and clipped into spheres, surrounding smaller regularly spaced plants. That, in essence, is what Kip shows in his usual loving detail.

We know a great deal about the making of the garden from Colchester's account book for the period 1696-1705, which survives in the Gloucestershire Record Office. This has been the source of indispensable information for the National Trust's restoration. Not only does it give detailed builder's bills but also the names, quantities and prices of the plants that were bought. The heart of this garden as Colchester made it, and the first part of it to be built, was the dominating Long Canal, 135m/450ft long by 6.6m/22ft wide. The first bills record payments for digging this canal in 1696, only two years after Colchester had come into the estate. At first he had simply canalized an existing stream, subsequently diverting it eastwards to its present position, the Westbury Brook which today separates the garden from the picnic area. Early on, too, there are bills for very substantial quantities of plants. In 1699 1,000 yews and 1,000 hollies were planted, probably for the hedges flanking the canal, which today have been replanted with yew punctuated with holly finials. There is a bill for £21 9s. 8d. – 'Pd. Tho. Wintle in full for laying 120,800 bricks.' The *clairvoyée* at the north-western end of the Long Canal, with its 'pineapples & pillers', also dates from Maynard Colchester's time. In walled gardens built

on a flat site this was an ornamental means of allowing outside views. In this case, with the garden sited on a busy road, it also allowed curious passers-by a glimpse of the garden within.

The pavilion also dates from this early period of the garden and was completed by 1704. This, too, has a Dutch character and resembles a pavilion shown in a painting by Pieter de Hoogh (1629-84) called *A Game of Ninepins* which hangs at Waddesdon Manor in Buckinghamshire. In Holland such lofty pavilions were built to provide views over the flat landscape. Here the pavilion allowed an axial view of the new formal garden not possible from the old house which was separate from the water garden. It also allows glimpses of the river Severn over the flat country beyond the road.

Maynard Colchester died in 1715 and his nephew, Maynard Colchester II, succeeded to the estate. It seems that he, too, took an intense interest in the garden and developed what his uncle had started, and it is probable that he was responsible for the additions to the garden made after the Kip engraving was done. In his time an additional T-shaped canal was added, parallel to the Long Canal. In the centre of the crosspiece of the T Colchester put a mid-seventeenth-century stone statue of Neptune riding a dolphin which remains to this day. Aligned with this new canal was a second *clairvoyée* with elegant urns. He also built a charming brick summer-house with handsome stone embellishments, and the little walled garden which it overlooks, in the far north-eastern corner of the formal garden.

When the National Trust took over in 1967, although the essential layout was still visible, it was in a catastrophic state of neglect. This was partly due to a prolonged lack of maintenance and partly to the decay of the garden's fabric. The linings of the canals had for a long time leaked; a serious flood had caused the roots of the flanking yews to become waterlogged and many of them had died. Everywhere plants had grown too big, weeds proliferated and the canals had become choked. In some gardens this kind

Mediterranean area in the late sixteenth century. Mysteriously it is not, however, shown in Kip's engraving, so its age has perhaps been overstated. On the other hand it is possible that Kip used his artist's licence to delete a feature that did not fit the formality of the rest. Another fine surviving tree, of no great age, is a tulip tree (*Liriodendron tulipifera*) near the holm oak.

The immediate task was to remove dead and dying plants – which included practically all the old yew hedging – and to dredge the canals which were clogged with the accumulated silt of hundreds of years. 1,000 cubic yards of it were excavated and spread on the ground to the east of the T-canal to form a nutritious foundation for later planting. The original stone lining of the canals had decayed and no longer held water efficiently. This had to be rebuilt and made as waterproof as possible.

The yew hedges flanking the long canal, as shown in Kip, were replanted in 1970. Being seedlings, the yew plants show considerable variation of colour. In some circumstances uniformity of colour would have been thought of as essential, but here, where formality is tempered by rusticity, this colour variation strikes the right note. Furthermore, in the seventeenth century it would have been quite usual practice to propagate by seed rather than by cuttings. Every seventh plant has been allowed to grow above the top of the hedge and has been clipped into a cone. These alternate with 'lollipops' of common holly (*Ilex aquifolium*). The plants got off to a variable start, probably because of the mixing of clayey subsoil with the topsoil when the ground was being reshaped with a bulldozer after the building works were complete.

By the time the Trust took over, the pedimented pavilion overlooking the south-west end of the long canal was in an advanced state of collapse. It had been much altered in the nineteenth century when a new house had been built incorporating it. The pavilion needed complete rebuilding and in the course of this, the original pillars, which had formed a loggia on the ground floor, were discovered to have survived. These pillars are, incidentally, referred to

of picturesque decay has a certain romantic charm. At Westbury, where crisply orchestrated formality is such an important ingredient, this is certainly not the case. The garden buildings and walls had also suffered and needed urgent attention. Very little old planting was healthy enough to be preserved, although one very remarkable exception is an extraordinary holm oak (*Quercus ilex*) at the south-western extremity of the garden, outside the formal arrangement. It has, by several feet, the greatest girth of any holm oak in England. It is estimated to have been planted no later than 1600, which in itself would be remarkable, for the tree was only introduced from the

A stone figure of Neptune – dating from the 1740s – restored to its position at the north-east end of the T Canal.

in the Colchester accounts in a bill from a mason called James Fox – '6 pillers & 2 pillasters & 36 quine [= quoin] stones'. All these details are visible in the restoration. When dismantling the remains of the roof it was discovered that there were still beams in place to support a lantern of exactly the type shown by Kip which had, at some later date, been removed and a very unsatisfactory sloping roof substituted. The lantern is now surmounted by a characteristic Dutch feature, a gleaming gold ball, which in the Low Countries could be seen at a great distance. At the back of the pavilion, clearly shown in Kip's engraving, there was a wall with sloping shoulders at each end, and with a pair of benches flanking the pavilion. All this has been restored. Not shown by Kip, but thoroughly in keeping with the character of the garden, are the terracotta pots containing tender 'exoticks' which are used to flank the entrance gate by the pavilion and elsewhere in the garden. The 'exoticks' in this case are agaves and oleanders, both of which are fairly early introductions to England and are mentioned in *The Garden Book of Sir Thomas Hanmer* written in 1659.

The long brick wall forming the north-western boundary of the water garden (which survived in its original state until it was demolished by a builder just before the Trust took over) has been replaced. It is now planted with a large collection of pre-1700 varieties of apple, pear and plum which are espaliered against the wall. They are kept to a height of 1.8m/6ft and the branches are trained to wires fastened with vine-eyes at intervals of 300mm/1ft. The plants are spaced at intervals of between 4.5m/15ft and 5.4m/18ft. The use of fruit trees in an ornamental way was common in formal gardens of the period from the Restoration until the mid eighteenth century. It is also a feature of Dutch gardens and in more than one of William of Orange's palace gardens, miniature clipped apple trees were used in parterres. Maynard Colchester's account books show that he bought a wide range of plants of all kinds – ornamental bulbs as well as shrubs, fruit trees and other trees. This passion for plants, allied to a formal

layout, is characteristic of Dutch garden style of this era. Contemporary French formal gardens, for example, used a more limited range of plants.

A narrow bed runs along the north-west wall, broken by three evenly spaced *clairvoyées*, with ornamental plants known to have been in cultivation by 1700. These include annuals, herbaceous plants, bulbs, shrubs and climbers. It is often wrongly thought that annuals are modern introductions to the garden. The showy love-lies-bleeding (*Amaranthus caudatus*), for example, was a very early introduction in the sixteenth century from tropical South America. The great herbalist John Rea records that in 1665

The entrance to the walled garden where, in the seventeenth century, especially rare and precious 'florist's' flowers would have been kept secure. It has been restored as a formal giardino segreto with period planting.

'country women' knew it by its modern common name. Here, too, is the pot marigold (*Calendula officinalis*), one of the earliest recorded European garden plants, described in the fourth century by Palladius. Love-in-a-mist (*Nigella damascena*) from southern Europe appears in Gerard's *Herball* (1597) – 'faire and pleasant'. Clumps of southernwood (*Artemisia abrotanum*) and sweet bay (*Laurus nobilis*) frame each *clairvoyée*. These, and repeated plants of *Cistus salviifolius*, form a rhythmically repeated pattern and are underplanted with many bulbs – old varieties of daffodil, fritillary, hyacinth and tulip. In Maynard Colchester's accounts for 1702 there is an item, 'Pd. Coz. Colchester in full 100 iris's 50 junquills 50 hyacynths double 50 double narcissus's 50 anemonys 50 ranunculus's 150 tulips.' Exotic tulips came to the west from Turkey in the middle of the sixteenth century and by the early seventeenth century had become an extraordinary craze in Holland. By Colchester's time tulipomania was well past its peak but a very large range of tulips was widely available. Tulips, incidentally, were, with pinks, the first group of flowers to be given cultivar names.

Planting of the period is continued along the north-east wall with old English lavender, rue (*Ruta graveolens*) and old roses such as the apothecary's rose (*Rosa gallica officinalis*), of great antiquity, and the true musk rose (*R. moschata*). This last, a native of southern Europe and the

*A*bove: *Inside the walled garden a gazebo of the 1740s overlooks box-edged beds. Opposite: In the north-eastern wall* clairvoyées, *flanked by stone urns, allow outsiders to view the garden.*

Middle East but known in England since the early sixteenth century, was thought to have been lost, but was rediscovered in a dazzling feat of horticultural detective work by Graham Stuart Thomas. Trained against this wall are various old species of climbing or wall-plants such as Christ's thorn (*Paliurus spina-christi*, 1597), summer jasmine (*Jasminum officinale*, 1548) and *Vitex agnus-castus* (early 1500s), known as the chaste plant because its seeds were supposedly anaphrodisiac. Planted at the feet of these are many herbaceous plants – valerian, cranesbills, soapwort, Jacob's ladder (*Polemonium caeruleum*), species peonies (both *P. mascula* and *P. officinalis*) and many irises. These plants, many now rare in gardens, show what riches were available to a discerning gardener before 1700.

In the north-east corner there is a small garden entirely enclosed by brick walls and overlooked by the summer-house. Originally this would probably have been for the cultivation of choice florists' flowers. It was restored in 1972 as a formal *giardino segreto* with square box-edged beds, gravel paths, vine arbours and honeysuckle trained over iron hoops. With the exception of a few nineteenth-century roses the planting here, too, is in period and it constitutes a fairly representative collection of pre-1700 chiefly herbaceous plants of which, in this small area, there is an astonishingly rich diversity. Many of these are of the kind associated with 'cottage' gardens – the dusky cranesbill (*Geranium phaeum*), great masterwort (*Astrantia major*), Jacob's ladder and so on. But in addition to these there are more aristocratic plants which, although garden plants of ancient use, have fallen out of favour. The white false helleborine (*Veratrum album*), for example, is a plant of outstanding beauty which has been grown at least since 1548. It has deep green pleated foliage like an exotic hosta and, in late summer, spires of white flowers brushed with green. Dittany (*Dictamnus albus*), in cultivation since Roman times, is another formerly very popular plant, with its spikes of white flowers in June and its foliage smelling of lemon when bruised. A special virtue, too, is made of the use of English natives such as ox-eye daisies

(*Leucanthemum vulgare*), tansy (*Tanacetum vulgare*), sea campion (*Silene uniflora*), the charming miniature foxglove, *Digitalis lutea*, and many others.

Outside the walled garden there is a collection of old pinks (*Dianthus* species and cultivars) of great interest. These include 'Caesar's Mantle' (sixteenth century), 'Prince of Denmark' (early eighteenth century), 'Green Eyes' (also known as 'Musgrave's Pink', *c.*1730), 'Old Salmon Clove' (sixteenth century), and 'Bat's Double Red' (1700). By the early seventeenth century there were already several varieties of pinks of which very few still exist. The survival of cultivars of short-lived garden plants is a chancy business depending, as it almost invariably does, on artificial propagation by gardeners.

Shown in Kip's engraving, near the original house and on a site that falls outside the boundaries of the garden today, is an ornamental parterre. This is mentioned in Colchester's accounts – 'paid Thos. Hall towards the knots in the garden £4-14-6'. The word 'knot' continued to be used for this kind of parterre well into the eighteenth century. The Trust has re-created part of it on land to the east of the T-canal, taking the detail from Kip's engraving and judging the scale from human figures shown in the engraving. The symmetrical pattern of low hedges of dwarf box (*Buxus sempervirens* 'Suffruticosa') is punctuated with topiary shapes of spheres and cones in common box. Within the beds are massed plantings of pre-1700 plants – *Nigella damascena* (by 1570), the shrubby candytuft (*Iberis sempervirens*, by 1597) with *Lilium pyrenaicum* (by 1633) growing through it, pot marigold (*Calendula officinalis*, by 1573) and the half-hardy annual sage (*Salvia viridis*, syn. *S. horminum*, by 1500). At either end of the parterre there is a formal quincunx of clipped Portugal laurel (*Prunus lusitanica*). The Portugal laurel has been in cultivation at least since 1648 and was recommended in the seventeenth century by Sir William Temple as a hardy plant that could take the place of citrus plants in British gardens. The quincunx is an ancient way of arranging trees in a pattern resembling the spots on the 'five' of a die. At the centre of

*T*op: *A froth of* Salvia viridis *erupts from a compartment of the Parterre, re-created from the 1720
engraving by Kip. Bottom: Portugal laurel (*Prunus lusitanicus*) – trained as a standard and clipped
into an umbrella shape – is a characteristic seventeenth-century plant.*

each group of Portugal laurels there is a clipped mound of the grey-leaved shrub *Phillyrea angustifolia* ('phillereys' are mentioned in Maynard Colchester's accounts and have been used in England at least since 1597). Planted nearby are other ornamental trees of ancient use – several thorns including the azarole (*Crataegus azarolus*, seventeenth century), *C. pedicellata* (1683), the service tree (*Sorbus domestica*, 1678) and the quince (*Cydonia oblonga*, of very ancient introduction). It is very rare that the garden visitor has an opportunity of seeing groups of trees of this sort, all in use before 1700.

Very recently a dashing new bench has been put in place at the southern end of the broad turf walk that separates the two canals. It is an elaborate concoction with appropriately Dutch cabriole legs and a swagger scalloped canopy supported on a high back. There is no evidence that a bench of this sort was ever in the garden but it looks entirely at home. Sitting on it the visitor may look north-east along a restful vista of rows of clipped box cones backed by yew hedges and convincingly imagine himself transported back to the late seventeenth century.

THE ESSENCE OF WESTBURY

The anonymous author of an article in *Country Life* in 1908, when the garden was still impeccably cared for, wrote of Westbury Court, 'There is . . . no lack of effective variety and changing scene in this garden of pure formality, perfect flatness and simple design. It is at once dignified and enjoyable, satisfying and alluring.' There is

The clairvoyée *aligned with the Long Canal and the Pavilion. The carved stone 'pineapples' are mentioned in a bill dated 1704.*

also about Westbury the unmistakable charm of the provincial garden. Although decidedly elegant it is a comfortable, inward-looking garden made for the delight of its owner rather than to impress his friends. Its intimacy and charm have been successfully preserved and enhanced by the restoration. Despite its air of privacy, it does not shut itself off entirely from its surroundings: the *clairvoyées* on the north-eastern side of the garden which borders the old Gloucester-Chepstow road allow passers-by delicious glimpses of the garden.

This, a quintessentially formal garden, is very far from being cold and severe, for the formality is alleviated by all kinds of light-hearted decorative touches and by the richness and variety of the flower beds. There are the ornamental topiary finials – lollipops of holly and cones of yew – that run along the crest of the yew hedges that flank the long canal. Although the fruit trees grown along the walls are trained into formal espaliers and fans, the trees themselves bring the character of a country orchard. At the feet of the espaliers and in the beds of the walled garden there is a lively profusion of ornamental plants.

The character of the planting in general makes an emphatic contribution to the whole atmosphere of the garden. Apart from a handful of nineteenth-century roses, all the plants, including most particularly the fruit trees, date from before 1700. This is not just a matter of historical pedantry, for the soft colours of the flowers and the natural character of these ornamental plants (many of which are English natives) are wholly in tune with the provincial and unsophisticated charm of the garden. This is seen at its most striking in the walled garden where the country formality of honeysuckle and vine trained over iron arches and arbours and the formal beds edged with box and separated by gravel paths provide a contrast to the planting with its hedgerow and woodland character.

The fruit of the old varieties will come as a surprise to visitors nourished on large, uniformly symmetrical, brightly anaemic 'Golden Delicious' apples. These old kinds have irregular shapes, flattened or pear-shaped, and

often brilliant colours. At Westbury there are many different kinds of pre-1700 apples alone.

To see a collection of plants of that time, in an authentic period setting, is an unusual experience. The whole garden is all of a piece, for nothing of consequence survived from later times that might have prevented a restoration to a single historic moment.

Lastly, the water itself forms the very heart of the garden. The canals give firm structure to the layout but their surfaces also reflect the decorative features of the garden – the pavilion, topiary and the handsome piers of the *clairvoyées*. In a circumscribed area the reflections of sky and trees introduce an airy spaciousness. This use of water as a mirror (*miroir d'eau*) was an essential part of the vocabulary of the French formal garden in the time of Le Nôtre. On a windless day the canals reflect their formal and decorative surroundings. When a breeze gets up, the surface is ruffled, introducing a lively note. But it is misleading, perhaps, to mention the name of Le Nôtre, for his gardens show the triumph of intellect over fancy. At Westbury the overwhelming atmosphere is one of fancy kept in check by light-hearted formality.

Maynard Colchester was a devoted plantsman. Many early cultivars of garden plants have been used in the restoration of his garden; here, the tulip 'Louis XIV'.

ERDDIG

---

*T*HE Yorke family, who made Erddig, was particularly odd. Reading about its members gives the uncanny feeling of reading a novel by an unusually inventive author with a connoisseur's taste for the eccentric. Not only did the Yorkes really exist, but their lives are copiously documented – which gives the history of their house and garden an exceptional richness. In a way, too, it was the eccentricity of the family, and its contempt for fleeting fashion, which meant that the house and garden at Erddig survived essentially unchanged. Landscaping was done but only to the north and west of the house, well beyond the walls of the pleasure garden. Thus the garden, a formal layout of the early eighteenth century, is one of the very few in Britain to have escaped the

*A*bove: *Screens of pleached lime were used to replace brick walls in the formal garden.*
Opposite: Wrought-iron gates, made in the 1720s by Robert Davies, make a focal point for the central vista in the formal garden.

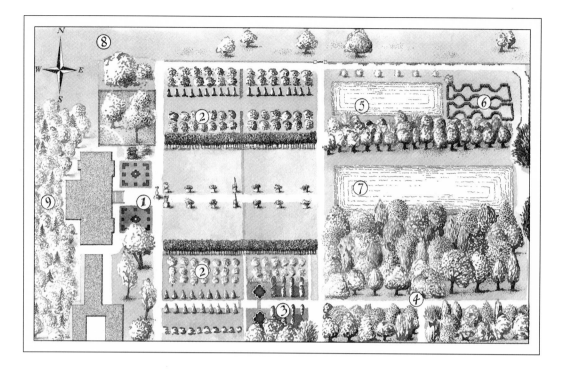

landscaping craze of the later eighteenth century. An aerial photograph taken in 1973 shows the relationship between house and garden, and their general character, to be much as it was depicted in an engraving by Badeslade in 1740. Time has stood still and it is this continuity, and the nature of the Yorke family, that form the essential background to the National Trust's restoration of the estate.

The house at Erddig in Clwyd, long and low, is built of handsome rosy brick. To the square and upright late seventeenth-century building were added rather ungainly wings, making the east façade, giving on to the garden, excessively broad for its height. Later still, the west front, from which one entered the house, was redesigned in the 1770s by James Wyatt with the addition of new stone facing. This was done partly to make the house grander and partly to resist the driving rain from the west.

The estate passed into the ownership of the Yorke family in 1733 when Simon Yorke inherited it from his uncle John Meller. It remained the property of the Yorkes

until 1973 when Philip Yorke III (the head of the family was called either Simon or Philip for over two hundred years) gave it to the National Trust with an estate of almost 2,000 acres. The continuity of ownership in this period, and the reluctance of the family to throw anything away, provides a unique background to the history of the estate.

One of the many and attractive curiosities of the Yorkes was their intense interest in their servants. The layout of the house shows how little separated were the staff and their masters – 'above stairs' and 'below stairs' scarcely existed. The servants' hall overlooked the main entrance courtyard giving them, very unusually, a clear view of visiting grandees. There was, literally it seems, no green baize door at Erddig and it must be the only country house where the billiard room was 'below stairs'. The first Philip Yorke (1743-1804) had great affection for his staff but even before his time, under John Meller, the practice was started of commissioning portraits of the servants to hang at the house. This was not a custom unique to Erddig

1. Parterre 2. Orchard 3. Dutch Garden 4. Moss Walk
5. Pool 6. Yew Niches 7. Canal
8. Park 9. Woods

but the collection there is exceptional: indeed, there are far more portraits of servants than there are of the family. Philip's great grandson, Philip Yorke II (1849-1922), added to the portraits verse descriptions of the qualities of the servants. Written in a relentlessly jaunty doggerel, and sometimes allowing art to triumph over boringly literal accuracy, they are charming in small doses. Here is part of his description of Albert Gillam, Head Gardener before the Great War:

> When those who view our gardens ask
> Who undertakes the arduous task
> Of tending all the spacious ground
> And that which is within it found,
> To such we joyfully confess
> In Gillam we a prize possess,
> And, tho' but recent on the scene,
> He a great power for good has been.

This affection for the servants, celebrated in portraits and in verse, extended into an intense interest in all the details of their life. It meant also that records of these relationships were carefully preserved at the house and give an irreplaceable insight into the history of the estate.

Merlin Waterson was one of those who helped ease the transfer of Erddig from the last Philip Yorke to the National Trust in 1973. By this time the house was semi-derelict, severely weakened by subsidence caused by coal mining, and the garden had long since been more or less totally neglected – Mr Yorke's 'gardeners' consisted of sheep that grazed peacefully up to the very walls of the house. Merlin Waterson described his first visit in 1971: 'the lodge at the entrance was derelict and roofless except for a few clinging tiles . . . Inside the park the road disintegrated into a ridge of mud flanked by almost continuous potholes . . . Most of the shutters were closed, many of the windows broken and whole sashes were missing. It was the death mask of a house which faced the two vast slag heaps in the park.' But lurking just below the surface of this desolation were the bones of the original garden shown in the 1740 engraving. There was general neglect

and the earlier planting had either become excessively overgrown or had been overlaid by subsequent schemes. Nevertheless, everything lay more or less within the unchanged framework of the original early eighteenth-century formal garden.

Badeslade's picture shows the house from the west with the neatly regimented garden sweeping away behind the house. Central to it is the axis of gravel path followed by narrow canal which are aligned on the centre of the house. This vista is closed by a *clairvoyée* at the end of the canal giving views of the countryside beyond. Broad gravel walks lie on each side flanked by brick walls and formal orchards, with the trees regularly spaced, and further brick walls flank the formal garden on either side. To the north, outside the walls, there are more formal rows of trees lying parallel to the main axis and beyond them woodland with walks among the trees. This part of the garden, Big Wood, as seen in Badeslade's engraving, with its winding paths skirting the motte of the Norman

*Clipped Portugal laurels (*Prunus lusitanicus*) seem to be planted in Versailles boxes – in fact they are planted in the ground. Portugal laurels were used in formal gardens of this period as hardy substitutes for citrus plants.*

castle of Wristlesham, has something of the character of a pioneer exercise in the picturesque. The position of the paths today, incidentally, is remarkably similar to that shown in Badeslade's picture and there remain sprawling plants of box and yew that could be the remains of hedges lining the walks. The magnificent hanging beech woods were famous in the eighteenth century. When Simon Yorke was presented at court, George III said how rarely he had seen Yorke's father Philip there, but added, 'I am not surprised at it; I have heard of his beautiful wood at Erthig.'

The formal layout was made between 1718 and 1732, that is to say, when Erddig was owned by John Meller. It was, for its time, an old-fashioned garden and this must have been a deliberate choice as Meller, a successful lawyer in London, would certainly have been in a position to know about the latest fashions in garden layout. From this early period there survive two invaluable lists (dated 1718 and 1724) of fruit grown in the garden. These include apples and pears in many varieties, apricots, peaches, nectarines, plums and grapes. Their very names have a fruity allure – who could resist a plum called 'Gush Madam', 'Green Impardigall' or 'Blue Pedrigon'? Most of the varieties listed have long since disappeared from cultivation.

The next substantial change at Erddig was the landscaping of the park by William Emes (1730-1803), a provincial landscape designer much of whose work was done in the borders between England and Wales. He had started his career as Head Gardener to Nathaniel Curzon at the time his great Adam house at Kedleston in Derbyshire was being built. He later went on to design landscape parks at, among many other places, Chirk Castle, quite near Erddig, and Powis Castle farther south. Between 1767 and 1789 Emes made repeated visits to Erddig and bills survive for the work he carried out – 'planting scattered trees of tolerable size . . . at the foot of the Hill, west front' – £211 1s. 9d. in 1778. Emes was a more than competent landscape designer and was thought of in his day as an entirely acceptable substitute for 'Capability' Brown whose only commissions in Emes's territory were for the nobility, whereas Emes specialized in the gentry. Emes was known for his plantings of naturalistic clumps of trees and careful attention to the approaches to a house by sinuous paths that afforded glimpses of the building from different angles. He did this at Erddig but, unfortunately, the visitor today usually leaves by the route which Emes planned as the entrance. Emes shared with 'Capability' Brown a particular interest in the use of water. He diverted a stream at Erddig, the Black Brook, and made a series of romantic cascades which culminated in a curious

*Avenue-like rows of eighteenth-century lime trees (*Tilia × europaea*) flank the canal. They still bear signs of having been pleached in their youth.*

feature, the 'cup and saucer', which he made in the park in 1774 to the north-west of the house. Here the swirling waters of the stream are gathered into a saucer-shaped basin at the centre of which is a wide hole through which the waters flow in a cylindrical cascade. Near by is a nine-teenth-century hydraulic ram, an ingenious device in which a flow of water provides the power for a simple kind of pump. Here it took water all the way to the house half a mile away and still has sufficient pressure to provide water for the fountains in the parterre under the east front.

The eighteenth-century landscaping activities were confined, however, to the north and west of the house. The formal garden to the east was untouched and it is likely that this conservatism was due to the antiquarian tastes of Philip Yorke I (1743-1804). For the same reason, too, no doubt, the garden front of the house was left plainly finished in brick when in the 1770s the west front was given its swagger new façade of stone. The Yorkes repeatedly showed this streak of independent conservatism. Simon Yorke III (1811-94), for example, took great delight in his Head Gardener James Phillips, who was contemptuous of foreign plant names:

Old-fashioned, in his notions, he
With foreign names did not agree
'Quatre-Saisons' 'Quarter-Sessions' meant,
The 'Bijou' as the 'By Joe' went;
'Glory to die John' was the rose,
Which each as 'Gloire de Dijon' knows . . .

Badeslade's engraving shows to the west of the house an imposing entrance – forecourts with, in the centre, an elaborate wrought-iron screen and gates. All this was swept away in Emes's landscaping to allow the park to run up to the house. The screen and gates were made in the 1720s by Robert Davies of Bersham. In 1721 Richard Jones, the agent, had written to John Meller, 'Robt. Davis the Smith has been ill of an Ague or the Iron Gate had been up before this time.' Davies was a smith of genius and although the gates he made for Erddig were lost, others survived and, as we shall see, came to Erddig.

Towards the end of the eighteenth century the walls flanking the central vista were removed and in their place hedges of beech (*Fagus sylvatica*) were planted. At about the same time, in the 1770s, rows of limes (*Tilia × europaea*) were planted by Philip Yorke I on either side of the canal, making the vista even more emphatic. These limes survive and there are some signs that they were pleached or clipped to form 'walls'.

The next important changes in the garden took place in 1857 when a new avenue of Irish yews (*Taxus baccata* 'Fastigiata') was planted flanking a new vista south of the

*L*ooking west across the pool towards the house. The tall tree in the centre, showing its fine autumn colour, is a swamp cypress (Taxodium distichum).

central gravel walk. At the same time a decorative brick alcove with a seat was made to open the new vista from the house end. At the end of the yew avenue steps lead up to a formal rose garden of 'Dutch design'. Before the end of the nineteenth century standard-trained Portugal laurels (*Prunus lusitanica*) in Versailles boxes were planted flanking the main vista looking towards the canal.

In the very early twentieth century new parterres were made under the windows of the east front, with a pattern of L-shaped beds, mounds of box and fountains with moulded stone surrounds. The fountains are much earlier; supplied by Blashfield's in 1861, they formed part of a previous formal scheme on the same site. Later still, in 1912–13, the walls to the south and north of the new parterres were given very ornamental scalloped Dutch gables so that they resembled garden pavilions. As many contemporary photographs show, the garden remained well cared for until World War II. The war was a decisive event in the history of many gardens, a watershed after which neglect set in, weeds flourished, walls crumbled and trees went unpruned.

In 1973, the National Trust's report on Erddig made terrifying reading – the house was 'undermined by coal extraction . . . severe subsidence. Dry rot, damaged stonework, leaking roof and collapsed garden walls.' Its rescue was acknowledged to be 'the most ambitious, extensive and difficult ever undertaken by the Trust'. The house alone, despite its wonderful contents, was not, perhaps, architecturally sufficiently distinguished to justify the rescue. What *did* justify it was the value of the ensemble – house, contents and garden, all of which bore the stamp of the Yorke family and which, to an exceptional degree, preserved different periods of the past. The guiding philosophy behind the restoration of the house and garden was to honour the Yorke family, in its full and glorious eccentricity, and to keep intact the varying stylistic overlays. A further limitation was that the restoration of the garden was restricted to what could subsequently be properly maintained.

Overgrown nineteenth-century Irish yews (Taxus baccata 'Fastigiata') *were cut down to stumps but have resumed their elegant shape. They form an avenue leading to the Dutch Garden and the Moss Walk.*

Apart from the essential task of giving order to chaos there were difficult problems from the start. It was decided to revert, as far as the main structure of the garden was concerned, to the formal garden as shown in Badeslade's engraving. Many of the formal ingredients survived – the canal and its flanking pool, the central vista (even though choked with overgrown planting) and the enclosing old brick walls (even though gravely dilapidated). Many of the later additions fitted in with the essential principles of the original formal garden – for example the rows of limes on either side of the canal and the Victorian yew walk and the new south vista. All these have been retained but their role in the formal layout has been sharpened, given more purpose.

In Emes's park, the carefully orchestrated setting for approaches to the house from the west, land subsidence had changed the lie of the land, creating precipitous hollows where none had been before, and had also caused the Black Brook to wander from its true, artfully meandering path, which thus affected the water supply to the 'cup and saucer'. The expense of reshaping the land to its original contours was out of the question. The stream was redirected back to its original course by banking up the ground at strategic points. The land in the park was in fairly good shape as it had been used for grazing sheep. Many of Emes's trees survived – chiefly lime, horse chestnut and oak now in splendid maturity. But there were many dead or dying trees and much surgery had to be carried out on mutilated or diseased specimens. The alteration in the water table caused by subsidence had deprived many trees of water, with the result that much of the topmost growth had died, giving the trees a characteristic stag's-head appearance. Nearer the house there were some very large wellingtonias (*Sequoiadendron giganteum*) and other conifers. Some of these were felled but, although they were trees that Emes could not have known, many were left as fine trees and representative examples of characteristically Victorian planting.

Immediately north of the formal garden, in Big Wood,

there was much clearing of congested planting, particularly of larch (*Larix decidua*), revealing splendid limes which must date from Emes's time. Once dead timber and excessive saplings were cleared it was possible once again to follow the paths exactly as they are shown in the Badeslade engraving.

Within the formal garden there were great problems to be faced. Some of the trees fringing the central vista had grown very large, among them some elderly beeches, the remains of the late eighteenth-century hedges. Three-quarters of these were on their last legs and required for reasons of safety to be removed as soon as possible. The remainder, however, were in the prime of ripe old age and in a different context would certainly have been earmarked for preservation. But to retain these mature beeches, fine trees in the wrong place, would have made it impossible to restore the formal layout of orchards. Furthermore, restoration must always take the long-term view; and the life expectancy of these beeches was not great. Their removal in 1974 was an instructive example of the complicated problems that can arise in garden restoration. First, it was decided that the whole trees, roots and all, should be taken out. A JCB digger excavated deeply round the roots and the trees were pulled over with a metal hawser attached to a winch on a crane. The wood was then sawn up, retaining what was good for timber. Disposing of the remaining stumps – each of which weighed between ten and fifteen tons – was a tricky business. They were lifted with the crane on to a dumper truck which took them to a field east of the Formal Garden to be buried.

It was foreseen that the removal of this very substantial windbreak could expose the rows of old limes flanking the canal, so when the beeches were felled, the limes were lopped by 9m/30ft to reduce their exposure. This proved successful and none has suffered. What was not foreseen was that the removal of the beeches allowed surplus water to gather in the soil – which had previously been absorbed by the immense root systems of the old trees – and this has meant installing quite extensive drainage *after* the formal

*T*op: *The apple orchard on the north side of the formal garden.*
Bottom: Planting in the Dutch Garden closely follows a 1900 description –
Clematis × jackmanii, Acer negundo *'Variegatum' and agapanthus.*

in 1908 at the Forest Lodge entrance to the estate. During World War II, when the American army occupied the park, the gates were threatened by large army lorries and were dismantled and stored. The Trust restored them, again in the original blacksmith's shop, and they were placed at the east end of the canal where they elegantly close the formal vista. They are painted a handsome dark blue-grey picked out in gold – exactly the colours for ironwork approved of by Celia Fiennes – 'blew with gold tops'.

It was possible to restore some of the later features of the garden whose layout had essentially survived. Much was known about the Edwardian parterres under the east front from old photographs and other documents and, indeed, the shapes of the original beds were still visible, slightly sunken, in the turf. Lying on either side of a gravel path that leads up to the garden doors of the house, the parterres consist of a pattern of L-shaped and square beds interspersed with mounds of box (*Buxus sempervirens*) which survive from the original planting and were clipped back into shape. At the centre of each parterre is a Victorian fountain surrounded by scalloped stone surrounds. In the past the planting here would have been almost entirely of bedding plants but this was thought too labour-intensive and a compromise of permanent and seasonal bedding is used. The square beds each have a square cushion of *Santolina chamaecyparissus* fringed with the sinister black grass-like *Ophiopogon planiscapus nigrescens*. Each of the L-shaped beds is edged with silver-leaved *Festuca glauca*. Seasonal planting, put in place for spring and summer, may vary from year to year but typical planting in each of the L-shaped beds might be lily-flowered tulips emerging from forget-me-nots. The summer bedding usually consists of impatiens, antirrhinums and heliotrope, all of which, without being minutely authentic, give a jolly Edwardian flavour. Adding to this character are several climbing roses trained to the flanking pavilion walls, most of which date from the late nineteenth and early twentieth centuries. Among them are 'May Queen' (1898), 'Violette' (1921) and 'Goldfinch' (1907).

The so-called 'Dutch Garden' on the south side of the formal garden dates from the same period as the east parterres. This has been restored with the help of a description in the *Journal of Horticulture and Home Farmer* that appeared in 1909. It reads, 'The garden on the South Side is of Dutch design, the display being made chiefly by Roses and annuals. A pretty feature also is the Jackmani Clematises and Dorothy Perkins Roses trained over Negundo aceroides.' These beds have been replanted using all the plants mentioned. The beds are 7m/23ft square and a pair of them lies on either side of the path that forms part of the south vista. Each pair of beds is set in grass and backed by yew hedges. In the centre of each there is an *Acer negundo* 'Variegatum' and, climbing up it, *Clematis × jackmanii* and the rose 'Dorothy Perkins' which, incidentally, was introduced only in 1902 and thus made its way to north Wales with almost indecent haste. The whole bed is edged in pink thrift (*Armeria maritima*), divided into a grid by strips of London pride, and within the spaces thus formed are blocks of low-growing modern 'patio' roses, 'Marlena' and 'Kim'. In each corner there is a 2.4m/8ft pillar with, trained up it, *Clematis × jackmanii* and 'Dorothy Perkins', and clumps of agapanthus ('Loch Hope' and 'Ben Hope') at its feet.

Immediately preceding these flower beds the path is flanked by scalloped pool-like enclosures with exactly the same shape of moulding as those in the east parterres. These had been part of the original scheme but it is not known if they ever contained water and they are now planted with the Hybrid Perpetual rose 'Reine des Violettes' which is trained to a horizontal framework of bamboos that fills the pool. This horizontal training means, also, that the surface of the pool is covered with vigorous upward-growing flowering shoots. Looking down the long south vista all this is invisible, for it is hidden behind buttresses of yew and is suddenly revealed as one climbs the gentle steps that lead to it. It is bold planting in an otherwise calm setting and certainly provides what the Edwardians would have called a *coup d'oeil*. A path continues the vista east into the woods along the Victorian Moss Walk which had been a sombre place full of holly, laurel and yew, considered appropriately gloomy for melancholy walks.

Clothing the brick wall that runs along the southern edge of this walk are many varieties of ivy which have a decidedly late-Victorian atmosphere appropriate to that part of the garden. Erddig holds the National Collection of *Hedera* cultivars and it is a good example of such a collection, both helping the cause of the conservation of garden plants and finding a home where it makes a contribution to the character and interest of the garden.

THE ESSENCE OF ERDDIG

Looking back towards the broad east front of the house, long and low, across the mirror-like canal, there is the unmistakable impression of something French. It is a country squire's vision of Versailles but with no nonsense, transported to the wilds of north Wales. The house itself is firmly related to the formal garden: the central vista is aligned on the garden doors and stairs on the east front, and the flanking parallel vistas are also pinned down by architectural features – a pedimented pavilion and the ornamental gateway leading into a walled garden. This gives the house and garden a peaceful unity which is not interrupted as it flows harmoniously into the landscape. It is a unity that allows, also, the easy accommodation of later and possibly heterogeneous features – the Edwardian parterres, the walls of pyramid-trained fruit trees and pleached limes and, a startling oddity in this context, the soaring swamp cypress that pops up with such insouciant cheek alongside the north vista.

The sound rule, rarely broken satisfactorily, that the more formal ingredients of a garden should be placed near the house and the layout should become increasingly informal as it approaches the countryside, is certainly exemplified at Erddig. At the garden end of the south vista a curved wooden bench, in the shade of a brick pavilion

built into the garden wall, commands an axial view. A gravel path runs down an avenue of Irish yews on either side of which is a low box hedge forming a Greek 'key' pattern. At the end of the yew avenue steps rise to an arrangement of simple square parterres. The gravel path continues, momentarily interrupted by further steps flanked by buttresses of clipped yew, and then plunges into the Moss Walk and the woodland; at the far end, where the wood stops and fields begin, there is a distant view of countryside. This simple path, like the plain thread of a necklace, makes a solid link for the various decorative devices which are strung together along it.

The airy walls of pleached lime give a feeling of firmness of purpose without the definitive enclosure that brick walls make. The formal part of the garden is, in fact, surrounded by brick walls, but the hardness of their lines is modulated by the espaliered fruit trees and climbing plants that clothe them. The special quality of country formality which at Erddig is a distinctive ingredient is dignified without being solemn for cheerfulness keeps breaking in; in spring, with the blossom of fruit and daffodils in full flow, and in winter, when the sparkling variegated leaves of the pyramid hollies that run along the south vista, and the burnished leaves of the clipped Portugal laurels down the central vista, introduce a sprightly note amid the gentlemanly formality.

The Moss Walk was a Victorian idea – a shady place of evergreens, holly and laurel, in which the visitor could indulge agreeably gloomy thoughts.

CLAREMONT LANDSCAPE GARDEN

*T*HE garden at Claremont has all sorts of claims on our interest. It is an extremely attractive 'forgotten' garden recently brought back to life in a remarkable restoration; it dates from that period in the history of gardening when a revolution in taste created the English landscape garden; and several of the best eighteenth-century gardeners influenced it. A description of what happened at Claremont in the early eighteenth century vividly traces a decisive change in garden taste and much of the evidence for it can still be seen by visitors to the garden today. In addition, the subsequent development of the garden and the way in which earlier features were suppressed tells a fascinating story about changes in garden fashion. The fact that many ingredients

Above: Vanbrugh's Belvedere commands views down a beech-hedged walk to the Bowling Green.
Opposite: Charles Bridgeman's turf amphitheatre was completely hidden by undergrowth
and large trees when restoration started.

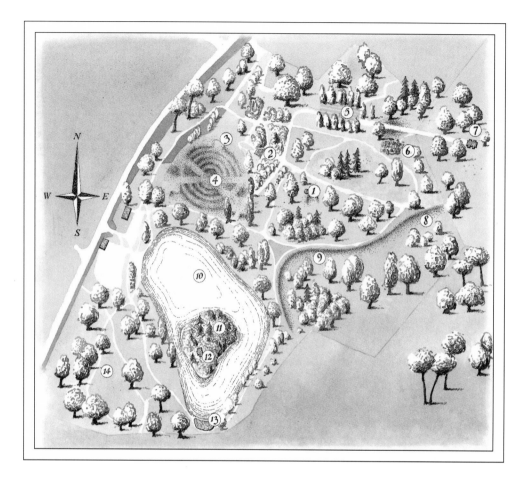

have been introduced by different hands at different periods has also made its restoration an especially interesting one. In its day it was one of the most famous gardens in England and, although it was all but lost, the various stages of its development are extremely well documented, which has been crucial for its restoration.

The first person to leave a mark on the garden was Sir John Vanbrugh, the Restoration playwright and architect, who bought the estate for his own use in about 1710 in order to be near his aged mother at Claygate. The estate, near Esher in Surrey, commended itself to Vanbrugh, 'the situation being singularly Romantik'. As it happened, his mother died very shortly afterwards and he sold the estate

to Sir Thomas Pelham-Holles who in 1714 became Earl of Clare and Duke of Newcastle in the following year. It was he who gave the estate its new name – Clare-mont. He retained Vanbrugh, who built a gigantic mansion and in the hills above it at the highest point of the estate a battlemented prospect tower or belvedere of a distinctly medieval character. Little is known about what Vanbrugh himself did in the layout of gardens but he certainly had a very vivid sense of the monumental presence of buildings in a landscape, as he had shown at Blenheim Palace in Oxfordshire and at Castle Howard in North Yorkshire. A poem by Sir Samuel Garth gives a lively contemporary opinion of his magical powers:

1. Round House 2. Nine Pin Steps 3. Viewpoint 4. Amphitheatre 5. Bowling Green
6. Camellia Terrace 7. Belvedere 8. Brown's Ha-Ha 9. Kent's Ha-Ha 10. Lake
11. Island 12. Temple 13. Grotto 14. Viewpoint

If, by Apollo taught, he touch the lyre
Stones mount in columns, palaces aspire,
And rocks are animated by his fire,
'Tis he can paint in verse those rising hills
Their gentle valleys, and their silver rills.

Vanbrugh formed close associations with a number of garden designers, one of whom, Charles Bridgeman, was consulted in 1716 about laying out the garden at Claremont. They had already worked together at Grimsthorpe in Lincolnshire, at Stowe in Buckinghamshire and at Eastbury in Dorset.

Bridgeman, whose 'Fancy could not be bounded', was a key figure in the early days of English landscape design. He was breaking away from the rigidity of avenues, alleys and parterres which we see in Kip's engravings, though he was still devoted to formality. But he was aware that views of the surrounding countryside were part of a garden's charm and at Claremont, north-west of the house and completely unrelated to it, he built bastions which formed platforms for viewing the scenery. Some time before 1726 he added, on a slope above his bastions, an extraordinary turfed amphitheatre which sweeps down the hill in a series of terraces at first concave and then convex. This feature, extremely rare in English gardens, was both a dramatic piece of landscaping and also provided a series of changing vantage points from which to admire other parts of the garden. In Italian Renaissance gardens there are many examples of stage-like settings, and the Claremont amphitheatre closely resembles that which was built at the Vatican Belvedere in the early sixteenth century. Below the amphitheatre Bridgeman made a pool, a perfect circle, showing that he certainly had not thrown off all formality. An engraving of about 1725 shows the pool encircled by a double avenue of trees with an obelisk in the centre.

Shortly after all this was completed, Vanbrugh died and the Duke of Newcastle turned to William Kent – 'the wild Goth' as Alexander Pope called him. Kent was a dazzling figure who, with no advantages of education or birth, was adopted by the circle of Lord Burlington and was deeply influential on it. He was an artist, architect and garden designer of whom Horace Walpole said in a famous phrase, 'He leaped the fence, and saw that all nature was a garden.' For Kent gardening was a kind of picture-making using natural features – trees, water and the lie of the land – together with ornaments and buildings, to direct the eye and to form the composition. Sir Thomas Robinson's remark of 1734 – 'There is a new taste in gardening just arisen . . . Mr Kent's notion of gardening, viz., to lay them out and work without either line or level' – gives the idea of an artist confronting a canvas. Robinson added that, 'This method of gardening is the more agreeable as, when finished, it has the appearance of beautiful nature.'

When Kent started work at Claremont in 1729, he was chiefly concerned with making Bridgeman's garden much less formal. The viewing bastion that Bridgeman had made to the south was removed and in this part of the garden Kent introduced 'sunk paths', as they are called on his drawing for the garden. This was a sinuous ha-ha which wound its way along the boundary separating the park from the grazing land beyond.

The frenzy of gardening activity that went on at Claremont between Bridgeman's starting in 1716 and the completion of Kent's work in the 1740s is chronicled in several exceptionally valuable plans and pictures. An engraving from *Vitruvius Britannicus* of 1725 shows the culmination of Bridgeman's work. In 1738 John Rocque made a very detailed engraved plan of the garden, bordered by detailed views of many of the garden buildings, which is a priceless record of the work done by Kent. A subsequent plan by Rocque done in 1750, by which time Kent's new plantings had blurred the formal outline, strikingly demonstrates the effects of Kent's deformalizing. The crisp outlines of, for example, the bowling green, have been eroded by Kent's plantings (often of beeches) and he had opened up the rigid plan of the garden to create harmonious passages from one part to another. Furthermore, a series of five oil paintings dating from the 1740s give a wonderfully vivid account of the garden in this transitional period.

The many new buildings introduced by Kent, some of them carefully fitted into existing arrangements, served the purpose both of providing ornament and of emphasizing some scene worth contemplating. For example, running north downhill from the mount of Vanbrugh's belvedere was an avenue interrupted by the large rectangular bowling green. Here, on the west side, Kent introduced a little classical pavilion which greatly animated that part of the garden. Many of his buildings are provided with a stage-like setting, a small apron of grass and 'wings' of trees which gives a sense of drama.

The work Kent did on Bridgeman's formal pool shows exactly the change that was overcoming garden styles at this period. He remodelled the pool, removing Bridgeman's formal double circle of trees, and made it into a serpentine lake with an island connected to the shore by an elegant bridge. On the island he built a classical pavilion, called The New House on Rocque's 1738 plan, which was intended for picnicking and fishing. On the southwest shore of the lake Kent made a cascade over which the stream feeding the lake flowed. His drawing for it, dated between 1729 and 1734, shows a classical pedimented building from which water gushes in three elegant arches.

Kent died in 1748 and in the years after his death little changed in the garden except that his cascade was altered into a picturesque grotto ornamented with spars and stalactites. Grottoes had become fashionable features in landscape gardens by the second half of the eighteenth century. Alexander Pope had built an early example for his Twickenham villa in 1719-21 but it was not until the 1740s that the craze for grottoes set in. It is very possible that the Claremont grotto was made by the most famous grotto-makers of the day, Josiah Lane and his son Joseph, who came from Wiltshire where they worked on the grottoes at Stourhead, Bowood and at Fonthill. They also created a grotto at Painshill in the early 1760s, and they may have made the nearby Claremont grotto at the same time.

The Duke of Newcastle died in 1768 and the following year the estate was sold to Lord Clive – 'Clive of India'. He demolished the Vanbrugh mansion and in 1769 commissioned a new house from 'Capability' Brown and Henry Holland. Brown also worked on the grounds – obscuring the amphitheatre with new planting and altering the route of the Portsmouth road to take it farther away from the lake. By 1786 when Claremont was visited by Thomas Jefferson, the future President of the United States, these new arrangements must have been fairly immature. At all events Jefferson, a discerning garden visitor, was unimpressed and all he recorded of it in his journal was: 'Ld. Clive's. Nothing remarkable.'

After Lord Clive's death the estate changed hands several times until in 1816 it became the home of the Prince Regent's daughter Princess Charlotte, on her marriage to Prince Leopold of Saxe-Coburg. Princess Charlotte died the following year but Prince Leopold remained at Claremont where he made many changes. In the garden he built a large camellia house which was described by J.C. Loudon in 1830 in his usual robust fashion: 'a greenhouse on an eminence in a very bad style; it is composed of large painted windows and fan lights like an assemblage of shop fronts.' The camellia house was designed by John Papworth who also designed a Gothic summer-house, gateways and an aviary. Some of the camellias remain and the surviving terrace has a railing which bears Prince Leopold's cipher.

It was under Prince Leopold that much distinctively Victorian planting was added to the garden. Two plants in particular, which came to dominate the garden, date from this time: the dangerously invasive *Rhododendron ponticum*, introduced in 1763 but not widely used until the nineteenth century; and laurel (*Prunus laurocerasus*), the archetypal spreading evergreen of gloomy Victorian shrubberies. He also planted some outstanding specimens of recently introduced conifers such as the Chinese fir (*Cunninghamia lanceolata*), which was introduced in 1804 and is one of the best specimens in England, and the Japanese red

cedar (*Cryptomeria japonica*) which was introduced in 1842.

Claremont subsequently became a favourite place of Prince Leopold's niece, later Queen Victoria, and it remained in the ownership of the royal family until 1922. However, after the Stock Market collapse in 1929 the estate was broken up. The great house, never closely related to the landscape garden, became a school and the remainder of the estate passed through various hands. In 1949 the pleasure grounds were acquired by the National Trust and were managed by the local council. In 1975 a benefactor donated £65,000 for the restoration of the grounds.

When work started there was, except for a sea of rhododendrons and laurel, very little that was visible in the garden. The belvedere stood proud above the tree tops – 'High on the wooded hill,' as Dorothy Stroud wrote at the time, 'the belvedere ravaged by time and vandals, stands as a defiant reminder of Vanbrugh's affection for "Something of the Castle Air".' The lake was all but concealed in densely tangled thickets of undergrowth and the park had reverted to nature, congested with countless birches, sprung up from seed blown across from Esher common. In the absence of the ruling hand of art nature had reimposed itself – the laurels and Pontic rhododendrons had seen their chance and let rip, swamping less robust plantings. At this time Claremont, despite its great fame in the first half of the eighteenth century, was a forgotten garden. A booklet published by Dorothy Stroud gave the essential history of the garden and served as a reminder of its past glories.

The first task of the restoration was to clear the undergrowth to see what was there. When the outlines of the original layout become so blurred, it is easy to destroy the very evidence that one is looking for – the pattern of original planting. At Claremont the restorers proceeded cautiously. For example, the laurels and rhododendrons were cut back to 600mm/2ft stumps – from which, if necessary for the layout that was revealed, they would

A simple grotto looks out towards William Kent's island in the lake.
The crisply defined island edges accord with the 1740s
paintings shown on pages 26–7.

quickly grow again. As this work progressed and as successive layers of the garden design revealed themselves, it was surprising to find how much of the earliest work of Vanbrugh and Bridgeman survived. The original approach to Vanbrugh's belvedere had been totally obscured, but trees remained from that period. The essential lie of the land had remained, too, allowing restoration to the appearance of Rocque's 1738 plan before the effects of Kent's remodelling were fully visible. The belvedere lies on land belonging to Claremont School, who allowed the National Trust to plant new beech hedges on either side of the grassy walk that sweeps uphill from the bowling green to the belvedere. At the bottom of the last 'step' before the belvedere Vanbrugh had made two flanking platforms of turf, like ancient earthworks, as a dramatic prelude to his castellated building. These bastions, of appropriately medieval aspect, were reshaped and turfed. The bowling green itself was cleared and levelled and surrounded with yew which is being clipped into hedges. Continuing this vista downhill, an avenue of common lime (*Tilia* × *europaea*) was planted. All this reasserts the essential formality shown in the plan. The main axis, although formal in execution, actually follows the spine of the hill, a happy marriage of art and nature. Here, in an area relatively untouched by subsequent schemes, it was fairly straightforward to revert to a single moment in the history of the garden. Elsewhere, however, things were much more difficult.

As work continued clearing the ground, a tree survey was done, plotting all good trees on a map. It was also possible to produce a composite map showing these trees and the existing layout and the chief features from the *Vitruvius Britannicus* plan, the Rocque surveys and a plan dating from 1820. This revealed very clearly how much survived from each period. In the clearing, large areas were left untouched to avoid the loss of scale which total felling can cause. There were also certain modern housing developments fringing the garden which it was thought best to leave well concealed and, in one case, quick remedial

*The island pavilion was designed by William Kent for fishing and picnicking parties. The tall beeches (*Fagus sylvatica*) shading it date from the 1740s.*

*T*op: *The invasive* Rhododendron ponticum *was a nineteenth-century addition to the planting about the lake. Bottom: A grove of sweet chestnuts (*Castanea sativa*) was planted in the eighteenth century on the slopes east of the lake.*

planting of a belt of western hemlock (*Tsuga heterophylla*) swiftly obliterated the view of an especially unfortunate modern estate that was perilously close to the garden east of the lake.

The most exciting discovery of all as clearing progressed was that of faint but definite terracing that followed the shape of Bridgeman's turf amphitheatre. On either side the original flanking bastions of Bridgeman's layout were also discovered concealed by dense undergrowth. At the foot of the amphitheatre there were several cedars of Lebanon (*Cedrus libani*) which would have interfered with a complete restoration to Bridgeman's design and these were felled; but others, nearer the lake, were left. From the felled trees it was discovered by ring-counting that they were planted in 1770 – thus dating from 'Capability' Brown's work in this part of the garden. Once the amphitheatre had been cleared completely, the surviving outlines were carefully marked out and a JCB with a grading-blade was used to reshape the terraces. When this was completed the soil was prepared for grass-seeding and a hard-wearing general grass-mix was sown. With today's much greater numbers of visitors to the garden than was ever the case in its heyday, access to the amphitheatre has to be restricted. Wooden benches, painted very pale grey and copied from those in the 1740s paintings, have been placed at the top of the amphitheatre and on each of the bastion platforms. The double semi-circular avenues of trees sweeping down on either side of the amphitheatre, shown in contemporary paintings and plans, have been replanted with common limes which were identified from a few surviving trees. Seeing this area today, one of the most remarkable of all garden sights, it is unbelievable that fifteen years ago it was invisible, lost in a jungle of self-sown plants.

The restoration of the lake below the amphitheatre was a major task. Its shores were obscured by undergrowth rising to 4.8m/16ft and its banks were crumbling. The water was deeply silted up and the island and its pavilion were hidden with a confusion of overgrown plants.

One of the problems about removing undergrowth is that the ground below is exposed to erosion; the undergrowth had, in fact, served to preserve the essential outlines of the lake. The surroundings of the lake were cleared, leaving strategic clumps of planting here and there, and it was then comprehensively dredged. The lake had originally been fed by water piped from nearby common land, which had provided an abundant supply for Kent's dramatic cascade. Some time between the wars the pipe had been severed and the only supply of water was a trickle from nearby springs which in the summer was often insufficient. Furthermore the edges of the lake had become shallow and beach-like, exposing a margin of mud when the water was low in the summer. The margins of the lake and of the island were deeply dredged and the banks consolidated with elm boards, a procedure called campshedding. Elm at that time, the height of Dutch elm disease, was in plentiful and cheap supply.

An essential point of an ornamental lake in an eighteenth-century landscape garden is the idea of smooth turf sweeping down to the crisply defined banks which enclose sheets of mirror-like water. Indeed, in the 1740s paintings the banks of the lake at Claremont seem to be edged with neatly laid white stone. No trace of this was found in the restoration and the banks were redefined and strengthened with elm planks which were attached to iron anchor-plates fixed into banks. The dredgings were used to build up the shores of the lake, behind the elm boards, where they provided fertile ground for the resown turf. Elm has the reputation for great longevity when totally submerged but it has been found at Claremont that it rots quickly in a half-submerged position and it already needs replacing. A more satisfactory substitute is pressure-treated softwood.

The banks of the island were treated in the same way and much clearing of scrub was done. The very fine beeches (*Fagus sylvatica*) had become congested and a few were felled. Ring-counting showed that they dated from Kent's time in the garden. The pavilion – both an eyecatcher and a pleasure dome – was derelict and roofless and had to be rebuilt. The restoration complete, visitors could see how the pavilion, half veiled by the beautiful planting of beeches, gave the lake its purpose.

The grotto to the south of the lake well illustrates the paradox of buildings made to resemble ruins – they may in time become too ruinous and need restoration; as Dezallier d'Argenville wrote in 1712, 'Grottoes being ruinous in character . . . are very subject to ruin.' Here the roots of self-sown saplings had weakened the structure. They were all carefully removed, disturbing it as little as possible, and blocks of stone were put back and fixed with stainless-steel bars. Originally the path round the lake passed in front of the grotto, allowing the eighteenth-century visitor to step into the gloomy recesses and indulge an agreeably melancholy frisson. The numbers of visitors to the garden today would forbid that and instead the path now goes above the grotto and laurels are being encouraged to form a tunnel at that point to provide the transition from light to shade that is the essence of the grotto experience.

The manner in which the visitor proceeds about a landscape garden is a very important part of the way it weaves its spell. Paths must have purpose but they should not be aggressively dictatorial and they must, of course, lead the visitor to viewpoints and objects of interest. The paths at Claremont have been restored substantially to their eighteenth-century pattern. They have been resurfaced in a natural material, hoggin from Worms Heath near by, which corresponds closely to the material originally used for the paths. It consists of smooth pebbles and sand bound together with clay which makes not only a hard-wearing but also an attractive surface. Kent's ha-ha, in basically good condition, has been cleared out and sumps installed to improve drainage.

The atmosphere of the landscape garden at Claremont has now been reinstated. Details remain to be restored; Kent's temple, known as Nine Pin Alley, of which only the steps survive, must one day be replaced. Already well

over 1,000 new trees have been planted throughout the garden, and planting continues. Many landscape gardens have too much planting of a single period, and suddenly decline as the trees come to the end of their life. To give continuity, a constant programme of replanting and tree maintenance is needed.

THE ESSENCE OF CLAREMONT

'The whole is a place wherein to tarry with secure delight, or saunter with perpetual amusement,' wrote Thomas Whately in his *Observations on Modern Gardening* (1770). At Claremont there is never any feeling that the visitor must make a forced march ticking off its delights. There is both a feeling of repose and many places to sit, but also a feeling that there is plenty more to see.

A starting point from which to grasp the essence of Claremont is the gravelled Camellia Terrace with calm views across the park. On the slopes below are fine mature trees – beech, oak and Spanish chestnut – with mossy hillocks in the shade. There is no excitement of rare plants, and no statues or temples are to be seen. Behind, farther up the hill, winding paths lead to the Bowling Green, which is in turn linked to the belvedere hill by an alley of clipped beech hedges.

At the other end of the Bowling Green an avenue of limes continues down the hill. A further avenue joins it at an angle and continues down the hill where the wandering visitor may suddenly find himself at the top of the amphitheatre. This is the site of the mausoleum which Prince Leopold built for his wife, Princess Charlotte. On either side a semi-circular double avenue of young limes sweeps down the hill. The view is an unlikely one, with the land sculpted into giant grassy terraces forming a monumental geometric design.

At the foot of the amphitheatre, occupying centre stage, is the lake with its curving banks and wooded island emphasized by Kent's pavilion, tantalizingly half-concealed in foliage. But the stage is framed, dramatically, by giant cedars of Lebanon, some of the finest examples of the tree in Great Britain. Although they were introduced around the middle of the seventeenth century, most specimens were killed off in England by the disastrous winter of 1740. These examples are probably among the trees that 'Capability' Brown added in this part of the garden after 1769.

In the later history of the English landscape garden ornaments and buildings became increasingly less important elements and the ingredients were restricted to trees, water and the land itself. Here at Claremont, however, and in other landscape gardens of the first half of the eighteenth century, the placing of buildings and ornaments in relation to the naturalistic ingredients is an essential part of the art of garden-making. William Kent did this with consummate skill. He was aware both of the building in its immediate surroundings of trees and grass and of its effect on the larger setting.

The position of a building or ornament served also to direct the visitor's gaze to other beauties. At his great garden at Rousham in Oxfordshire, which is later than Claremont, statues and buildings look outwards, directing the view over the curving river Cherwell and the fields beyond. But Claremont is an inward-looking garden, and except for the grazing land beyond the ha-ha there were no views revealing what lay beyond its confines. Loudon disapproved of this, writing that the grounds 'are rather deficient in distant prospect'. But it is the very essence of Claremont that it is a self-contained world of its own in which nature is ordered according to the rules of art.

*A*n octagonal brick summer-house – with a hint
of the Gothic cottage – in a clearing
to the west of the lake.

PAINSWICK ROCOCO GARDEN

ARDENS may disappear with bewildering ease. It is possible for an outstanding garden to be lost, forgotten about and eventually re-discovered. That is what happened at Painswick and what enabled the present owner to embark on a remarkable private restoration. The story starts, rather obliquely, in 1972 with the rediscovery by the architectural historian John Harris of the paintings of Thomas Robins the Elder. Robins painted enchanting topographical views, delicately worked in watercolour and gouache on vellum. Frequently they are embellished with beautifully executed borders of flowers, shells and birds. Although he adopted a naive method of showing perspective, his paintings are full of valuable detail. He was a shadowy figure who was

*Eighteenth-century landscape gardens mixed Gothic and classical styles of architecture with relish.
Above: The Doric Seat, with its rusticated columns, is a classical garden building of gentlemanly
demeanour. Opposite: From the Fish Pond the ground rises towards the Gothic Red House.*

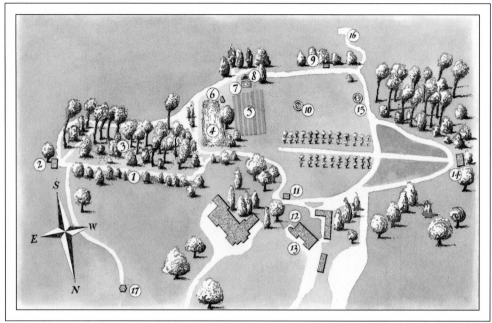

born in Charlton Kings near Cheltenham in 1716; he moved to Bath in 1760, where he died in 1770. He painted several houses and gardens in the Midlands and clearly enjoyed some success in his lifetime, but after his death he was forgotten. Few of his paintings survive but there remains a precious handful in the ownership of the family that built Painswick House.

Charles Hyett, a prosperous lawyer, came from a family anciently established in Gloucestershire and he built Painswick House in the 1730s. It was built on hilly land to the north of Painswick, commanding fine views over the village, and its airy position was reflected in its original name – Buenos Aires. Charles Hyett died in 1738 and his son Benjamin inherited it and made the garden at Painswick. Bishop Pococke visited it in 1757 and wrote, 'We came to Painswick, a market town prettily situated and on the side of a hill, and esteem'd an exceeding good air; just above it Mr Hyett built an house of hewn stone, in a fine situation, and made a very pretty garden; before it is a court with statues and sphynxes, and beyond that a lawn for the grand entrance; the garden is on an hanging ground

from the house in the vale, and on a rising ground on the other side and at the end; all are cut into walks through wood and adorn'd with water and buildings, and in one part is the kitchen garden.' The house and garden were painted by Thomas Robins in 1748 and this painting survives at Painswick, owned by Benjamin Hyett's descendant Lord Dickinson, who inherited the estate in 1955.

The painting shows a handsome Georgian house standing four-square with the land falling away in front of it. The garden corresponds to Bishop Pococke's description. At the front of the house, facing south, is an apron-shaped forecourt with statues. Behind the house, apparently rising up on vertiginously steep ground ('hanging' as Bishop Pococke says) is the rococo garden. In fact all this is hidden, enfolded in a narrow combe immediately behind the house and Robins's old-fashioned bird's-eye view gives a completely misleading impression. The site was protected from the prevailing south-westerly winds and provided the seclusion for a secret garden, visible only from the upper windows of the north façade of the house.

What kind of garden was it and how does it fit into the

1. Beech Walk 2. Gothic Alcove 3. Snowdrop Grove 4. Fish Pond 5. Bowling Green 6. Ram House 7. Plunge Pool 8. Spring Head 9. Doric Seat 10. Pond 11. Eagle House 12. Melon Ground 13. The Stables 14. Red House 15. Pond 16. Viewpoint 17. Pigeon House

early history of English landscape gardening? The garden in the painting shows a beguiling mixture of formality and asymmetry. There is a central axis on which lies an exotic Gothic exedra, and three aligned pools flanked by symmetrical beds. But there is also irregularity – a hedged alley cuts across at an angle and the lie of the land forbids symmetry. There are well-drilled rows of ornamental trees and winding paths amble through the enclosing woodland. It resembles the 'wilde Regularitie' described a hundred years earlier by Sir Henry Wotton who praised the idea of an irregular garden to contrast with the regularity of architecture. In a description that presages Painswick uncannily, he wrote, 'the first access was a high walke like a Terrace, from whence might be taken a general view of the whole Plott below; but rather in a delightfull confusion than with any plain Distinction of the Pieces.'

By the beginning of the eighteenth century, fashionable garden taste, led by Pope and Addison, turned away from the formal designs of the Restoration in which 'Grove nods at grove, each Alley has a brother', as Pope wrote, towards a more naturalistic style. Pope's own garden at Twickenham still had many traces of formality – avenues, quincunxes and symmetry – but it also had romantic paths winding through woodland, a wilderness and naturalistic groves. The garden at Painswick may be seen as belonging to the same hesitant phase in garden design, breaking away from strict formality towards what Pope called 'the amiable Simplicity of unadorned Nature'.

Painswick is called a 'rococo' garden but it is difficult to know how useful that term is. Robins's paintings with their delight in carefree ornamentation, their festoons of curlicues and delicacy of touch, certainly seem filled with the rococo spirit. But there is little rococo influence in England in the visual arts and certainly no tradition of rococo garden design. It makes more sense, perhaps, to think of Painswick as a fascinating example of a transitional landscape garden, filling the gap between the early experiments of Pope, Bridgeman and Kent, and the full-blown naturalism of 'Capability' Brown.

The event that convinced Lord Dickinson that the garden depicted by Thomas Robins substantially survived was the research of two architectural historians, Roger White and Tim Mowl, who published their findings in an article in the *Journal of Garden History* called 'Thomas Robins at Painswick'. When Tim Mowl first saw the garden in 1982 it was covered in brambles to shoulder height and it required great imagination to make the connection between what lay on the ground and what was to be seen in Robins's painting. But the connection was certainly there and this investigation revealed, for the first time, what had survived at Painswick, and analysed in detail its relationship with Robins's painting. They showed that the layout and many of the garden buildings depicted in the painting survived. Whether Robins himself was the designer of the garden and his painting was, in effect, a plan for it, or whether he merely painted the garden shortly after it was made, remains uncertain.

No one knows who designed the garden buildings. It is known, from a surviving catalogue of his library, that Benjamin Hyett possessed several of the architectural pattern books which inspired the design of so many of the garden buildings of the period, but these books contain nothing that served as the basis for the buildings at Painswick. Some of these are of exceptional interest. The

The remains of the crenellated Eagle House. It was originally crowned with an airy canopy of fretted wood which it is planned to restore.

curious Gothic Red House which lies to the north of the main area, commanding views down the hill, has two façades, slightly angled to face different vistas. Originally it was rendered and painted with red paint – hence its odd name. This serves to underline a characteristic quality of the garden, which is its painterliness. No other architect at the time would have dreamed of painting a building red. Was Robins himself the designer of this exotic and delightful building? Whatever Robins's role might have been in the creation of the garden and its buildings, there was no doubt that his painting served as a precious basis for the restoration of the garden.

Through the Garden History Society Lord Dickinson got in touch with Paul Edwards, a garden designer with a special interest in the restoration of historic gardens. Lord Dickinson's brief was flexible. He wanted to know what were the possibilities of restoration and he asked Paul Edwards to look into a minimal scheme whereby the ground would be sufficiently cleared to allow visitors to see the surviving garden buildings in the same sort of sequence that was indicated by the paths in the Robins painting. The other alternative was a complete programme of restoration.

At this time, in 1984, the whole garden was choked with fallen trees, blackberries and sapling trees. Furthermore, the central area which on Robins's painting includes a great diamond-shaped parterre, the bowling green and the main vista, had been planted with trees by Lord Dickinson himself when it had proved no longer possible to maintain it as a large-scale kitchen garden in the 1950s. Paul Edwards and the gardener, as an experiment, decided to try and clear one of the vistas shown in the painting. From a window of the Gothic Red House at the north-east end of the combe they projected a line in the direction shown by the painting and set about cutting through the undergrowth and trees with a chainsaw. At the end of the day they arrived at exactly the place shown in Robins's painting where the vista meets the corner of the fish pond. That evening Lord and Lady Dickinson joined them in the

The snowdrop grove in the woods to the east of the garden. At Painswick artifice merges harmoniously with surrounding nature.

Red House and, looking down the hill, they realized that the view that was newly revealed to them had not been seen before in their lifetime. That is one of the rare excitements of garden restoration, to reveal the living bones of an ancient garden design sleeping beneath the débris of time. Few things give a more vivid sense of intimate contact with the past.

Paul Edwards made detailed proposals for the restoration of the garden in November 1984. The most immediately urgent matter was the state of the woodland and a report on it was commissioned from a tree-surgeon. The report proved quite frightening. It was found not merely that many trees were dangerous to visitors but also that some of the garden buildings were threatened by overhanging trees. In the winter of 1984/5, the tree-surgeon was contracted to clear the trees in the central area and to carry out essential surgery on important older trees that were to be preserved and on any dangerous trees. Trees that were dangerously overhanging garden buildings, such as the horse chestnuts by the Gothic Alcove, were removed. Felling them was a tricky business and they had to be winched away carefully from the building.

As the central area forms such an important part of the garden shown in Robins's painting it was essential that all the stumps of felled trees should be removed. Long stems were left on them to make it easier to lever them out, leaving a gigantic pile of stumps which were burnt *in situ*. One of the agonizing problems of garden restoration is illustrated by the removal of these trees, many of which were very fine but dated from long after Robins's painting. None was an outstanding specimen of a rare tree but Lord Dickinson was understandably reluctant to see all the trees go. But it was plain that they formed no part of the layout shown by Robins, nor was there any evidence that they were part of any subsequent designed scheme.

In that first winter of work paths were cleared and restored. Once the undergrowth was cleared away it was surprisingly easy to trace the paths, which closely corresponded to the detail of Robins's painting. Their edges were frequently marked with small stones and traces of old gravel were found. They were resurfaced with gravel or wood chippings. Purist garden historians of a more delicate disposition may jib at this entirely modern surface. However, it is cheap, unobtrusive and, being very light, easy to barrow to inaccessible places. A further point should be borne in mind; the garden in its heyday was intended as a private place of recreation and delight and did not need to accommodate the heavy feet of many thousands of visitors a year, many of whom come specially to see the snowdrop grove in the late winter when dry paths are most necessary. One would have to be a purist indeed to insist upon the squelch of wet feet as an essential accompaniment to the snowdrop-viewing experience.

In 1985 the public were allowed to visit on the understanding that what they were seeing was a garden very much in the course of restoration. In this year, too, a proper survey was carried out on the state of the buildings. Many of the enchanting follies, temples and alcoves shown in Robins's painting survived more or less intact; of some there was no trace (and indeed no evidence that they had ever been there); others were in a very derelict or incomplete state. All the garden buildings had some purposeful presence in the garden scheme. At the northeasterly extremity of the valley is the Red House with its asymmetrical façade. Despite its oddness, there is no doubt that the building is complete, as it is locked so firmly into the layout of the paths.

Water is an essential ingredient in the garden design at Painswick – as it is in most eighteenth-century landscape gardens. Needing urgent attention was the fish pond which lies at the end of the main vista down the hill from the site of the Exedra Garden and which also ends another vista coming down at an oblique angle from the Red House in the woods. This was tackled in the winter of 1984/5. It had long been completely silted up and a large chestnut had fallen across it. Both the decorative cascade overflow (which had been made by Lord Dickinson) and the stream that fed it were choked. The pond was dug out

*A door of the Red House commands a view of the main
vista of the garden – east to the Fish Pond and
the woods beyond.*

very carefully with a HyMac scoop, great care being taken not to damage the original puddled clay lining. The cascade overflow was also repaired. The water supply for the fish pond comes from the Plunge Pool to its north which is fed direct from a spring. The Plunge Pool is a common ingredient of eighteenth-century landscape gardens – one of the same date exists at Rousham, for example. There is, however, no sign of the pool in Robins's painting. Later on, the central pool, which Robins *does* show, was revealed and that, too, was cleared and relined with the help of a grant from English Heritage. The original stone moulding was carefully preserved and a new waterproof base made of concrete.

The involvement of English Heritage (or the Historic Buildings and Monuments Commission for England, to give its full, resounding name) was of great help in the restoration. They gave financial help and advice in the restoration of the garden buildings and monuments. They insist, naturally, on an expert professional assessment of what restoration is needed and monitor the execution of the work. A local architect, familiar with vernacular building materials and styles, was recruited to supervise the restoration of the buildings, some of which presented difficulties. The Eagle House, for example, was incomplete. This is a curious building, half partly submerged grotto and half airy belvedere. A painting by Thomas Robins shows vivid detail of it. However, only the lower half survived and the interpretation of this, because of Robins's puzzling ways with perspective, was difficult. It is flanked by two wings, pierced with round-topped lancet windows, but the exact angle of the wings was impossible to judge from the painting. An expert excavation by the Bath Archaeological Trust in March 1988 revealed the exact position of the footings of the wings and provided essential information for their replacement.

This team of archaeologists, under the direction of Rob Bell, also excavated other parts of the garden with a view to establishing whether or not other features of the Robins painting had ever existed. By the time their work

*The Gothic Alcove forms an eyecatcher at the end of a replanted avenue of beech (*Fagus sylvatica*) which will, in time, form a Gothic tunnel to frame the Alcove.*

started the upper pool, north-east of the central circular pool, had been replaced, using the painting and the lie of the land alone as a basis for positioning. An excavation, however, discovered the site of the original pool, slightly farther up the hill and to the left. It also laid bare evidence of a water supply from a spring farther up the valley, which would have had sufficient pressure to power a handsome fountain in the fish pond farther down the valley. No foundations were discovered for the exedra which is such an important part of the upper pool in Robins's painting. Such very ornate garden ornaments were, however, frequently made of wood which had a short life and needed no substantial foundations. Further excavations in January 1989 were carried out to try and find some of the paths shown in the painting. These were found in exactly the right places, slightly cambered surfaces still bearing traces of gravel. Also found were some of the stake-holes supporting the intricate trellis-work fencing shown so clearly in the painting. It was an important moment in the restoration when it was realized that every single piece of evidence derived from the archaeological digs precisely confirmed the accuracy of Robins's painting. There was also a feeling that further digs might reduce the likelihood of the sort of mistake that had been made in the placing of the upper pool. This had been based on the evidence of Robins's painting and the existing pattern of paths, both of which had proved generally a very accurate basis for the restoration. It was just bad luck that, in this case, the assumptions were wrong. But in a garden of the intricacy of Painswick, where the features are so intimately interlocked, there can be a 'knock-on' effect as a small error becomes magnified in relation to the pattern of the parts.

The replanting of the garden was one of the most difficult parts of the restoration. The Robins painting, while clearly showing the position of plants, is not helpful in identifying them, nor does archaeology have much to contribute in the identification of plants that once were in the garden. The colours have faded so that, for example, the hedges forming part of the main north-south axis

appear completely brown. Nor is there any other documentary evidence about the planting except for Bishop Pococke's remark that there was a kitchen garden. It had been assumed that the central diamond-shaped area was a kitchen garden as it had been in Lord Dickinson's childhood and for a very long time before that. In the painting there certainly are narrow rows of plants which resemble the planting of a vegetable garden. In fact, in Robins's painting there is another area, in a more logical position nearer the house, which looks strikingly like the kitchen garden and could be the one to which Bishop Pococke referred. But that would have been north-facing and not, perhaps, the best place for a vegetable garden.

The small trees on either side of the yew hedge were, it is assumed, fruit trees, but that is entirely conjectural. However there is a long tradition of the use of fruit trees in the ornamental parts of gardens, as other gardens in this book such as Hatfield, Westbury Court and Erddig amply show. The varieties of apple and pear that have been planted on each side of the yew hedge are all eighteenth-century – 'Ribston Pippin', 'Reinette du Canada', 'Orleans Reinette', 'Wagener' and 'Louise Bonne of Jersey'. They are very decorative and Robins's painting does show trees planted here in orchard-like rows.

The replanting of the beech avenue leading to the restored Gothic Alcove was completed in 1988. Here there were remains of ancient and diseased trees which had to be removed, a tricky job on the north side of the walk where the land falls away abruptly into the valley. In the course of time the beeches will grow and eventually form, where they meet, that characteristic Gothic arch which one sees in old avenues.

The programme of restoration continues. So far the vast bulk of it has been paid for out of Lord Dickinson's own pocket. But now a charitable trust has been set up to help with the financing of the garden. This is essential if money is to be acquired from the many charitable organizations that, in principle, may help with garden restoration. Most of them give money *only* to registered charitable trusts. As soon as further funds are available another archaeological dig will be commissioned to establish the pattern of paths in the areas of the parterre-like diamond-shaped bed in the centre of the garden and the Exedra Garden. When that has been established the parterre will be planted as an ornamental *potager* to Paul Edwards's design. It is hoped to restore the decorative trellis railing surrounding the exedra, and shown in such detail in Robins's painting. In addition Lord Dickinson plans to restore the superstructure of the Eagle House. But much of the essential work is now complete – bringing the garden shown in Robins's painting vividly back to life.

THE ESSENCE OF PAINSWICK

The distinctive character of the landscape garden at Painswick is its domestic scale. This was not a garden made to impress the great or to advance a career – as many eighteenth-century landscape gardens were. It is a place of delight rather than of ostentation. It was made for the recreation of the Hyett family and their friends and is, in the best sense of the word, provincial – perfectly suited to the life of its owner and the world in which he lived. The garden buildings are intimate in character, there are no Olympian temples or other grand classical allusions. The size of the buildings is in scale with the intricacy of the landscape and their placing, both to be seen as ornaments and to be used as vantage points from which to admire a view, is carefully judged. There is nothing arbitrary here, nor is there any mechanical and obtrusive schematic plan.

The garden is completely enclosed, cut off from the surrounding rural countryside but constituting, itself, a piece of ideally ordered countryside. It is a hidden, secret garden – an atmosphere that has been very much preserved by the restoration. The new entrance to it is through a door pierced in the old brick wall of the Melon Ground. One is not prepared for anything special, nor is the garden immediately revealed as one enters it. It comes as a surprise – an enchanting sight that immediately invites exploration.

There is a harmonious linking of very different ingredients. The ambling paths that wind apparently inconsequentially up and down the wooded slopes gradually lead to a point where some neatly articulated view is revealed – a temple, seat or garden house. Each of the ornamental incidents seems to occur in a visually logical progression. This is plainly landscape gardening of a characteristic eighteenth-century kind, but if Stowe or Stourhead are full-blown symphonies, Painswick is lighthearted chamber music, seductively intimate.

A lead figure of Pan by the Flemish artist John Van Nost, the greatest of the early eighteenth-century sculptors specializing in garden statuary.

MONTICELLO

ALL good gardens have some unique quality that is distinctive to them. Monticello, the estate that Thomas Jefferson created in western Virginia, has so much that is original that it is hard to know where to start in describing it. Above all, the character of Jefferson himself imposed upon it, in all its detail, a personal stamp. He designed the house and gardens himself and although one can certainly trace influences on them, they have a striking individuality that derives partly from Jefferson's genius and partly from his readiness to consult the spirit of the place in their making. He was not a man to build some reach-me-down mansion borrowed from a pattern book, nor would he lay out a garden copied slavishly from what he read about, and saw for himself, in America or

Above: A rustic arbour, festooned with the rampant hyacinth bean (Dolichos lablab), edges the vegetable terrace. Opposite: Early-morning mist veils the west front of the house at Monticello.

in Europe. He must, too, have had a sense that, just as he was a prime instigator of the political independence of his country, so also was he making an estate that was distinctively American, not colonial. It would not have been very easy for him to regard the ossified tradition of the formal gardens of the colonial past as a model for the horticultural future. What one sees at Monticello today is not merely the restoration and re-creation of a fascinating garden from an early period of American horticultural history but it has the added interest of a garden made at the decisive moment of independence.

Thomas Jefferson, born in 1743, was the son of Peter Jefferson, a self-made and self-educated farmer who had cleared and worked virgin land in western Virginia. Thomas went to study law at the College of William and Mary in Williamsburg, the seat of government of the Colony of Virginia. He practised as a lawyer and started

building on the estate of Monticello in 1769 while he was still living near by at his father's house at Shadwell. But even before the building started, he had in 1768 planted a row of pear trees on the south-east side of the hill, where the replanted orchard may be seen today. By this time his political career had already begun when he was elected to represent his county, Albemarle, in the House of Burgesses. Henceforth his life was bound up with politics, often at the epicentre of affairs, until his retirement from the Presidency in 1809. His most arduous years as a politician were during the War of Independence (1774-6), as Governor of Virginia from 1779, as Secretary of State under George Washington in 1784-9 (spending most of that period as Minister in France) and serving as President for two terms of office in 1801-9. During all this time his mind and heart were never very far from his estate at Monticello. In his voluminous surviving correspondence

1. North Pavilion 2. West Front and Oval Flower Beds 3. South Pavilion 4. Roundabout Walk and Flower Border 5. Mulberry Row 6. Kitchen Garden 7. Garden Pavilion 8. Vineyard, Berry Squares and Submural Beds 9. Orchard 10. First Roundabout

– over 18,000 items – politics alone are a more frequent subject than gardening. But it was not until his second term as President that he was able to execute the considerable plans for his garden that had for so long been maturing in his mind's eye.

Jefferson took great pains in the design of his house. It was built and remodelled over a period of forty years and although its detail and intricacy are very much Jefferson's own, it was plainly inspired by Palladio. It is finely built of brick with decorative white-painted wooden balustrades, pediments and pillars and crowned with a distinctive segmental dome – the first domed house to be built in America. Two handsome pavilions (the southern of which served as Jefferson's first home) are connected to the house by L-shaped boarded walks railed with Chinoiserie balustrades. From these walks are fine prospects of garden and countryside. All this has a lightness of touch which shows Jefferson's architectural genius and, indeed, the house was considered remarkable in his lifetime. The Marquis de Chastellux, a Frenchman, thought it unique in America and recognized its happy combination of use and beauty when he wrote that 'Mr Jefferson is the first American who has consulted the Fine Arts to know how he should shelter himself from the weather.' The decorative house, occupying as it does a position at the peak of the hill, also constitutes a brilliant garden ornament which makes others superfluous.

As a site for a garden the hill was scarcely ideal although its height conferred two advantages. It certainly commanded handsome views; as Jefferson wrote in 1806: 'Of prospect I have a rich profusion and offering itself at every point of the compass. Mountains distant & near, smooth & shaggy, single & in ridges, a little river hiding itself in among the hills so as to shew in lagoons only.' The height of the hill also provided good frost drainage which sometimes mitigated damage from the severe late frosts which can be so devastating in this part of Virginia, even as late as the month of May. On 5 May 1774, for example, he noted in his *Garden Book* that a frost had destroyed

almost everything but remarks that 'in all other places the destruction of fruit was total.' A great and constant problem, however, was lack of water, despite the presence of several springs in the mountainside and a well that was dug in 1769 just south-west of the site of the house. Much later, with characteristic ingenuity, Jefferson made four giant cisterns, each holding over 3,000 gallons, which gathered water from the roofs of the house, outhouses and covered walkways. However, during all the years that Jefferson was at Monticello, all these sources together were often inadequate for the needs of his growing household. Jefferson was also aware of the problems of laying out a garden on such a site, as he wrote in 1806: 'The hill is generally too steep for direct ascent, but we make level walks successively along it's side, which in it's upper part encircle the hill & intersect these again by others of easy ascent in various parts.' Jefferson made a virtue of the problems of his site with these 'roundabouts', as he called them, which he made of two gradients, 1-in-10 and 1-in-20 which provided both 'easy ascent' and delicious walks in the 'native woods which are majestic'.

Little is known about ornamental gardening in America before the time of Jefferson. There is certainly not enough evidence to build any very detailed picture of the style of American gardens before the end of the eighteenth century. Whatever the influences on Jefferson's gardening ideas, Monticello is probably best thought of as less an American garden than a Jeffersonian one. As far as one can judge, what Jefferson did at Monticello was without precedent in America, nor was it any literal adaptation of what he knew about the latest European gardens, several of which he visited when he was Minister in France.

The garden that George Washington made for his house at Mount Vernon in north-eastern Virginia gives a clear idea, perhaps, of a garden made by a cultivated man within the American gardening tradition that Jefferson inherited. Washington returned to the family home in 1758 and took a great interest in embellishing both house and garden. He bought a copy of *New Principles of Gardening* by Batty Langley (1728) which recommended a softening of the rigidly formal schemes which had been the norm in early eighteenth-century English gardens. None the less, the garden that Washington made, which can be seen in Vaughan's contemporary plan of 1786, is entirely symmetrical with a regular bowling green edged by serpentine walks and flanked by two walled gardens which are divided into parterre-like divisions for ornamental plants (the Upper Garden) or vegetables (the Lower Garden). As Benjamin Latrobe described it on a visit in 1796, 'The ground on the west front of the house is laid out in a level lawn bounded on each side with a wide but extremely formal serpentine walk . . . on the side of this is a plain kitchen garden, on the other a neat flower garden laid out in squares and boxed with great precision.' This scheme has been meticulously followed in the restoration that visitors see today.

In a fascinating piece of research in local archives in south-east Maryland, Barbara Wells Sarudy has painted a vivid picture of gardening practices in the Chesapeake Bay area in the late eighteenth century. Here, as she writes, 'the gardening gentry . . . although well aware of the new English style and sometimes adding serpentine roadways as approaches to houses as well as paths through gardens, overwhelmingly chose to design their grounds to include traditional geometric parterres and classical terraced falls.' This kind of garden continued to be made well into the nineteenth century. For example at Bremo, on the James River 40 miles south of Monticello, the house built for General John Hartwell Cocke in 1817-20 had box-edged parterres and terraces – or 'falls' as they are called in these parts. This kind of formality would have been familiar to Thomas Jefferson who visited many gardens. In his view, 'the only rival . . . to what may be seen in England', by which he presumably meant a naturalistic garden, was the Woodlands, which had been made near Philadelphia by his friend William Hamilton. Jefferson was certainly a fervent admirer of English gardens as he discovered on his tour in 1786: 'The gardening in that country is the article

in which it surpasses all the earth. I mean their pleasure gardening. This, indeed, went far beyond my ideas.'

Our knowledge of Jefferson's gardening activities comes partly from his own *Garden Book* – which he kept, with occasional gaps, from 1769 to 1824. Here he recorded all kinds of observations of the weather, the flowering and fruiting of trees, plant-lists and, as his great kitchen garden evolved, meticulous planting plans for vegetables. In addition to the *Garden Book* there is a voluminous and lively correspondence in which gardening looms large, and various memoranda and accounts which, taken together, give the most complete picture of early American gardening that we possess.

By 1771, before the garden at Monticello was truly under way, Jefferson had read three important books in the history of the English movement – Lord Kames's *Elements of Criticism* (1762), William Shenstone's *Works in Verse and Prose* (1764) and Thomas Whateley's *Observations on Modern Gardening* (1770). He was a particular admirer of Whateley's book and took it with him in 1786 on his visits to English gardens recommended by Whateley. He found Whateley's descriptions 'models of perfect elegance . . . remarkable for their exactness'. Much of what he read in these books, and saw on his garden tour, clearly had an influence on schemes for his own garden. In 1771 he recorded various ideas in his *Account Book* for the garden at Monticello. Among these was to be a graveyard located in 'some unfrequented vale in the park' with a spiral of cedar or holly at the centre of which should be 'a Gothic temple of antique appearance' illuminated only by 'the feeble ray of an half extinguished lamp' on an altar of turf. Several other ideas, including the provision of a grotto, are explored in this memorandum, all of which would have been wholly congenial to the early landscape movement in England. None of these plans was carried out, and Jefferson certainly realized how different was the climate and rural landscape of western Virginia from that of England. He would have read, too, Whateley's words in the summing up at the end of *Observations on Modern Gardening*:

'the genius of the place must always be particularly considered; to force it is hazardous; and an attempt to contradict it always unsuccessful.'

The flower garden at Monticello evolved over a long period. A drawing from the 1770s shows an early plan with a pair of rectilinear beds flanking the portico on the west side of the house but, as far as is known, these were never made. Other plans were considered and there are many records of the acquisition of ornamental plants but nothing is known of what was actually laid out until 1807. A drawing by Jefferson from this year shows an arrangement of oval flower beds on the east and west sides of the house. Those by the west portico are in the same place in which, in 1772, he had contemplated a more formal arrangement. These new beds, planted up 18 April, contained mostly herbaceous plants – among them pinks, sweet Williams, the everlasting pea (*Lathyrus latifolius*), lychnis, *Lobelia cardinalis* and 'the yellow lilly of Columbia' (*Fritillaria pudica*). All these would conform to Jefferson's principle that ornamental plants should be 'either handsome or fragrant'. All are European natives, or garden forms of them, with the exception of the lobelia and the fritillary; both of these are American natives of which Jefferson had had seed from a gardener and nurseryman of central importance in American horticulture, Bernard McMahon.

McMahon was an Irishman who came to America in

*T*he west front of Jefferson's Palladian villa reflected in one of the fish ponds. The large trees flanking the house are tulip trees (Liriodendron tulipifera*), a Virginian native, which date from Jefferson's time.*

1796 and settled in Philadelphia. Here he started a nursery garden and wrote *The American Gardener's Calendar*, which was published in 1806 and is among the first books to give detailed advice on gardening in America. It is not merely a manual of practical horticulture but it also gives advice on garden design, some of the principles of which may be seen at Monticello. From the botanical point of view also, McMahon was of great importance for it was he who was chosen by Jefferson to hold seeds and plants (among them the Oregon grape, *Mahonia aquifolium*, named after McMahon) brought back from the west by the great voyage of exploration conducted by Lewis and Clark. Captain Meriwether Lewis had been Jefferson's secretary and was charged in 1803 with leading the expedition whose purpose was to explore 'the Missouri & whatever river, heading with that, leads into the western ocean'. Lewis was chosen for his general capabilities rather than any specialist knowledge – he was 'brave, prudent, habituated to the woods, & familiar with Indian manners and character'. But he and Clark acquired enough botanical knowledge to recognize and collect unfamiliar plants and their expedition immensely enriched knowledge of American indigenous flora.

To have in his garden plants that were ornamental and increased understanding of American natural history was something that certainly attracted Jefferson. He grew many natives at Monticello – among herbaceous plants alone were the columbine *Aquilegia canadensis*, the lady's slipper orchid (*Cypripedium acaule*, which Jefferson called the 'Mockaseen'), the twinleaf *Jeffersonia diphylla* (named after him and flowering at about the time of his birthday, 13 April) and the Virginia bluebell (*Mertensia virginica*). As I shall show later, Jefferson was equally aware of the garden merits of the astonishing riches of American woody plants, some of them Virginian natives.

Specifically to display flowering plants Jefferson laid out a serpentine path edging an expansive oval lawn beyond the new arrangement of oval beds immediately west of the house. A plan dated 1807 survives for this but

The great vegetable terrace was an important part of Jefferson's garden. He saw it as both decorative and productive and arranged the plants in an ornamental fashion. It has been restored with early varieties of vegetables.

the work was not actually done until the following year. The serpentine walk – unlike, for example, that at Mount Vernon – is asymmetrical, and within each loop, to give variety, Jefferson planned large oval beds for shrubs. This arrangement follows very closely the advice on 'modern gardening' given in McMahon's *The American Gardener's Calendar* which Jefferson had received from the author as soon as it was published in 1806: 'In designs for a Pleasure-ground, according to modern gardening; consulting rural disposition, in imitation of nature; all too formal works being almost abolished, such as long straight walks, regular intersections, square grass-plats, corresponding parterres, quadrangular and angular spaces, and other uniformities, as in ancient design; instead of which, are now adopted, rural open spaces of grass-ground, of varied forms and dimensions, and winding walks, all bounded with plantations of trees, shrubs, and flowers, in various clumps.' Jefferson's plan was specifically designed to increase space for flowering plants, as he explained in a letter to his granddaughter Anne Randolph: 'I have resumed an idea . . . for a winding walk surrounding the lawn before the house, with a narrow border of flowers on each side. This would give us abundant room for a great variety.' The idea was that the borders should be continuous on either side of the path. Although from Jefferson's correspondence we know that the work was done in 1808,

A 'roundabout walk' encircles the lawn west of the house. It is edged with narrow beds containing a wide range of plants – herbaceous perennials and annuals – with special emphasis on American natives and un-hybridized forms.

there are unfortunately no entries in the *Garden Book* for that year and we do not know exactly what was planted.

To the west of the lawn and its roundabout walk, where the ground begins to slope downwards, Jefferson planned his Grove. In a drawing dated 1806 showing the top of Monticello hill a large area is marked 'Grove'. In a letter of 1806 to his friend William Hamilton, another knowledgeable gardener who received plants and seed from the Lewis and Clark expedition, he describes his ideas for this area. He admires the English landscape style above all others but realizes that it is inappropriate to Virginia because of the need for shade from 'the beaming, constant and almost vertical sun'. He therefore proposes an ingenious method for making a version of the naturalistic landscape style, with its characteristic clumps of trees: 'Let your ground be covered with trees of the loftiest stature. Trim up their bodies as high . . . as the tree will bear, but so as that their tops shall still unite & yield dense shade. A wood, so open below, will have nearly the appearance of open grounds. Then, when in the open ground you would plant a clump of trees, place a thicket of shrubs.' Apart from the beauty of such a setting, Jefferson might also have had in mind Bernard McMahon's detailed advice on planting shady walks which, apart from shelter from sun and wind, also provide 'opportunity for private and contemplative walking'. No planting plan survives for the Grove but he wrote a memorandum in 1804 in which he describes the ingredients. The large trees should be poplar, oak, elm, maple, ash, hickory, chestnut, linden, Weymouth pine and sycamore. The thickets of broom, calycanthus, magnolia and fringe tree should be arranged in a spiral, with plants becoming taller towards the centre, at which there should be a temple or seat. It seems also that Jefferson wanted to create effects of contrasting foliage and colour. On a visit to Monticello in 1823 Jane Blair Smith referred to 'the many-tinted grove'.

The evolution of the orchards and kitchen garden at Monticello preoccupied Jefferson more than any other single horticultural activity. His *Garden Book* devotes far more space to the cultivation of vegetables and fruit than to any other topic and fruit trees were the very first plants cultivated at Monticello. Reading Jefferson's accounts of his persistent experiments with the cultivation of fruit puts one in mind of an ardent and persevering lover repeatedly rejected by the object of his desire. On 10 March 1775, for example, after remarking on an exceptionally mild winter he notes that the peach trees are in blossom. Later that month he writes that 'there came very cold weather, which killed every peach at Monticello'. On 14 March 1806, he notes, 'The cherries & peaches are completely killed this year.'

He started making a terraced vegetable garden just below the summit of the hill on its south-east slopes in 1806 and by 1812 it consisted of a vast area, divided into three 'platforms' with a total of twenty-four beds. Entries in the *Garden Book* for later years are exclusively taken up with planting plans and calendars for this elaborate and productive garden which was so important to Jefferson that he often referred to it merely as 'the garden'. Here were grown many different kinds of vegetable. A wide range of vegetables was available from nurserymen in America by the end of the eighteenth century. Bernard McMahon, for example, listed twenty-one varieties of pea, eight cucumbers, seventeen cabbages and even ten varieties of radish. Jefferson grew seventeen varieties of his favourite peas and took part in the annual competition to see who could serve a dish of peas from the garden earliest in the year.

Early on in the making of the vegetable garden Jefferson had the idea for a series of four pavilions, each designed in a different architectural style, on the walk along the south-east edge of the terrace. This walk was to be shaded by an arbour of 'locust [i.e. *Robinia pseudoacacia*] posts set in the ground crossed by poles at the top, & lathes on these'. This was to be planted with vines but the sides should remain 'quite open' to afford views of the plain below. He rejected this, however, noting that 'after all, the kitchen garden is not the place for ornaments of this

kind. Bowers & treillages suit that better.' He did, however, make a small pavilion which was described by Henry D. Gilpin in 1827 shortly after it had been destroyed in a storm, 'On a point of the mountain . . . there is an eminence where Mr. Jefferson had erected a little Grecian temple & which was a favourite spot with him to read & sit in.'

South of the vegetable garden lay a vineyard and orchard. Jefferson had first attempted to cultivate the vine in 1770 and later recorded, 'For more than 50 years I labored to establish viniculture on the Monticello hillside but often with little success and considerable frustration.' His first vineyard, for example, was almost completely destroyed by a late frost on 5 May 1774 ('a frost which destroyed almost every thing'). He recruited the aid of an Italian, Philip Mazzei, who came to Virginia with ten vignerons and with Jefferson's help settled on a farm near Monticello. Jefferson was especially keen to cultivate the native Fox grape (*Vitis labrusca*) and the 'Scuppernong' (which is derived from the muscadine, *V. rotundifolia*) but he also experimented with many varieties of *V. vinifera* from which all European wine and dessert grape varieties are derived. Although Jefferson's vineyard obeyed the Virgilian directive – 'plant your vines towards the rising sun' – the capricious late frosts and the problems of importing living plants proved insuperable.

In the orchard laid out near the vineyard Jefferson grew a very wide range of fruit. By the end of the eighteenth century several varieties were available from American nurserymen, a number of them of domestic origin. The Prince nursery, which was established on Long Island in 1737 – the first in America – supplied many fruit trees to Monticello. Jefferson grew seventeen varieties of apple of which most were American strains, including the incomparable 'Newtown Pippin' (which originated on Long Island). Benjamin Franklin took this apple to England and in the nineteenth century it became a favourite of Queen Victoria. There was an astonishing growth in the selection of different strains of apple, and in the nineteenth century more than 17,000 varieties are named in American pomological literature. By March 1811 there were 384 trees in the south orchard at Monticello, including 160 peaches, apples, cherries, apricots, nectarines, quinces, pears and plums.

When Thomas Jefferson died in 1826 the estate had already suffered from lack of his supervision and in 1831 it was sold to pay off his debts. The house and grounds decayed rapidly and when Frank Stockton, a family friend, visited in 1827 he noted that the 'orchards and terraced garden, the serpentine flower borders on the west lawn and the beautiful roundabout walks and drives have all disappeared.' In 1839, when J. Bayard H. Smith saw the grounds, she reported, 'Around me I beheld nothing but ruin and change, rotting terraces, broken cabins, the lawn ploughed up and cattle wandering among Italian mouldering vases, and the place seemed the true representation of the fallen fortunes of the great man and his family.' The estate was bought by a retired apothecary, James Barclay, who reputedly ploughed the west lawn to grow corn and cleared the Grove in an attempt to start a silkworm farm which soon failed. It was bought in 1836 by Uriah Phillips Levy and remained in his family until it was bought by the Thomas Jefferson Memorial Foundation in 1923. During

Above: Jefferson liked to sit in his elegant pavilion and admire the 'sea-view' – hills shrouded in the distinctive blue haze of the region. Previous pages: Maples (on the left the sugar maple, Acer saccharum) *give spectacular autumn colour on the slopes of the Monticello mountain.*

all this time the estate had decayed, especially during the Civil War when the house was unoccupied for long periods. A late nineteenth-century photograph shows the east front of the house with white marble figures eyeing each other across fallen leaves as though they were in some forsaken and gloomy Italian *giardino inglese*.

The first restoration of the garden was organized by the Garden Club of Virginia and completed in 1940. This was confined to one of the best-documented parts of the garden – the west lawn with its 'roundabout' walk and the 'ellipse' of trees and shrubs immediately to the east of the house. At that time virtually nothing survived from Jefferson's garden. There was a handful of trees – two magnificent tulip trees (*Liriodendron tulipifera*) and two copper beeches (*Fagus sylvatica purpurea* – since blown down) near the house and a few about the west lawn – a sugar maple (*Acer saccharum*), a red cedar (*Juniperus virginica*) and a European larch (*Larix decidua*). There also remained some of the original plantings of bulbs which served to trace the borders that edged the path. Using in addition Jefferson's plan of 1807 it was possible to retrace the route of the roundabout walk, and his small fishpond near the south pavilion was excavated and restored. In the replanting of the narrow borders edging the serpentine path it was decided not to have them continuous, nor were the large oval beds in the loops of the walk replaced. We do not know in detail what Jefferson planted in the narrow borders but we do know what plants he liked. Here are planted only bulbs, herbaceous perennials and summer annuals. Since the original restoration the plants here have been refined as knowledge of historic plants has increased. In the spring there are repeated plantings of varieties of tulips which have been chosen to resemble old cultivars of the sort that Jefferson would have known. There are many native plants – the very decorative red and yellow *Aquilegia canadensis*, the May apple (*Podophyllum peltatum*), the elegant Atamasco lily (*Zephyranthes atamasco*) and the American 'columbo' (*Swertia caroliniensis*). Among the many summer bedding plants are the native cardinal flower (*Lobelia cardinalis*), the species prickly poppy (*Argemone mexicana*) and *Mimosa pudica*, the sensitive plant. Other annuals include several species of plants which are more commonly seen as some dazzling garden variety such as the species marigolds (*Tagetes erecta* and *T. patula*) and the species zinnia (*Zinnia peruviana*, which was not mentioned in Jefferson's writings but was known in North America in his time).

The character of this part of the garden is, as Jefferson intended, that of an agreeable walk affording displays of ornamental flowering plants. Although it is not known whether the larger oval beds of shrubs in the loops of the walk were ever made they would, in my view, be a valuable addition. They would serve to relieve the linearity of the path and would give the sort of visual variety which Jefferson advocated in a different context. In the letter of 1806 to William Hamilton, describing his ideas for the Grove, he talks about excesses of the same view: 'To prevent a satiety of this is the principal difficulty. It may be successively offered, & in different portions through vistas, or which will be better, between thickets so disposed as to serve as vistas, with the advantage of shifting the scenes as you advance on your way.' Such an arrangement on the west lawn would 'shift the scenes' of the lovely house, now hidden, now revealed, and of the path, flower beds and the trees and shrubs that lie about the perimeter.

The restoration of the remainder of the garden has been achieved since 1978. An archaeological investigation of the kitchen garden site in 1958 had discovered the exact position of the great retaining wall, most of which had long since disappeared, and of the 'little Grecian temple' on the edge of the terrace. A much more elaborate excavation in this area and on the slopes below where there had been orchards and vineyards was carried out from 1979 to 1980. The results, as is often the case, did not add to our knowledge of the ingredients of the garden but they yielded valuable information about the exact location of features and gave independent corroboration to the surviving documentary evidence. For example, it was known that Jefferson had fenced the whole area of vegetable terrace, orchard and vineyard – more than eight acres – with 'a paling 10 feet high'. Post holes, and indeed fragments of locust timber, were discovered which confirmed that the fence had indeed been built and showed exactly where it ran. It was not possible to trace the original pattern of beds and paths in the vegetable garden – the ground had been too deeply ploughed. But it was possible to determine the extent of the terrace – it is 350m/1,000ft long and 25m/80ft wide – retained by a dry-stone wall which rises to a height of 3.35m/11ft. This has been rebuilt of exactly the same kind of stone as the original and laid in the same rough-hewn fashion. Using Jefferson's memoranda of 1810 and 1821 it was possible to reconstruct the pattern of beds which are now separated by walks of mown grass. In the replanting it was estimated that only about 30 per cent of the 250 varieties of vegetable grown by Jefferson survive in cultivation. As many as possible of the original varieties, many of which are hidden behind modern cultivar names (for example the pea which he called 'Leadman's Dwarf' is the modern 'Dwarf White Sugar'), were planted and in addition a good collection of nineteenth-century varieties of the sort described in the first book on American kitchen gardening, published in 1863, *The Field and Garden Vegetables of America* by Fearing Burr Jnr.

Archaeologists also confirmed the foundations of the pavilion that Jefferson built on the terrace. No drawing of it survives but Jefferson did leave very detailed notes on its construction and these were used for the rebuilding which was completed in 1984. Although no sign was found of an adjacent arbour, the evidence of which could have been obliterated by ploughing, a simple locust arbour has been made. Climbing beans – the scarlet-flowered runner bean (*Phaseolus coccineus*) and the hyacinth bean (*Dolichos lablab*) – festoon the superstructure and form in high summer a shady tunnel. Jefferson was certainly aware of the decorative possibilities of vegetable beds; he planted a border of okra (*Hibiscus esculentus*) which has decorative yellow flowers, about his tomatoes. He also planted a succession

of red, white and green broccoli (all of which, incidentally, were sold by Bernard McMahon).

One of the most exciting archaeological discoveries was that of the planting holes of many of the fruit trees in the orchard below the vegetable terrace. These corresponded closely with the detailed planting plans – showing both spacing and varieties – which Jefferson had made. Part of the orchard has been replanted with old varieties reflecting as closely as possible Jefferson's well-documented interests. Among the American apples are the local 'Albemarle Pippin', 'Esopus Spitzenburg' and 'Roxbury Russet'. Of the 38 varieties of peach grown by Jefferson twelve have been traced and replanted, including 'Heath Cling', 'Indian Blood Cling' and 'Oldmixon Free'. The Italian 'Poppa di Venere' was retrieved from an Italian source but is still languishing in the four-year period of quarantine demanded by the U.S. Department of Agriculture. In some cases peaches survived under different names. For example 'Kennedy Caroline', mentioned in 1807, is called 'large yellow pine apple' in William Coxe's *A View Toward the Cultivation of Fruit Trees* (Philadelphia, 1817 – the first American book on fruit growing in the New World). The same peach is easily available today under the name 'Lemon Cling'. Even more easily available was the excellent late eighteenth-century 'Seckel' pear, new stock of which was bought in a supermarket in Charlottesville.

Archaeology revealed a puzzling irregular pattern of post holes on the site of the vineyard. In 1984 this area was replanted using many of the varieties that Jefferson struggled with for so long – native cultivars (including the 'Scuppernong') as well as table and wine grapes of the European kind. Little is known of the method of training and pruning vines in America in Jefferson's time but they have been espaliered on a high fence-like framework of locust uprights and cedar crosspieces taken from Edward Antill's 'Essay on the Cultivation of the Vine', published in Philadelphia in 1769.

Jefferson's Grove, lying to the west and north of the west lawn, was the subject of a programme of re-creation

A magnificent specimen of the western Catalpa (C. speciosa) on the north side of the roundabout walk. Behind it are the white flowers of the native dogwood Cornus florida.

from 1977 onwards. Here, within the Grove proper, there were no survivals from any original planting (if, indeed, Jefferson had made any) nor was there any other evidence of past use on the ground. The essential documents in the restoration were Jefferson's manuscript memorandum of about 1804 on the 'Garden or pleasure grounds' and his 1806 letter to William Hamilton in which he describes his spiral thickets artfully disposed among tall trees. Part of the mountainside is native forest with many fine trees – tulip trees, red oak (*Quercus rubra*) and American chestnut (*Castanea dentata*). There is also a wonderfully rich carpet of wild herbaceous plants – *Geranium maculatum*, May apple, twinleaf and *Cimicifuga racemosa*. Parts of the upper part of the Grove have been cleared and loose spirals of thickets planted with many of the plants recommended by Jefferson including mountain laurel (*Kalmia latifolia*), the wild European barberry (*Berberis vulgaris*), the east coast *Ceanothus americana* (with dull white insignificant flowers – a retiring cousin of the showy Californian ceanothus) and wild American azalea (*Rhododendron periclymenoides*). The unobservant visitor might overlook the artfulness of these thickets and they have not been planted as tightly as Jefferson's drawing indicates nor have the plants been graded in size, becoming taller towards the centre, as Jefferson proposed. Instead of a temple or a seat one of the spirals has a mossy rock at its centre.

The west front of the house seen under a canopy of the spring flowering native Virginian fringe tree (Chionanthus virginicus)*. Jefferson called it 'the snowdrop tree'.*

The part of the Grove that abuts on the western extremity of the west lawn has been replanted with many trees that Jefferson liked – the native American crab apple (*Malus coronaria*), the Chinese bead tree (*Melia azedarach*, known as the 'Chainyball' in the American south where it flourishes like a weed) which is doubtfully hardy in western Virginia, umbrella magnolia (*M. tripetala*) and the Virginian sweet bay magnolia (*M. virginiana*).

There are still many questions and possibilities at Monticello. Would it be possible to re-create the *ferme ornée* on the northern slopes of the mountainside in which Jefferson tantalizingly described 'articles of husbandry' intermingling with 'the attributes of a garden'? How interesting it would be to see in full action the 'submural' beds which were made at the foot of the great retaining wall of the vegetable terrace whose stone accumulated heat and warmed the beds for tender plants. Could the archaeologists reveal the oval beds that may once have flanked the serpentine walk round the west lawn?

The work on restoring the gardens has achieved an immense amount since 1978. Jefferson's original ideas of garden design, his eclectic taste in ornamental plants and his passion for the produce of the kitchen garden are all now more vividly displayed than they have been since his death.

THE ESSENCE OF MONTICELLO

From the airy pavilion that overlooks the terraced kitchen garden the ground falls away sharply at the foot of the vast retaining wall that supports it. Spreading out on either side of the pavilion, herbs and vegetables are marshalled with crisp precision. Husbandry – the productive and well-ordered life – is vividly displayed. Farther up the hill the smart brick and white-painted woodwork of Jefferson's house is just visible through a tracery of foliage. On the slopes below the pavilion are the replanted berry square and, to its east, the vineyard. Beyond these the re-created orchard sweeps down the hill and seems to merge with woodland. Richly wooded land extends towards a distant and broad horizon which is often shrouded in the characteristic blue haze of this part of western Virginia. Because of this, Jefferson himself called this prospect 'sea-view'. All this corresponds to the ideal Renaissance garden described in Alberti's *De Re Aedificatoria* (1452) in which a hillside setting is recommended for a villa to provide views 'that overlook . . . the owner's land, the sea or a great plain and familiar hills or mountains . . . in the fore ground there should be a delicacy of gardens'. On such a site as Monticello in sixteenth-century Tuscany a Renaissance Jefferson would have laid out balustraded terraces, rich with statues and fountains and punctuated with Italian cypresses. Instead Jefferson made his great vegetable garden retained by a wall of uncut stone. For the pergola of marble columns recommended by Alberti, Jefferson had a wooden pergola of vines; instead of topiary clipped 'in the charming habit of the ancients', he had the patterns of vegetables in rows. In all this he must have remembered Whateley's words, 'one of the latest improvements has been to blend the useful with the agreeable.'

Here, domestic harmony merges easily with the wilder rhythms of the natural landscape. Jefferson's interests in gardening were part of a larger view in which the house and its setting in the landscape, and the atmosphere of their dramatic surroundings, were made harmonious. The pleasure grounds to the west of the house were edged in trees and shrubs which gave way, to the west and north, to the naturalistic woodland groves that provided a connection between garden and countryside. The very planting merged with nature because Jefferson used so many native Virginian plants in his garden. He had admired William Hamilton's house near Philadelphia 'embosomed' in mature trees and wanted to see his own house framed by trees in this way, so that it would not obtrude too starkly in the landscape. He had read William Shenstone and no doubt fully shared his idea that 'Art should never be allowed to set foot in the province of nature, otherwise than clandestinely and by night.'

GRAVETYE MANOR

THERE are few gardens where the presence of one man is so strongly felt as at Gravetye Manor in Sussex. Although its maker, William Robinson, died over fifty years ago and although the garden has survived only by the skin of its teeth, it is still powerfully redolent of Robinson's character. It was the first and only garden he made and he brought to it the experience of thinking and writing about gardening for almost thirty years. It remains today, thanks to a restoration undertaken when such things were almost unheard of, the only place where a visitor may see what a true Robinsonian garden really looks like.

William Robinson was born in Ireland in 1838, the son of a land-agent, and worked

Above: In the Kitchen Garden a Venetian well-head is surrounded by flowering mint.
Opposite: The west front of the Manor, swathed in Virginia creeper (Parthenocissus quinquefolia), seen from the Flower Garden.

as a garden boy for the Marquis of Waterford at Curragh-more. Later he worked for Sir Henry Johnson-Walsh at Ballykilcavan where he rose to be in charge of the glass-houses. The legend is that after a row with one of his colleagues he allowed the glasshouse stoves to go out and, realizing that all the tender plants would die in the night, set off immediately for Dublin. He then went to London and was given a job with the herbaceous department of the Royal Botanic Society's garden in Regent's Park, where he rose rapidly and was elected a Fellow of the Linnean Society in 1866. He had started garden journalism and in 1867 was sent to Paris by *The Times* to cover the International Exhibition.

This experience in France gave him the material for his first book, *Gleanings from French Gardens* (1868). At this early stage many of his opinions were already formed. He writes, 'our love for rude colour has led us to ignore the exquisite and inexhaustible way in which plants are naturally arranged – fern, flower, grass, shrub and tree,

sheltering, supporting and relieving each other.' This way of planting, learning from nature but not imitating it slavishly, is the hallmark of Robinson's style. In this book he approves of the use of tender plants such as palms, cannas and dracaenas but points out that similar effects, in which the striking shape of the foliage is the essence, can be achieved using hardy plants such as pampas grass, *Crambe cordifolia* and the large-leaved *Rheum palmatum*.

Robinson saw much to admire in France and was especially impressed by the quality of city parks in Paris and the excellence of kitchen gardens, especially of fruit growing. But he also visited the huge formal gardens of Le Nôtre which were to remain throughout his life the very definition of everything that he found repellent in gardens. He wrote of Le Nôtre's grand layout at St Cloud, for example, 'It is, perhaps, one of the most uninteresting gardens known. It is, however, worth seeing, if only to get an idea of how much "the genius of Le Notre" may do to spoil a place naturally beautiful.'

*1. Flower Garden 2. Azalea Bank 3. The Long Lawn
4. Alpine Meadow 5. Trout Lane 6. Drive 7. East Garden
8. Wild Garden 9. Magnolia Walk 10. Kitchen Garden*

Through his writings Robinson became extremely well known and influential. Of his earlier books by far the most important was *The Wild Garden* (1870) which had the subtitle 'Our groves and shrubberies made beautiful by the naturalization of hardy exotic plants'; by 'exotic' he meant plants introduced from foreign countries. The book also had a chapter on the use of British wild flowers in the garden which, outside the humble cottage garden, was a distinctly novel idea. At this time, too, he founded the first of many periodicals – *The Garden* (from 1871) which brought him to the attention of a wide readership and published the early work of many gardening writers who together defined advanced gardening taste at that period. Among his contributors was Gertrude Jekyll whose gardening philosophy had much in common with Robinson's. That magazine was aimed at the owners of larger gardens but his later *Gardening Illustrated* (from 1879) introduced the new way of gardening to an increasingly numerous type of gardener – owners of newly built suburban houses who wanted a different kind of garden for a new way of life.

In 1883 he published his most influential book, *The English Flower Garden*, which passed through twenty-four printings in his lifetime and has continued to infuriate and delight long after his death. The book is still intensely readable, especially for Robinson's acute descriptions of plants based on his own close observation.

William Robinson was a rare pioneer, a decisive influence on the way we garden today. Many of his theories and interests are particularly important today for he was, in a nutshell, an ecologist long before such things were fashionable. He thought that the most important thing about planting a garden was to choose hardy plants and put them in sites that corresponded as closely as possible to those of their natural habitats. Only by knowing the lie of the land intimately could one ever make a good garden – 'I believe that the best results can only be got by the owner who knows and loves his ground. The great evil is the stereotyped plan ... his picture can only come from

constant thought as to the ground itself.' He repeatedly emphasized the importance of the whole concept of a garden rather than the superficial decorative trimmings – one should consider 'The picture before the frame', as he put it.

When Robinson started gardening in the 1850s the prevailing fashion in large gardens was for formal arrangements which were dependent on vast seasonal bedding schemes, spring and summer, and this style of gardening was very widely practised until World War II. Robinson himself approved of bedding schemes in his early career but came to reject them completely. In 1872 he went to see the parterre at Cliveden and said it was 'one of the most repulsive examples of the extra formal school, [thrusting] itself in a rather awkward manner into the grand landscape'. This very elaborate parterre had been replanted in the 1850s by John Fleming and in spring alone 20,000 plants were bedded out together with 10,000 tulips. Conservatories and heated glasshouses for the cultivation of tender plants needed for bedding were essential features of early Victorian gardens. But Robinson's view was that not only would plants grow better if planted in the correct site but also they *looked* better. 'The vegetation that clusters round the lake', he wrote of his own lake at Gravetye, 'is, apart from native trees which come where they will, that which belongs to the waterside. Poplar, willow in

A fountain in the South Garden where many aromatic plants flourish – among them sage, artemisia and lavender.

variety and trees with pointed leaves.' He also realized that an artificial environment like a glasshouse tended to conceal a plant's true needs. He was among the first to understand, for example, that camellias were perfectly hardy and to plant them unprotected in the garden instead of under glass. He was violently opposed to topiary and clipping in general – what he called 'barber's gardening' – 'Hundreds of gardens in England are disfigured by this ignorant and stupid practice. Half the beauty of the evergreen trees – ilex and yew – is owing to form and movement in the wind.'

'Some years ago I came into possession of an old Manor, built in 1596, with much to be done to it,' wrote William Robinson in 1917. He bought Gravetye Manor in 1885 and almost immediately began to make his garden. The house was a handsome gabled manor house in an exceptionally fine position in rolling land in West Sussex, enclosed by old woodland but with open views to the south across a wide valley – a wonderful setting for a house and garden.

Robinson is often regarded, somewhat unthinkingly, as the sworn foe of all formality and an unyielding devotee of the wild garden. In fact, there was much formality in his garden. One of the first things he made at Gravetye, in 1885, was a long formal rectangular tennis lawn immediately north-west of the house. He was careful, however, here and elsewhere, to fit such things in with the natural lie of the land and to preserve any particularly good trees. The Flower Garden, for example, which he made immediately to the west of the house, had some fine old yews, which are still there, but their view was blocked by some poor cedars which he felled.

The Flower Garden evolved according to Robinson's changing ideas. When it was first laid out it consisted of an open rectangular lawn with a surrounding gravel path and a large collection of Tea roses about the perimeter. Robinson 'thought that these most beautiful kinds of Roses had been much neglected, and resolved to grow them in the open air'. The Tea roses had started to come from China in the early nineteenth century but many of them are not reliably hardy and in Robinson's time they were usually grown in heated greenhouses or as pot plants. By the 1880s they were being crossed with Hybrid Perpetual roses to produce the large-flowered Hybrid Teas which became the first truly mass-market garden roses. Although some of the less hardy Tea roses were cut to the ground in severe winters they sprouted again from the base and provided magnificent flowers late in the season, continuing to September and October.

In the eastern corners of the Flower Garden lawn Robinson added beds of what he called 'Tufted' pansies which were hybrids between the alpine horned pansy (*Viola cornuta*) and native heartsease (*V. tricolor*). Judging from contemporary photographs these were rather fussy little beds although Robinson insisted on planting them in 'colonies and bold groups . . . never in lines and never dotted about singly'. So while the form and position of these beds was wholly artificial, the planting within them was naturalistic. There is a charming photograph of him sprawled on the lawn with the beds in the background. Later still, a grid of York-flagged paths was laid down separating rectangular beds with stone edgings. This was painted by Beatrice Parsons in 1912 and she shows rich mixed plantings of roses, campanulas, agapanthus and profuse edgings of carnations. By this stage the Flower Garden had become completely different in character from Robinson's rather chaste and fiddly first inspiration; it was richly colourful but with the controlling discipline of a firm framework of paths and symmetrically arranged beds. It was also, incidentally, in direct opposition to the view he expressed in *The English Flower Garden* – 'One purpose of this book is to help uproot the common notion that a flower garden is necessarily a set pattern – usually geometrical – placed on the side of the house.' By the early twentieth century his own Flower Garden exactly conformed to 'the set pattern'. Later still, metal arches were added at the end of each of the beds, and railings down the middle of them, to support roses and clematis.

On Robinson's death in 1935 the Gravetye Estate was

*In the enclosed South Garden, full of Robinsonian plants, the colour
scheme is cool and soothing – grey, blue and violet with
occasional warmer notes of pink.*

left to a trust. The house and thirty acres of garden and woodland was let as a private estate on a long lease and the Forestry Commission was charged with the responsibility for the remaining 1,000 acres of woodland. The garden, large, complicated and demanding knowledgeable attention, gradually decayed, greatly accelerated by the shortage of labour during World War II. By the late 1950s it was derelict and when the lease was bought by Peter Herbert in 1957 no gardening at all had been done for two years. It was his plan to convert the house into a luxurious country hotel and he saw that an attractive garden would give

much pleasure to the hotel guests. He knew, of course, of the connection between Gravetye and William Robinson but knew little about his garden philosophy. By that time Robinson was not exactly forgotten but the battles that he had fought seemed distant history and many of his ideas had become the normal practice of countless gardeners who had never heard of him. Also the subject of garden history itself, and the very idea of restoring a garden, had scarcely developed.

When Peter Herbert arrived he found the garden 'in a pitiful state . . . The great peach tree stood dead in the conservatory . . . the York stone paths had disappeared under a welter of weeds – unmown lawns were a tangle of rotting grass.' He began work on restoring the garden by clearing manually the Flower Garden to the west of the house. At this time almost all his energies were devoted to making the hotel work but he was able to garden at weekends and do one day's work per week to help the single full-time gardener.

With the Flower Garden Peter Herbert encountered a general problem of garden restoration which Gravetye Manor illustrates particularly vividly. William Robinson lived at Gravetye for over fifty years, in which time the garden changed as his ideas evolved. Although he had all sorts of vigorously expressed principles they were by no means unchanging. For example, in his book *Home Landscapes* (1914) he wrote that iron fencing was 'the most infernal outrage ever done to the landscape beauty of England'. Yet he himself, in an attempt to keep out rabbits, installed hundreds of yards of iron fencing about the perimeter of his garden and it may still be seen. In the case of the Flower Garden, with such a complicated history of changes, there was no single point of historical reference and it seemed sensible, first of all, to clear the ground, most of which was done laboriously by hand, preserving anything of value.

Peter Herbert was very lucky to have as a near neighbour the great plantsman Will Ingwersen who had known Robinson, and he gave valuable advice on replanting.

*By the South Garden steps self-sown valerian (*Centranthus ruber*), 'a handsome, hardy plant', thought William Robinson, contrasts with the white and silver of* Convolvulus cneorum.

Rather than attempting to reproduce any known scheme of William Robinson's, Mr Herbert followed the principle of immersing himself in Robinson's writings. One of the most valuable of his books was *Gravetye Manor; or Twenty Years' Work round an Old Manor House* (1911) which was a selection of notes from Robinson's gardening journals which he kept from the moment he started the garden in 1885. This describes specific work that Robinson undertook in the garden and gives immensely valuable information about his way of gardening. It is also reassuringly candid about failures. Robinson mentions, for example, planting some lady's slipper orchids, sent specially from Philadelphia, and adds a footnote – 'Never could find a trace of the plants since.'

When the choked mass of weeds was removed the layout of flagged paths and stone-edged beds was found to be as shown in Beatrice Parsons's painting. In the south-west corner the yew trees which Robinson had so admired were still there. Mr Herbert removed the metal arches and railings in the beds, finding them – especially in the winter – gaunt and gallows-like. In replanting the beds advice was given both by Will Ingwersen and by Graham Stuart Thomas who has also taken a helpful interest. The pattern of beds has been kept and the essential character of Robinson's arrangement as seen in Beatrice Parsons's painting has been successfully retained. The sundial, found hidden in the undergrowth, has been restored to its place at the centre of a cruciform pattern of paved paths which divide a large central lawn. Rectangular beds parallel with the sides of the lawn are intensively planted with herbaceous and woody plants. Mr Herbert has not attempted to restrict himself to historically authentic plants although many of the plants are those used by Robinson – sedums (which Robinson used to underplant his Tea roses), pinks ('plants of the highest garden value'), many violas, the milk thistle (*Silybum marianum* – 'bright glistening green with broad white veins'), campanulas and hostas. Rising above these herbaceous plantings are shrub roses – 'Felicia', 'Honorine de Brabant', 'Belle de Crécy', 'Ferdinand Pichard' and many others. Mixed borders of this sort planted in a naturalistic way, with edgings of pinks and sedums and herbaceous plantings with pronounced foliage interest in association with rose bushes have become almost universal. It is hard to realize how novel this kind of informal mixed planting was in Robinson's time and how completely his style of gardening has entered into and remained in English gardens.

North of this, the Azalea Walk was in a desperate state when Mr Herbert came. The original plantings of azaleas had become congested and it was infested with weeds.

Gradually this has been restored with fine gravel paths wandering through varied plantings of azaleas, rhododendrons and Japanese maples which are underplanted with a ground-cover of ferns, pulmonaria, comfrey and sheets of cyclamen. Robinson described this area after planting it in 1890 – 'Planted a variety of azaleas on the slope above the flower gardens . . . so as to plant the bank in a shrubby way. This plan at the same time gives us nice spaces for pretty plants beneath and between the azaleas.' This effect has been exactly re-created. Running along the northern side of this part of the garden is Robinson's formal rectangular lawn beyond which woodland sweeps up the hill. On the lower slopes Mr Herbert has been establishing a Wild Garden in which grassy paths wind

*T*he Flower Garden was planned essentially for one season – high summer. Many old-fashioned roses are underplanted with a rich mixture of Robinsonian plants.

through old thorns, silver birch, many decorative Japanese maples and hazel-nuts. In Robinson's time all this had been a heather garden but they did not flourish here and the only survivors were a few gnarled *Erica arborea*. It now makes a convincingly Robinsonian preamble to the woodland beyond.

Immediately to the south of the house, protected by walls, is the little South Garden. In Robinson's time this was filled with border carnations arranged in narrow stone-edged beds. Robinson realized that his cold retentive soil was not what carnations liked, but here, at the top of a slope, he had one of the best-drained and sunniest sites in the garden. When Mr Herbert came, the original pattern of many small beds survived. The whole area was re-arranged to make secluded sitting areas and replanted with an immense range of plants to provide a cool and restful colour scheme of greys and silvers, with many plants which Robinson admired and described in his books. He thought *Perovskia atriplicifolia* was 'worth a place in the choicest garden for its graceful habit and long season of beauty'. *Melianthus major*, although known in England since the late seventeenth century, was revalued by Robinson who admired its 'finely-cut, large, glaucous leaves'. *Carpenteria californica* had been introduced to England as recently as 1880 when an American reader sent specimens

Above: The porch opening out on to the Flower Garden is garlanded with the rose 'Constance Spry'. Left: The naturalistic meadow setting to the south-east of the Manor in late summer.

Markham wrote books about clematis which, ironically, have never been very easy to grow at Gravetye. Markham, nevertheless, successfully bred clematis and many of his excellent cultivars are still in commerce – for example *Clematis macropetala* 'Markham's Pink', *C.* 'Ernest Markham' and *C.* 'Gravetye Beauty'.

To the south of the house is the area that Robinson called the Alpine Meadow, on a steep slope that runs down to the upper lake. Here Robinson naturalized huge quantities of scillas, erythroniums, anemones (including, of course, *A. nemorosa* 'Robinsoniana'), daffodils and fritillaries. To allow the seed to ripen, the grass was not cut until late into the summer. This kind of meadow gardening, now widely practised, was in Robinson's day revolutionary. He took great care in the actual planting of the bulbs to avoid any air of artificiality; of narcissi he wrote, for example, 'All were planted as far as possible in free "natural" looking colonies, the centre somewhat closely massed with outlying fringes and groups.' He also chose particular species carefully for their setting. For example, here he planted the 'common English sorts' of daffodil by the shore of the upper lake but reserved the poet's daffodil (*Narcissus poeticus*) for drifts that fringed a romantic grove of oaks to the west of the Alpine Meadow. This meadow, untouched by fertilizer or weedkiller since Robinson's day, has been impeccably preserved and many of the plants that Robinson planted are still here. When Mr Herbert came a path went straight across the meadow, rather too abruptly, and he has made a more leisurely path that follows the contours in a natural way.

The lakes, upper and lower, were part of the garden in which Robinson took an especial interest. The upper lake, long and thin, was newly made in Robinson's time and he remodelled it, removing an island ('prim and too artificial') and planting its banks with suitable plants, especially the white willow (*Salix alba*) which he thought was the most beautiful of all trees of the northern hemisphere. Later on when one of the gardeners was drowned Robinson drained the lake, which never again held water in his

to Robinson's journal *The Garden*. 'A lovely hardy shrub for walls in southern districts', it first flowered in Miss Jekyll's garden at Munstead in 1885. Here too are many sages – 'few plants are more useful, with their showy spikes of flowers.' All these are planted in proper Robinsonian fashion in a place that suits them well. In addition there are many plants with striking foliage – *Macleaya cordata*, cardoons (*Cynara cardunculus*), *Phormium tenax* – with climbers festooning the walls. Among these are several kinds of clematis honouring the memory of Robinson's Head Gardener Ernest Markham. Both Robinson and

*A swathe of common catmint (*Nepeta mussinii*) in front of a pergola draped with* Wisteria floribunda *'Alba' at the west end of the Flower Garden.*

lifetime. Mr Herbert has now reinstated it, which was a major operation. Robinson had built an iron fence down the middle of the site and planted large numbers of his favourite white willow. The fence, with very solid footings, was removed with a bulldozer and over a hundred willows had to be uprooted, the ground cleared and the bottom of the lake dredged. The sluice which separates the upper and lower lakes was put back in position and in three weeks the lake had filled with water and once again assumed its original appearance. To Mr Herbert's surprise many of the original water plants re-emerged, including *Potamogeton crispus* and *Egeria densa* which now need annual reduction. The near side of the lake is kept fairly simply but the far side is densely planted with bamboos (*Shibataea kumasasa* and *Phyllostachys viridi-glaucescens*) and the giant reed *Arundo donax*.

The lower lake was infested with pond weed and for many years weekend guests were commandeered to help clear it by dragging a weed-cutter through the water. This was a 1.8m/6ft alloy blade to which a rope could be fixed at each end. Above the blade and at right angles to it a grid gathered the severed weed, allowing it to be dragged to the shore where it was piled up, so that water-snails and other pond creatures were able to fall back into the water. The weed was left on the bank where it rotted down very quickly. It was discovered that some of the weed, *Egeria densa* for example, thrived on this cutting and was better left to its own devices.

It was in the course of weed-clearing that an attractive old wrought-iron garden bench was found which is now in position on the north side of the lake. The paths also were cleared to reveal the views intended by Robinson. These paths had originally been made in 1903 and, as Robinson wrote, their purpose was to make 'effects of water better, and of the plantings too'. Mr Herbert has restocked the lakes with trout, brown and rainbow, as they were in Robinson's day.

In October 1987 the woodland at Gravetye was shattered by the great storm which devastated many gardens

in the south-east of England. The drive to the house was blocked by over one hundred fallen trees. To the north-west of the house swathes of Robinson's original tree planting were obliterated. He had planted a huge grove of Corsican pines (*Pinus nigra* var. *maritima*) of which two hundred – some of which were 30m/110ft tall – were felled by the storm. A handful survive and the spot is poignantly marked by Robinson's original cast-iron label with the words 'Corsican W.R. 1888'. The damage at Gravetye was on a spectacular scale and it took almost six months to clear up the fallen trees and the damaged fencing.

The new borders below the south side of the house contain chiefly herbaceous plants with striking foliage – among them, variegated hostas, Helichrysum petiolare *and the giant thistle* Onopordon arabicum.

South of the Corsican pines many other old conifers were blown down and Mr Herbert has been quick to make good in a thoroughly Robinsonian fashion. The removal of all these mature trees in this very clayey area created severe problems of drainage and new land-drains had to be installed before any replanting could be done. Here 100mm/4in Agripipe flexible drains were laid in 450mm/18in trenches filled with gravel. Mr Herbert has replanted many ornamental trees and shrubs in bold groups of the sort Robinson would have liked. Here are *Liquidambar styraciflua* ('a very beautiful summer-leaving maple-like tree from Florida westwards' as Robinson called it, characteristically telling his reader what it looks like, what it does and where it comes from); a grove of aristocratic magnolias (*M. wilsonii*, *M. × loebneri* and *M. × soulangeana*); maples (*Acer palmatum* 'Senkaki' and *A. davidii* 'George Forrest'). To the west of all this a belt of common holly has been planted which will in time protect these new plantings from storms to come. And what did Robinson think of common holly? – 'It would be difficult to exaggerate the value of this plant, whether as an evergreen tree, the best of all fence-shelters for our fields, or as a lovely ornament of our gardens.'

The kitchen garden, to the north-west of the wild garden, has been thoroughly restored. Robinson made this kitchen garden on a south-facing slope and enclosed it in a gigantic oval of stone walls. It had been totally neglected and was a terrifying sea of mare's tails which Mr Herbert's children were encouraged to dig up, with prizes for the longest specimens. The spring which provided all the water for the house originates here and is marked by a fine Venetian well-head. This is a thoroughly watery part of the garden and fluctuations in the water-table had damaged the stone walls which have been tied with irons and bolted through. The only plant to survive from Robinson's time is a large mulberry which flops over the wall on the northern side providing shade for a stone bench. Many fruit trees have been espaliered round the south-facing walls, a very wide range of vegetables and

soft fruits is grown and the garden is now immensely productive. Ernest Markham wrote a book on *Raspberries and Kindred Fruits* with the subtitle 'How to obtain fresh supplies daily from June to November' and the kitchen garden at Gravetye is once again able to do that. A new project is the restoration of the peach house, upon which Mr Herbert intends shortly to embark.

Robinson saw his garden and woodland as a richly varied estate – in which the beauty of flowering plants and of trees in appropriate settings was allied to the ideas of domestic rural economy. His own produce was served at table; his own wood heated the house in fireplaces designed by himself to be smoke-free; the house was provided with his own spring water. All this is once again true of Gravetye.

THE ESSENCE OF GRAVETYE MANOR

A curving drive through rich woodland leads the visitor to Gravetye Manor. The garden proper starts with a set of iron gates beyond which the drive is edged with deep verges of mown grass which from time to time penetrate in broad swathes into the groups of shrubs and ornamental trees that lie on either side. In the grass are clumps of William Robinson's *Leucojum aestivum* 'Gravetye Giant'. Many of the plants here date from Robinson's time – fine old Japanese maples, *Aesculus indica*, rhododendrons, *Robinia pseudoacacia* and skimmias. There is nothing either wild or natural about it, but it is a carefully controlled passage between the woodland outside and the formalities within.

From a gravel forecourt in front of the manor a path leads south through a pergola with massive stone pillars, draped with a vast wisteria, making a shady but monumental tunnel leading through to the garden – 'the pergola should always have a use and meaning in its direction,' as Robinson wrote in *Home Landscapes*. An idyllic valley scene to the south is framed by the pergola – the land falls away, a grassy meadow sweeps down to the lake on the other side of which the land rises steeply in densely wooded slopes. A path leads along to the west with the Alpine Meadow to the left and the house to the right. Stone flags lead up to a little enclosed South Garden where the visitor may sit surrounded by an aromatic jungle and glimpse the Alpine Meadow through a gap in the foliage.

On the west side of the South Garden an arch leads through to the Flower Garden which has an air of parterre-like formality and, furthermore, occupies exactly the position that such an arrangement would have had in a Tudor garden – below the windows of the house. The formal pattern of paths here was made by Robinson partly so that parts of the garden could be visited, and plants admired, in wet weather. It is too easy to cast Robinson in the role of the wild man of gardening, damning all formality and loving only the natural garden. In fact, near the house, as can be seen vividly today at Gravetye, formality is entirely permissible; indeed, apart from the practical matter of dry feet, it is necessary to mediate between the symmetry and formality of the house and the wilder

gardens beyond. And it is here that we can learn the essential Robinsonian lesson, not far off the Renaissance ideal of the harmony between house and garden; but Robinson wanted to continue this idea into a harmony of garden with the landscape that surrounded it.

Looking north from the Flower Garden the ground slopes gently upwards and the view is directed to the sky-line with its few remaining Corsican pines, Scots pine (*Pinus sylvestris*) and silver birch (*Betula pendula*) and, in the middle ground, *Nyssa sylvatica*, old specimens of *Davidia involucrata* and a bold clump of pampas grass (*Cortaderia selloana*). This last, so often seen in small suburban front gardens, needs space to be appreciated and Robinson liked to see it in a woodland setting.

Many visitors to Gravetye will be happy to revel in the rich plantings and idyllic views. But the whole garden is an object-lesson in Robinsonian planting with appropriate schemes in different places and the whole accommodated to the surrounding countryside with perfect harmony.

The view from the south side of the Manor. A meadow – in which Robinson naturalized many plants – sweeps down to the restored upper lake.

HESTERCOMBE HOUSE

$\mathscr{I}$N a position of unspoilt beauty with wide views of the Vale of Taunton looking towards the Blackdown Hills, Hestercombe in Somerset is an ancient place and its name dates back to an Anglo-Saxon charter of 854. The Domesday survey describes it as a substantial estate – 'Worth forty shillings, now fifty shillings', that is to say, between five and six hundred acres. There was a house here in the Middle Ages owned by the Warre family, from whom the estate passed by marriage to John Bampfylde whose son Coplestone Warre Bampfylde succeeded in 1750. Bampfylde was an artist, interested in gardening and an intimate of Henry Hoare, the maker of Stourhead. Bampfylde did several paintings in 1770 of the recently made landscape garden at Stourhead, which

Above: The Pergola is planted with clematis and roses in violet, blue and pink. Opposite: The Rotunda pool was designed by Lutyens as a simple mirror to reflect its decorative surroundings. Walls are planted with wintersweet (Chimonanthus praecox) and the rose 'Climbing Little White Pet'.

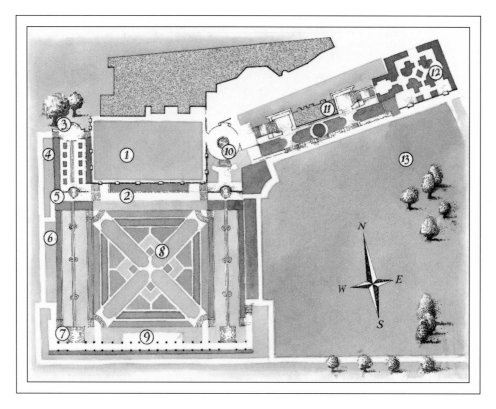

remain among the most valuable pictures of the garden in its early stages. Under the spell of Stourhead he made a romantic garden of his own in the valley behind Hester-combe House, of which traces remain today – some fine mature trees, the remains of a handsome brick and stone arbour and a temple and part of an ornamental lake. The figure of a witch painted on a wall of the arbour was referred to in a contemporary poem about the garden written by Dr Langhorne, the Vicar of Blagdon in Somerset:

O'er Bamfylde's woods, by various nature graced,

A Witch presides, but then that Witch is taste.

In the late eighteenth century Bampfylde's garden, now forgotten, was one of the most famous in the west country. It was the first garden made on this site of bewitching possibilities.

The estate was sold in 1872 to the first Viscount Port-man who rebuilt John Bampfylde's handsome Queen Anne house in 1874-7 under the direction of the architect Henry Hall. An article in *Country Life* in 1908 cruelly but accurately described Hall as 'one of that large class of Victorian architects who did not understand what style was and who lacked feeling both for form or surface. It is uninformed and uninspired clerk's work.' Lord Portman gave the estate to his grandson, The Hon. E.W.B. Port-man, as a wedding present. It was he who in 1903 commissioned Edwin Lutyens to make a garden on a new site on sloping meadows to the south of the house. Lutyens was then thirty-four and already firmly embarked on the golden career that made him the most successful and the finest architect of the Edwardian period and, in collaboration with Gertrude Jekyll, the greatest garden designer of his time. They had first met in 1889 – 'at a tea-table, the silver kettle and the conversation reflecting rhododen-drons,' as Lutyens described it. He was twenty-six years

1. Nineteenth-century Terrace 2. The Grey Walk 3. Arbour 4. Rose Garden
5. Pool 6. Rill Terrace 7. Pool 8. The Plat 9. Pergola 10. Rotunda
11. Orangery 12. Dutch Garden 13. Orangery Lawn

her junior and she, an accomplished artist now afflicted with severe myopia, had abandoned art and turned whole-heartedly to gardening. It was an unlikely partnership but it produced astonishing gardens.

By the time Lutyens was asked to design the new garden at Hestercombe he had been collaborating with Miss Jekyll for twelve years. They had evolved a style which was quite distinctive and yet it drew its inspiration from traditional forms of architecture and planting. Lutyens was deeply interested in vernacular architecture and the use of local building materials. Miss Jekyll trained as an artist and took a knowledgeable interest in the new ideas of colour theory that influenced Impressionist painters. She met both John Ruskin and William Morris and was immensely knowledgeable about the countryside, particularly about traditional crafts. She shared with Lutyens the conviction that house and garden should be thought of as a unity. In her ideas on planting Miss Jekyll had much in common with William Robinson. The discipline of Lutyens's formal architectural garden designs provided the ideal framework for Miss Jekyll's planting. To see one of their great gardens today is a curious experience, for they seem at once startlingly original and oddly familiar. The familiarity comes from the classical principles underlying the architecture and the materials in which it is executed. The originality lies in Lutyens's brilliant variations on these familiar ingredients and in the rich but controlled planting at which Miss Jekyll excelled.

Although Miss Jekyll had designed several gardens before she met Lutyens, there is no doubt that her best were made in collaboration with him. By the time they started at Hestercombe they had achieved a perfectly harmonious working relationship and made several gardens of exquisite quality – including Marsh Court in Hampshire, and Folly Farm and Deanery Garden, both in Berkshire. But the results of their work at Hestercombe surpassed all of these. 'The Hestercombe gardens', in the words of Lutyens's biographer Christopher Hussey, 'represent the peak of the collaboration with Miss Jekyll and

his first application of her genius to classical garden design on a grand scale . . . The whole conception of the Hestercombe gardens, with the brilliant handling of varying levels to produce at once a lucid and an intricate horticultural drama, is entirely mature, indeed unsurpassed in Lutyens's garden repertory.'

At Hestercombe they had a wonderful site. The land slopes gently south from Lord Portman's rebuilt house, forbidding and undistinguished. Lutyens's design firmly turns its back on the gloomy mansion and all attention is focused on the garden in its rural setting and the wide, open views that lie beyond it. It is a rare example of an unworthy house being adorned with a masterly garden.

In essence, the garden consists of three giant terraces. The first, immediately to the south of the house, running its whole width, is a deep balustraded terrace made in the nineteenth century and probably part of Hall's rebuilding. Originally it had Victorian scrolled parterres and Lutyens left this unaltered. Today the parterres have gone and the spacious lawned area provides a kind of visual no-man's-land between the new garden and the house. Its firm rectangular shape enabled Lutyens to relate his garden in a logical way to the idiosyncratic, asymmetric south façade of the house. The second terrace is the Grey Walk which lies below the nineteenth-century terrace, with beds on either side. It overlooks the third terrace, a square parterre exactly the same width as the Grey Walk, called the Great Plat. This in turn is raised up from the fields that lie beyond it. Flanking the Great Plat, on the same level as the Grey Walk, are two identical water gardens. Miss Jekyll described these in her book *Wall and Water Gardens*: 'The planted rill may be considered the invention of Mr E.L.Lutyens. The one in the garden at Hestercombe shows the most typical form. The wide, paved ledges make pleasant walking ways; at even intervals they turn, after the manner of the gathered ribbon strapwork of ancient needlework, and enclose circular tanklets, giving the opportunity of a distinct punctuation with important plants.' Each rill is fed from a pool cut into the terrace wall

from which carved masks in the keystones spout water. At the other end the water drops into rectangular lily-ponds. Running across the southern extremity, and linking these two ponds, is a pergola, built in characteristic Lutyens fashion of alternating square and rounded pillars of rough stone supporting oak cross-pieces. All this is perfectly symmetrical but it is much enlivened by a dash of asymmetry on each side of the nineteenth-century terrace.

To the west is a rose garden, a pattern of small rectangular beds on either side of a stone path. At its head is a spacious and shady arbour of wych elm (*Ulmus glabra*) – one of the very few original plants remaining in the garden – enfolding a bench designed by Lutyens. On the east side of that terrace is a spectacular Lutyens *coup de théâtre*. The Rotunda is a circular enclosure with high stone walls and a circular pool at the centre. It has three entrances linking the nineteenth-century terrace, steps down to the East Water Garden and a path leading to Lutyens's orangery. The orangery and the Dutch Garden that lies beyond it run parallel to the awkwardly shaped façade of the house; that is to say they form a dog-leg axis jutting out at an odd angle to the main axes of the rest of the garden. The Rotunda enabled Lutyens to link these things painlessly and, typically, he made something special of it. So, far from seeming to be the contrived solution to a tricky problem, it becomes an essential and attractive feature with the character of complete inevitability. Lined with winter-sweet (*Chimonanthus praecox*) – the original plants survive – and roses 'Little White Pet', 'Perle d'Or' and the Rugosa 'Blanche Double de Coubert', in winter and in high summer it is bathed in scent. Miss Jekyll had an acute sense of smell which, as her eyesight began to fail, became increasingly important to her. She liked to place fragrant plants – rosemary and myrtle were favourites – at entrances, against which one might brush in passing.

The orangery, in Lutyens's most dashing 'Wrenaissance' style, is made of Ham stone, ornamented with richly carved details but calmed down with soothing bands of grey Devonian clay limestone. Steps lead up to

The east rill where irises flourish in damp beds enclosed in loops of stone – 'The planted rill may be considered the invention of Mr E.L.Lutyens,' wrote Miss Jekyll.

the Dutch Garden, formerly a rubbish dump which Lutyens smoothed and made into a beguiling paved parterre of lavender, roses and catmint.

Lutyens selected with his habitual care the material for the walls, terraces, paths and garden buildings. He built the walls of self-splitting unworked local stone, quarried in the combe, and thus made a visual link with the pinkish-brown earth of that part of Somerset. The walls have deeply recessed mortar, made of a weak mix of stone-dust and lime, giving them the rustic and rough-hewn character of Somerset dry-stone walls. The walls have finely cut

ashlar coping made of the lovely golden limestone from nearby Hamdon Hill – always called, somewhat confusingly, Ham Hill or Ham stone. Paths are made of slabs of morce slate, a warm grey with a reflecting, shiny surface. The slabs are roughly shaped and laid in lively patterns, enriched at turning points with mill-stones laid among them – a characteristic Lutyens motif. Nearer the house – in the detail of the orangery, the Rotunda, the lily-ponds and in doorcases and stairs, Lutyens allowed himself the luxury of beautifully carved ornamentation – masks, brackets, swags and spandrels – worked in Ham Hill stone. Farther from the house, the details of stonework are less sophisticated, so that the pergola, which runs along the southern extremity of the Great Plat, is made of roughly shaped stone columns and simple oak beams.

The beauty of the site and the rural landscape that surrounds it imposed limitations which Lutyens solved with characteristic ingenuity. The countryside is very much part of the garden, an essential view to which the design of the garden frequently directs one's attention – thus it was important that the garden should harmonize with its setting. Nor was Lutyens oblivious to the splendid remains of Bampfylde's eighteenth-century landscape. Christopher Hussey, writing about the garden in its heyday, describes Bampfylde's Scots pines which Lutyens took care to work 'so effectively into almost every view'. Apart from their intrinsic beauty these had made the house less conspicuous and anchored house and garden more firmly to the landscape.

Work had started on the garden in 1904. By 1908 it was substantially finished and a long article was published in *Country Life* with many photographs showing the planting in its complete state. The gardens are described as 'a work of art to be admired and an example to be followed. They prove that an architect can be in unison with Nature, that a formal garden can form part of a landscape.' A further long article, by Christopher Hussey, appeared in *Country Life* in 1927 showing the garden at its zenith: Hestercombe was at its peak between the wars when eighteen

The Polyanthus rose 'Nathalie Nypels'- not originally planted at Hestercombe – set off by the rich purple of Lavandula angustifolia 'Munstead'.

gardeners were employed to tend it and it was at the centre of a busy social life.

During World War II the house was occupied by the American Army and the garden fell into serious neglect. In 1944 the house and garden were ceded to the Crown Commissioners in lieu of estate duty and after the war many very fine trees to the north and east, doubtless part of Bampfylde's eighteenth-century planting, were felled. Subsequently, the house was let to the Somerset County Council to be used as headquarters by the County Fire Brigade and under the terms of the lease the County was responsible for the upkeep of the garden. It was maintained, but increasingly the old planting was replaced with inappropriate introductions. In this period only one gardener was in full-time employment, with a further gardener working eighteen hours a week.

In 1970, the Somerset County Council (prompted by William Mount, a landscape architect working in the County Architect's Department) set up a working party 'to consider the possibility of reinstating the Hestercombe Gardens to the original standards and plans of Sir Edwin Lutyens and Miss Jekyll'. It was a critical moment in the history of the garden. By 1972 a detailed survey of the existing planting showed that most beds had none of their original planting and only two retained more than ten per cent of it. Miss Jekyll's exquisite borders had simply disappeared. A few important pieces of planting survived, including the wych elm arbour. This was injected against Dutch elm disease with apparent success. It was feared that holes drilled in the relatively slender trunk might weaken it further but this was not the case and it now grows vigorously. The state of the masonry had become almost irretrievably perilous and a survey estimated that 'another 10 winters would see the total destruction of the Ham Stone balustrading', of which there is a very large expanse. A further problem was that, in 1952, there had been an auction sale of the garden ornaments and furniture – pots for the Dutch Garden, statues and the distinctive benches designed by Lutyens himself. In a Lutyens garden

these things are not merely items of decoration, wheeled on adventitiously; they are an essential part of it.

By the spring of 1973 a programme of restoration was worked out which was to start with the Grey Walk and to tackle the northern segment of the Great Plat in the winter of that year. It was an early decision to restore complete, relatively small, sections of the garden one by one – a tactic which is both psychologically more satisfying, and often more instructive. There were other considerations which had more to do with horticultural diplomacy. For example, the garden had in its declining period been open

Carved stone masks, fringed with grapevines, spout water into curved basins at the head of each rill. Lutyens was a master of the decorative use of stonework.

to visitors who deplored the removal of plants they loved, however incorrect and un-Jekyllesque they were. Thus, initial plantings were much denser than proposed either by Miss Jekyll's plans or by the usual rules of planting. But they helped appease critics; they smothered weeds; and, no doubt, they impressed the controllers of the purse-strings at County Hall. Gradually, as the plantings matured, they were thinned out to their correct density.

An amazing stroke of good luck, and possibly an omen of the future, had been the discovery of Miss Jekyll's planting plans, in her own hand, pinned up in the potting shed. These were not complete but gaps were filled with the help of the Reef Point Gardens Collection at the University of California, which possesses a vast archive of Gertrude Jekyll material. Thus most of the plans, the essential 'score' for the garden, survived.

Miss Jekyll's plans are meticulously drawn showing an exact understanding of the site (which at Hestercombe, as far as we know, she never visited) and the planting possibilities. Although the plans show clearly the location and the density of the planting there were still many problems to solve about the exact identity of the plants specified by her. It was not merely that their names had changed but in many cases the exact species or variety of the plant was not given. It was only by a thorough immersion in Miss Jekyll's writings that it was possible to judge which plants she would have used in certain circumstances. Her writings, too, are rich in information on her horticultural techniques, so vital to an understanding of the appearance of her gardens. To give one example – she abhorred the use of bamboos or stakes to support herbaceous plants. She thought that they were an unnecessarily artificial and harsh vertical presence in the foliage and she advocated the use of brush-wood instead.

Early in the planning stage of the restoration there was much debate about whether to go for complete authenticity or to aim at a reconstruction honouring Miss Jekyll's spirit but reducing maintenance. It was the latter course that was chosen. The county was acutely conscious of the importance of arriving at a garden that would not have additional burdens of maintenance and there is no point in restoring a garden if it then cannot be kept up. Besides, it was simply impossible to know exactly which plants Miss Jekyll intended. On her plans she could be provocatively vague, writing, for example, 'Seven pink paeonies' in her elegant, spindly handwriting. Her books and contemporary nurserymen's lists were carefully read in order to discover exactly the cultivars she might have used. But in the end it was decided to choose plants which were Jekyllian in spirit but which also reduced maintenance. There was the further problem that it seems that some parts of her design were never actually executed in the form she proposed. In the Great Plat, judging from the photographs taken in 1908, it is plain that Miss Jekyll's plans had not been carried out. For example, the plans specify canna lilies but none is visible in the photographs. Thus the restored planting was based on the evidence of photographs together with the original plans, with some variations determined by the need to reduce maintenance. For example, Miss Jekyll had specified 'Mr Sutton's variegated maize' (*Zea mays* 'Variegata'), a favourite plant of hers. A problem at Hestercombe is that the old walled gardens, and glasshouses, are now in the separate ownership of the Crown Commissioners. Thus, apart from the consideration of labour, there are no longer the facilities for propagating annuals of which, contrary to belief, Miss Jekyll was very fond. Here the perennial grass *Miscanthus sinensis* 'Gracillimus' has been used instead of the annual variegated sweet-corn.

Although there is not an enormous number of different species and varieties of plants in the garden – the complete plant list has less than 300 names – Miss Jekyll did depend on the multiple or repeated use of plants. Her genius lay less in the restless pursuit of botanical novelties than in a very exact understanding of the specific values of plants and how to use them effectively in the garden. Many of the plants chosen in the restoration reflect this spirit. For example, Miss Jekyll specified the silvery

The Grey Walk is planted with mounds of Santolina chamaecyparissus nana, Nepeta mussinii, Stachys byzantina *'Silver Carpet' and, in the wall, clouds of a distinctively Jekyllesque plant,* Erigeron karvinskianus.

lamb's tongue, *Stachys byzantina* (syn. *S. lanata*) as an edging in many parts of the garden. Miss Jekyll removed the pink flowers to encourage the plant to spread. For the restoration a modern non-flowering cultivar, 'Silver Carpet', has been used. Although this did not exist in Miss Jekyll's lifetime it seems a perfectly acceptable substitute. Instead of white pinks, snow-in-summer (*Cerastium tomentosum*) has been substituted in the Grey Walk. This also has white flowers and pale foliage – and it is of the same family as the pink. The pink, however, needs much more care and attention, requiring dividing every three or four years. In the Great Plat modern cultivars of delphinium such as *Delphinium × belladonna* 'Blue Bees', have been used. They have smaller heads than those used by Miss Jekyll and thus do not need laborious staking in this rather windswept site. The purist may jib at these deviations from total authenticity but they are simply unavoidable in a garden with far fewer staff than it was designed for.

A very substantial labour in the early days was the removal of incorrect planting, the eradication of weeds and the introduction of much new soil. When the garden was made all the soil was brought in and the pH level varies but the average is around 6.5. All the clearing and weeding was done by hand and there were infestations of perennial weeds – especially ground elder, bindweed and oxalis. The extensive masonry – paths and walls – meant that there were many inaccessible places where the deep roots of perennial weeds could luxuriate in moist seclusion. There still remain a few recalcitrant patches in particularly tricky places. The use of weedkillers has always been very sparing. Simazine has been used occasionally to control annual weeds in rose beds, but it is thought that regular doses would cause a dangerous accumulation of chemicals in the soil. Weeding the paths is a labour-intensive burden which in the past was done by 'weeder women' who came in from the village. The gardeners are now experimenting with Nomix which has an electric spray with a pressure control that can be varied according to the walking speed of the user. In Hestercombe's heyday some of the garden staff of eighteen would certainly have worked on the vegetable garden, which does not exist today, and there would have been more intensive gardening in the woodland; however, it is a very different picture compared with the two gardeners today.

By September 1974 the restoration of the Grey Walk was complete. This was an important event, for this part of the garden is not only a *tour de force* of Jekyll planting but it is an essential prelude to the garden. A broad grass path edged with stone forms the walk, with a bed on either side. That to the north is backed by the high wall of the nineteenth-century terrace; that to the south runs to the brink of a wall which forms the northern boundary of the Great Plat. In the main bed are shrubs with grey or glaucous foliage and flower colour is subdued. There are cistus (*C. × corbariensis* and *C. × purpureus*), the Munstead form of lavender, the Polyantha rose 'Nathalie Nypels' (introduced in 1919 and thus not authentic), the form of rosemary called 'Miss Jessopp's Upright', the dwarf form of cotton lavender (*Santolina chamaecyparissus nana*) and different forms of yucca giving solid architectural shape. Among the woody plants are many herbaceous plants of typical Jekyllian character – catmint (*Nepeta mussinii*), the ghostly pale-flowered loosestrife (*Lysimachia clethroides*), and giant thistles. At each end of this border are solid clumps of the shiny-leaved *Choisya ternata* which survive from the original planting of the garden. The wall planting in the Grey Walk was a distinctively Jekyllian invention – making borders and walls into a continuous flow of plants – and she specified it on her plans with just the same care as she did for the borders. Here the restored planting included many pinks, *Cerastium tomentosum, Tanacetum argenteum* (syn. *Achillea argentea*), *Sedum spathulifolium* 'Cape Blanco' and *Campanula carpatica* 'Bressingham White'.

The pergola running along the south side of the Great Plat is an essential and distinctive feature of the garden. The timbers were restored in the winter of 1973/4. The stringers – running between the beams – were replaced with new ones. But the beams supporting them had rotted

*T*op: *Lutyens's richly decorated orangery with the Dutch Garden
beyond. Bottom: A terracotta vase in the Dutch Garden copied from
Lutyens's original design and based on a few surviving fragments.*

badly on the top edge. These were originally cut to a gentle and harmonious curve – Christopher Hussey writing about the pergola in 1927 describes the 'beams that rise slightly to their centres, giving that spring to the spans that the eye, as well as the weight of the rafters, requires'. To replace them would have been extremely expensive: each one would have had to be cut from a block of oak. Instead, the rotted surface was cut away, thus regrettably flattening out the curve.

Miss Jekyll's planting plans for the pergola did not survive and when it was replanted there was virtually nothing remaining from her day – a few vines and some forsythia. It was replanted with many different roses with an emphasis on subdued pink flowers – including 'Madame Grégoire Staechelin', 'Climbing Cécile Brunner' and 'François Juranville'. Here there is, perhaps, more latitude in the choice of plants than when planting a border and certainly some of the restored plants could not have been used by Miss Jekyll.

A problem throughout the garden has been the condition of the masonry. The whole formal part of the garden when it was first made had to be raised up above the surrounding ground but, unfortunately, the original foundations were of poor quality. When the paths were originally made the flags were laid directly on to earth which had not been very solidly firmed down, with the result that irregular subsidence has occurred throughout the garden. There has been a continuous programme of relaying the paths and the gardeners became skilful at it. The paths are made of random slabs, neatly fitted together. When they are relaid, about ten to twelve stones are numbered with chalk, a sketch plan made of their arrangement, and they are then lifted and put to one side. The correct level is then established with reference to some firm point – the top or bottom of the steps or the base or top of a wall. A new level area is pegged out with the help of a spirit-level and a firm straight-edged board. The ground is excavated to a level of 100mm/4in and a new base material brought in and firmed down hard. The mixture used is

The Great Plat with bold clumps of the feathery Miscanthus sinensis *'Gracillimus' and edgings of the shining evergreen leaves of* Bergenia × schmidtii, *a favourite plant of Miss Jekyll's.*

equal parts of sand and fine grit with a very small amount of builder's lime and cement. The paving stones are bedded into this mixture and levelled up. Sometimes a relaid path will reveal subsidence in an adjacent border which will be built up to the correct level with new earth. This work has continued over many years and in 1988 English Heritage gave £200,000 to complete work on restoring the balustrades and ashlar coping.

In Lutyens's design for Hestercombe, water is an essential ingredient. The source of water was a reservoir up in the combe behind the house at a distance of about a mile. Over the years, however, the pools which fed the reservoir silted up and the pipes carrying the water deteriorated. Eventually the water supply stopped altogether. An especial problem in restoring the supply was the fact that the land on which the reservoir lies is now in the separate ownership of the Crown Commissioners. After some negotiations it was possible to repair the pipes and reopen the supply of water which flowed once again in 1988. This water supplies the masks at the head of each of the rill gardens which spout water into the semi-circular lily-ponds below. From here it should trickle out and flow down the rills to the square lily-ponds at the far end. It was essential to Lutyens's plan that the water should flow gently over the stones lining the bottom of the rill, giving an effect similar to the water-chutes, or *chadars*, of Mughal gardens. In the past the bottom of the rills was plugged with clay which was renewed every year. Work has now been started to raise the stones lining the bottom and put down an impermeable surface.

One further part of the garden where water played an essential part is the circular pool in the Rotunda. Originally, as is shown in early photographs, this was supposed to be filled to the very brim, forming a cool mirror-like disc on the floor of the Rotunda. Alas, because of the poor foundations which I have referred to already, the pool has sunk on one side making it impossible to fill it to the brim. The whole Rotunda floor and the lining of the pool itself will eventually have to be taken up and relaid.

Although the restoration of Hestercombe is nearly complete there is still work to do. I have already mentioned the unhappy dispersal of the garden ornaments in a sale in 1952. It is hoped that these will gradually be replaced. In the Dutch Garden there were large ornamental earthenware pots. These have been beautifully reconstructed by Philip Thomason using some fragments from one of the originals together with photographs, and were replaced in 1989. There were leaden figures on the tops of the columns of the Rotunda and amorini in the Dutch garden – all of which need replacing.

The restoration of Hestercombe started in 1973 in an economic climate, and a climate of opinion, very different from today. It is in many ways a pioneer of garden restoration: when it started, people needed convincing of the importance of a garden designed by Lutyens and Jekyll. Looking at the garden today it seems so strikingly obvious that this is an enchanting masterpiece that it is hard to believe that anyone needed persuading of its importance. But before the restoration started the garden was a dim shadow of its former – and future – splendour. Since then garden conservation has made great ground and our knowledge of garden history has enormously increased. But gardens are still effectively unprotected by law and there will be many more battles to be fought.

THE ESSENCE OF HESTERCOMBE

Hestercombe is a very easy garden to be in. The Great Plat combines liveliness and peacefulness and must have made an out-of-doors drawing-room that was entirely satisfying to Lutyens's clients. There are plenty of places to sit – some secluded for intimate conversations; some commanding long views to the countryside; all situated carefully within the scheme of the garden and all turned away from the clumsy house. It is also a garden in which to walk. Although not at all large by Edwardian standards, the intricate patterns of paths, steps and changing levels means that the ingredients of the garden may be viewed from many different angles. Gardens very much smaller than Hestercombe may also be given diversity by similar careful planning. The interest of a limited range of plants and planting schemes is also immensely magnified by the shifting views afforded by different heights and angles.

Another source of architectural harmony at Hestercombe is the subtle interplay of similar shapes. For example, at the head of the two water terraces, the curves of the pool and its head are echoed in the flanking niches and the circular inlets strung out along the rill. Even the curve of the water falling from the mask in the keystone seems designed to fit in with the scheme. A contrasting inverted curve is found in the bold sweeping shoulders of the walls framing the pool from the south. The richness of the architectural detail is never obtrusive and it is firmly related to the overall scheme.

The same may also be said of the planting. Hestercombe is not at all a plantswoman's garden and Miss Jekyll used a restricted range of plants. But there is a confident simplicity in the planting and a soothing lack of fuss. Consider her use of bergenias edging the beds in the Great Plat: 'I am never tired of admiring the fine solid foliage of this family of plants, remaining as it does in beauty both winter and summer,' as she wrote. In her plans for the Great Plat she specified *Bergenia × schmidtii* (or *Megasea ligulata* as it was then called). Some of these plants survived from her original planting and the others have been replaced. They make a bold edging, decoratively flopping over the stone flags, and they are strong enough to have presence even when the beds are in the height of their summer flowering. In the winter their evergreen, shiny leaves sparkle with life and blur the crisp edges of stone. The full realization of the distinctive virtues of plants, often used in an inhabitual way, is a hallmark of Miss Jekyll's planting. She was able to make much more of often quite humble plants; among ordinary gardeners the reverse is usually true – they diminish the splendour of the most aristocratic plants with insensitive planting.

The retaining wall of the Grey Walk is richly planted with Cerastium tomentosum, Lavandula angustifolia *'Munstead'* and red and white valerian (Centranthus ruber).

NEWBY HALL

OLD country houses frequently occupy sites of exceptional beauty, but although aesthetic considerations may have influenced the choice of site they were rarely the determining factor. The really important things were practicalities – a strategic position on an eminence; the protection of hills to the north or views down slopes to provide warning of approaching trouble; or the proximity of water. At Newby Hall, hard by the cathedral city of Ripon in North Yorkshire, the vital attraction was the River Ure which from very early times provided an ideal setting for an estate. In the thirteenth century Newby belonged to the Nubie family who took their name from the place. Although the history of the present house and garden does not really begin until the estate was bought in 1689 by

Above: In the Statue Walk solemn figures, their feet swathed in Cotoneaster horizontalis, *are interspersed with Irish yews. Opposite: An eighteenth-century stone urn reposes in a sea of* Salvia viridis *and lavender.*

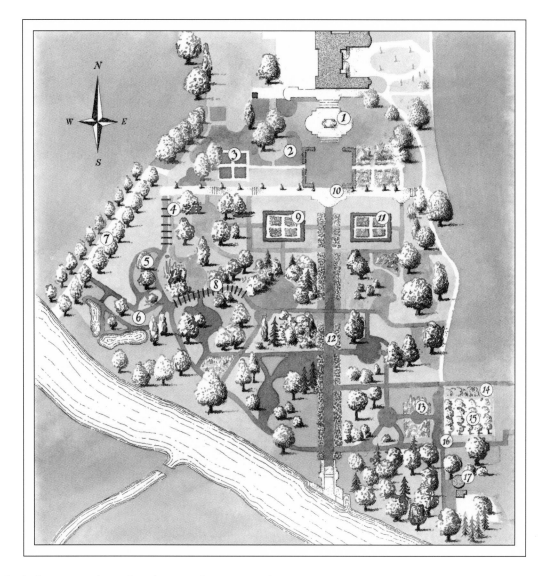

Sir Edward Blackett, Member of Parliament for Ripon, there remain signs of an earlier house on the very banks of the river.

This house was not considered grand enough and Sir Edward Blackett built his new house, completed in the 1690s, on an eminence slightly farther from the river than its predecessor. A persistent legend is that it was designed by Sir Christopher Wren but there are no documents to support this theory. The house is nevertheless a dazzling creation, built in a beguiling rosy brick with curved stone pediments and crowned with a dashing balustrade.

Sir Edward Blackett was clearly extremely interested in his garden and recruited an exceptional gardener, Peter Aram, who had been a pupil of George London, the most influential gardener of his day, at the Brompton nursery in London. He subsequently worked at Fulham Palace for

1. Lily Pond 2. The Wars of the Roses 3. Sylvia's Garden 4. Rose Pergola 5. Waterfall 6. Rock Garden 7. Lime Avenue 8. Curving Pergola 9. Rose Garden 10. Statue Walk 11. Autumn Garden 12. Herbaceous Borders 13. Circular Garden 14. White Garden 15. Orchard Gardens 16. Tropical Garden 17. Wheel House

Henry Compton, Bishop of London and an ancestor of the present family at Newby. It is not known exactly when Peter Aram went to Newby, but he was certainly there by 1694. By the time Celia Fiennes visited the estate in 1697 the garden had been made and, as we shall see, it is very likely that Aram himself was responsible for this new layout. Celia Fiennes wrote that Newby was 'the finest house I saw in Yorkshire' and her detailed description of the garden is very valuable. What she observed corroborates precisely the Kip engraving which was made only a few years after her visit. The accuracy of this engraving is, incidentally, further confirmed by an anonymous early eighteenth-century painting, still at Newby. It shows an elaborate formal garden, typical of that time. To the west, which was then the entrance side of the house, there are three great avenues arranged in a *patte d'oie*. The central avenue, aligned with the house, is double and the flanking avenue pointing to the north-west has as its focal point the cathedral of Ripon, three miles away. To the north of the house there is a vast area of orchard, laid out in squares (where the superb eighteenth-century stable-block by William Belwood now is). To the east, another double avenue extends towards the horizon. On the south side of the house there is a huge parterre with a central axis and flanked by regularly spaced rows of trees. It is a four-part arrangement of beds and statues, separated from the house by a broad walk. Celia Fiennes describes this area: 'fine gravel walks between grass plots 4 square with 5 brass Statues great and small in each Square, and full of borders of flowers and green banks with flower potts', all precisely as shown by Kip. This bold design, entirely typical of its period, firmly linked the house to the countryside and made the most of its surroundings, with fine views of the river and the distant cathedral. The sweeping curves of the river contrast with the linear formality of the layout. It is a tribute to the firmness of this design, and its easy logic, that it still exerts a powerful influence on the garden today, despite many changes and the passage of almost three hundred years.

Peter Aram was a man of parts and wrote more than competent verse, including a poem celebrating the charms of the neighbouring garden at Studley Royal, 'Studley Park'. He also wrote an extremely interesting book, *A Treatise of Flowers*, whose manuscript survives and has recently been published for the first time. A treasure trove of the horticultural practices of its time, it is full of lively practical detail and shows the author to have been a discerning plantsman. There also survives a drawing by him, dated 1716, showing a design for 'the North East quarter' of the garden at Newby. This is a virtuoso parterre with 'Pyramid Yews and round headed Variegated Holly together with Flow'ry Decorations intermxt', and it is not at all the sort of drawing the average head gardener could knock off on a rainy afternoon. These polished accomplishments, together with Aram's apprenticeship with George London, add to the likelihood that Aram was the author of the garden at Newby. Daniel Defoe described it in 1720 in its maturity: 'the Avenues, now the Trees are grown, are very fine, and the Gardens not only well laid out, but well planted, and as well kept; the statues are neat, the Parterre beautiful.'

In 1748 the estate was sold to William Weddell. He was a man of great cultivation, a member of the Dilettanti Club, and in touch with many distinguished architects of

At the centre of the Rose Garden a stone urn is fringed with the perpetual flowering Shrub rose 'Ballerina' and with a hedge of Santolina chamaecyparissus nana.

the day. He went on the Grand Tour in 1765/6 and made a fine collection of classical sculpture which is still kept at the house. It was he who commissioned John Carr of York to add the east wings, William Belwood to design the stable-block and, most dramatically, Robert Adam, a Grand Tour acquaintance, to design many new interiors of ravishing quality. Nothing is recorded of what changes Weddell made to the garden at Newby but he would certainly have involved himself with it. His memorial in Ripon Cathedral, a handsome marble bust by Nollekens, is surrounded by an airy columned rotunda designed by James 'Athenian' Stuart, remarkably similar to the Temple of Fame in the landscape park at Studley Royal. Weddell was related to the Aislabie family at Studley who were obsessive garden-makers and, with his interest in architecture and the arts, it is very likely that he shared their horticultural interests.

Of the subsequent history of the garden there are only tantalizing glimpses. An article in J.C.Loudon's *The Gardener's Magazine* in 1837 refers to the house's 'fair proportions' being 'barbarously altered by a modern addition of two excrescences in the form of the wings on the east front'. This plain-spoken criticism very much reflects Loudon's blunt editorial style although the article is not by him. It later says, 'A mass of flower-beds, enclosed by a wire fence, is extremely ill placed close to the west front of the house: these beds have nothing to recommend them, and it is seen at a glance that they have no business where they are.' At this time the garden lay almost exactly where it does today, between the house and the river. Here, in 1837, were fine specimens of Turkey oak (*Quercus cerris*) and the white oak (*Q. alba*). Also noted is a good '*Salisburia adiantifolia*' (now *Ginkgo biloba*), the maidenhair tree. The author of the article cautiously praises the new gardener, Mr Smith, who has made 'some judicious alterations in the pleasure ground, which, however, is still capable of being greatly improved'. His unqualified praise, however, is reserved only for a new form of straight cucumber, 'Walker's Improved'. Not all accounts of the

Giant double herbaceous borders sweep down a gentle south-facing slope to the river Ure. The stone balustrades and urns in the foreground are part of William Burges's nineteenth-century scheme.

and Frederick Vyner was murdered by the brigands as a result of a misunderstanding. Lady Mary commissioned William Burges to build a church, paid for with the ransom money, in honour of her son. This, consecrated in 1876, was Christ the Consoler, built in the park at Newby where it still stands, shrouded by mournful weeping beeches. Burges later built the church of St Mary at Studley Royal, for Frederick's sister Henrietta who had married the 1st Marquess of Ripon, then the owner of the Studley Royal estate. Here, Burges's church, considered his masterpiece, is explicitly related to the design of the garden, being the focal point of an avenue of limes at the other end of which Ripon Cathedral terminates the view.

Little is known about Burges's work as a garden designer but he certainly designed his own garden at the Tower House in Kensington, which survives, and a remarkable moat garden for Cardiff Castle which, alas, does not. At Newby Burges advised on the garden and in 1876/7 provided vases, garden seats, gates, statues and 'two Alcibiades dogs' which are now at Wrest Park which was owned by the de Grey family, related by marriage to the Vyners. By tradition Burges was also responsible for the Statue Walk forming the strong east–west axis that is still today a vital ingredient of the garden. Here handsome Venetian stone figures are flanked by Irish yews. A photograph in *The Gardener's Magazine* shows the arrangement in 1901 with the yews still quite young, dwarfed by the statues. Today the yews are splendidly mature. The original arrangement made a rather stark contrast between the yews and the figures, but the pedestals of the figures now emerge from a skirt of *Cotoneaster horizontalis* which makes a satisfyingly emphatic green base. At the west end of the Statue Walk Burges introduced a monumental bench, carved of Caen stone, with a curved back. The lines of the bench are echoed in the yew that is neatly clipped round the back of the bench following its lines. This makes a focal point to the walk, both imposing and restful. At its other end there is another stone bench, more whimsical, decorated with carved animals, that is also

garden at this time were so cantankerous. Halgrove's *History of Knaresborough* describes 'avenues, shrubberies, and walks disposed with much elegance'. This suggests the possible survival at that time of some of the formal elements shown in the Kip engraving.

On William Weddell's death in 1792 the estate passed to his cousin Thomas Robinson, Lord Grantham, whose daughter Mary married Henry Vyner. Newby was given to Lady Mary Vyner shortly after her marriage. Her son Frederick, travelling in Greece in 1870, was kidnapped by brigands. The ransom money was prepared but never paid

*In late summer, pampas grass (*Cortaderia selloana*) – an archetypal nineteenth-century plant – makes a handsome and appropriate foil for William Burges's stonework.*

from Burges's time. Between the Statue Walk and the south front of the house there were elaborate *parterres de broderie* and some handsome balustrades also from the same date. Rather later than all this, around the turn of the century, Miss Ellen Willmott advised on the making of a rock garden and a curved pergola, both of which survive and have been carefully restored. Miss Willmott, of Warley Place in Essex, lived from 1858 to 1934, and was one of the most extraordinary gardeners of her day. With a very large fortune, she also maintained gardens near Aix-les-Bains and on the Italian Riviera and was a great patron of the plant-collectors of the time, especially of E.H. 'Chinese' Wilson, some of whose discoveries are named after her.

In 1921 the estate passed to Major Compton, the father of the present owner. Between the wars he came to know Lawrence Johnston of Hidcote and visited the garden there in its heyday. This was an important influence when Major Compton began to reshape the garden. The essence of this was to make an emphatic axis, running gently downhill from the south front of the house to the river, at right angles to Burges's Statue Walk, flanked by deep herbaceous borders backed with hedges of yew. With the Statue Walk it formed a slightly lopsided cross, the quadrants of which made secluded sites for abundantly planted garden rooms, each at its best in a different season.

Major Compton died in 1977 and his son Robin took over the garden. By this time the garden had expanded in size and complexity beyond the capacity of the garden staff to look after it impeccably. There was a great deal of congested planting, especially in the woodland areas. Yet Mr and Mrs Compton felt the formal design of the garden lacked an element of romance and therefore more informal plantings were introduced. Furthermore, it was decided that the house and garden should be regularly open to the public, and extensive facilities were needed for their recreation. What Robin Compton has done is to juggle successfully with several different, and possibly irreconcilable, objectives. He wanted to restore and improve the garden *and* the house and defray the maintenance costs

from entrance charges. Today about 100,000 people visit between Easter and the end of October. Such a number of visitors has a great impact on the state of a garden and its maintenance. To give one example, the wear and tear on grass paths means that endless patching and replacement must be done. There is half-an-acre of turf maintained in the kitchen garden solely for this purpose.

At Newby the house and the garden together tell a vivid story of the family's successive enthusiasms and, to bring out the full character of the estate, both had to be restored together. Under Mrs Compton's supervision the

In the Rock Garden Welsh poppies (Meconopsis cambrica), London pride (Saxifraga × urbium) and ferns spread about the rocks.

Adam interiors of the house – 'among the finest of their date anywhere in Europe', according to Pevsner – have been superbly restored to their original colours and quality. The restoration of the garden has been an equally delicate task. Although superficially most of the garden dates from the last hundred years, and virtually all of the planting has been done since World War II, much of its character is derived from ancient bones.

The twin herbaceous borders make the word spectacular seem inadequate. Each is 4.5m/15ft wide and a 7.5m/25ft broad turf path runs between them. They are 300m/990ft long. On each side they are backed by yew hedges which, in the past, came right up to the beds. Apart from making hedge clipping difficult the shallow roots of the yews competed for nourishment with the border plants. Robin Compton solved this problem by making a new turf path, between the outer edge of the borders and the backing hedges, wide enough to allow easy mowing with a ride-on mower which also pulls a trailer from which hedge-cutters can be operated.

The planting of the herbaceous borders has been gradually restored by Mrs Compton. She has taken a section each year, divided some old plants, replaced others and enriched the soil. A recent and effective experiment is the use of wide-gauge plastic mesh stretched horizontally 750mm/2½ft high over the borders to support herbaceous plants as they grow through them. This is at least as effective as individual staking and very much less laborious to put into place.

Lying on either side of the borders, and linked visually, are the Autumn Garden on the east and the Rose Garden on the west. The Autumn Garden was planted in 1939 by Major Compton and replaced a croquet lawn. Some of the original planting survives but many new and exotic plants have been added. The garden is surrounded by wattle fencing with borders running in front. At the centre an urn rises from a sea of lavender and gravel paths separate four central beds. There is exuberant planting here but it is given discipline by regular structural

planting. At the centre of each bed is a *Eucalyptus gunnii* which is pruned back each year to 1.8m/6ft. This not only keeps a potentially very large tree within bounds but also means that there is a regular display of the especially handsome juvenile foliage. At each entrance to the Autumn Garden there are matching mounds of fuchsia. The use of different species of the same genus in this garden also gives harmony. The late-flowering sweetly scented *Clerodendrum trichotomum* flourishes in one corner and its more tender cousin, *C. bungei*, with exotic corymbs of reddish-purple flowers in September, is planted in the opposite corner. Several cultivars of *Buddleja davidii* are planted in the central beds, and the oak-leaved *Hydrangea quercifolia* and purple-flowered *H. aspera villosa* are growing in the surrounding beds.

Looking west from the Autumn Garden a vista cuts across the herbaceous borders, with narrow ramparts of *Helichrysum rosmarinifolium* on either side, and leads to the Rose Garden. The vista is continued beyond the Rose Garden and ends in a distant glade of beech and a very large variegated sycamore. At the centre of the glade a fine urn on a pedestal is backed by a semi-circle of glistening laurel (*Prunus laurocerasus*) and newly planted holly. This line existed before but it has now been given full emphasis by the careful use of planting and ornament. Garden 'rooms' in the tradition of Hidcote can seem claustrophobic unless their entrances and exits, and their relationship with the garden's other ingredients, are carefully contrived. The opening up of new vistas, and the emphasizing of existing ones, has been a very important part of the restoration and is an essential ingredient in the harmony between formal enclosures and woodland areas. For example, farther south down the herbaceous borders, Mr and Mrs Compton opened up, in 1978, a new cross axis towards a fine copper beech (*Fagus sylvatica purpurea*) which is now seen from the east, framed in a gap in the yew hedges with a white-painted bench at its base. Just because a copper beech is a common tree does not mean it is not worth looking at and a good specimen can, in this way, be given

*The bold foliage of bergenias flourishes in the dappled shade of the laburnum tunnel. Beyond,
Ceanothus thyrsiflorus repens flowers among ferns. Following pages: The south front of the house
seen from the broad path that separates the herbaceous borders.*

exciting emphasis. Flanking the vista on the other side of the herbaceous borders is another example of a distinctive kind of planting at Newby. Here two groups of maples, each of a single species, guard the opening in the yew hedge on the woodland side. To the south are several *Acer griseum* with decorative orange-brown peeling bark. The group to the north is of a snake-bark maple, *A. pensylvanicum*. Single exotic specimens may sometimes have an artificial obtrusiveness but, then, few gardens have the space to plant naturalistic groves in this striking way.

The enclosed Rose Garden to the west of the herbaceous borders and immediately south of the Statue Walk was completely renovated in 1979. This had been designed as a 'sunk' garden in the 1930s by Robin Compton's father. Unfortunately this meant excavating some 900mm/3ft into hungry and sandy subsoil and plants never flourished. For the restoration all the existing top soil was removed and replaced with humus-rich compost and all the roses were replanted. The garden is entirely surrounded with a hedge of copper beech 1.5m/4½ft high. This provides an excellent background colour to the predominantly pink roses and for the pale foliage of the weeping silver pears (*Pyrus salicifolia* 'Pendula') in each corner. The roses, planted in four beds separated by paths, are all of the older varieties with many Damasks - 'Blush Damask', York and Lancaster, the Holy Rose (*Rosa × richardii*) and Quatre Saisons and Bourbons such as 'Commandant Beaurepaire', 'Louise Odier' and 'Madame Pierre Oger'. All these are finely scented and in late June make an outstanding display. They are underplanted with purple-flowered *Viola cornuta* and its white form, *Geranium renardii* with its suede-soft foliage and white-veined flowers, and the spreading purple bugle *Ajuga reptans* 'Atropurpurea'. All these plants make labour-saving ground cover but here they have been chosen carefully to suit the intimate scale of their setting. Ground cover is used throughout the garden and always a sense of scale is preserved. In the woodland areas, for example, the bold foliage of bergenia and the elegant *Polygonum affine* 'Superbum' are used to excellent effect.

In the woodland garden a grove of the pale-barked Himalayan birch, Betula utilis jacquemontii, *is carpeted with candelabra primulas.*

To the north of the Rose Garden is Sylvia's Garden, named after Major Compton's wife. This is a sunken garden, surrounded by yew hedges, with York stone steps leading down to paths of bricks laid in a basket-weave pattern. In the centre is a decorative urn-like Byzantine corn-grinder which now emerges from a froth of the peppermint-scented *Calamintha nepeta* (syn. *C. nepetoides*). Originally the planting here depended on a lavish display of summer bedding with standard-trained cherry-pie (*Heliotropium* × *hybridum*) rising from an ocean of rich blue lobelia. It has been completely replanted by Robin Compton's wife with a scheme that provides interest throughout the year but is much less laborious to maintain. There is much interesting foliage colour in golden marjoram (*Origanum vulgare aureum*), the glaucous rue (*Ruta graveolens* 'Jackman's Blue') and the tender variegated perennial wall-flower (*Erysimum linifolium* 'Variegatum'). In each corner is the variegated form of the coralberry (*Symphoricarpos orbiculatus* 'Foliis Variegatis') which makes an airy mound of golden-edged foliage. The repeated use of different plants with grey, silver or variegated foliage gives harmony and structural pattern. Here are several unfamiliar lavenders such as *Lavandula stoechas pedunculata* and *L. multifida*, shrubby sages such as *Salvia officinalis* 'Icterina' and the spreading silver-leaved *Tanacetum densum*. The

planting in this garden reflects the present owners' intense interest in unusual plants but the use of the plants, and the harmony of colours, are subservient to the existing formal framework. Banging in rarities is often thought of, entirely erroneously, as an easy way to make an interesting garden. Much harder, and much more interesting, is the disciplined use of plants – familiar or rare – in a way that capitalizes on their characteristic virtues.

The fine wrought-iron gates to Sylvia's Garden have been painted the rich deep blue that Celia Fiennes commended when she praised 'blew railings' on her travels. The same colour, used on other pieces of metalwork in the garden, is far more flattering to good wrought iron than black, and fits in more harmoniously with planting.

At the far western end of the Statue Walk, behind Burges's curved stone seat, an exciting discovery was made in the winter of 1981. During especially hard weather, which limited work in the garden, one of the gardeners was up a ladder, pruning trees, from where he noticed several large mature limes (the common limes, *Tilia* × *europaea*) planted in two lines and regularly spaced. This proved to be part of the south-west avenue shown in Kip's engraving. The areas round the avenue have now been cleared and gaps made good with new young limes.

Running south from Burges's seat is a rose pergola which leads to a great Rock Garden, which was designed in about 1900 by Ellen Willmott. The central feature was a waterfall supplied by a tank above, but when Robin Compton took over the garden the water supply had long since failed. This was restored in 1980 and once again a cascade splashes down the rocks. Many moisture- and shade-loving plants flourish there – ferns, the spreading *Alchemilla alpina* and curse of Corsica (*Soleirolia soleirolii*). From the rockery a curving pergola, also designed by Miss Willmott, winds gently uphill. It was originally intended to display different forms of ivy but Major Compton replanted it with *Laburnum* × *watereri* 'Vossii', which in the spring, mixed with the crimson flowers of Japanese quince (*Chaenomeles japonica*), makes a spectacular tunnel of flowers.

*In Sylvia's Garden the calm atmosphere derives from symmetry and repeated plantings – among them, clumps of golden marjoram (*Origanum vulgare 'Aureum'*), irises and the ghostly blue* Veronica gentianoides.

Apart from restoring existing parts of the garden the Comptons have simplified many overgrown areas and added excellent ideas of their own – such as Mrs Compton's very successful white garden, which makes a soothing passage from the main garden to the restaurant. No garden can stand still and any keen gardener wants to do more than merely restore and maintain existing features. All over the garden there is evidence of the revaluation of old parts and the discerning addition of new ones.

THE ESSENCE OF NEWBY HALL

At the heart of the gardens at Newby is the house itself, with its balustraded terrace, rising like some celestial garden ornament. There is nothing forbidding or overbearing about the house. The garden immediately surrounding it has formality – York stone flagged walks, finely carved stone balustrades and a scalloped lily-pool. But farther from the house this gradually gives way to increasing informality with effortless ease. The great backbone of the garden, leading from the balustraded terrace running along the south front to the river's edge, is the grassy walk flanked by its virtuoso double herbaceous borders backed by yew hedges. Running across this, William Burges's Statue Walk provides a substantial cross axis and this firm grid allows the harmonious accommodation of a rich variety of garden effects. The formal arrangement of Autumn Garden and Rose Garden linked by a further axis; Sylvia's Garden and the late-Victorian drama of Ellen Willmott's shady rock garden and curving pergola – all this merges easily with woodland gardens with specimen trees rising from spreading pools of spring bulbs. As the garden nears the river, however, things become increasingly informal. Grass walks wind along the river shore and occasional pathways lead enticingly into the woodland.

Although the garden contains a very large number of different species (including the National Collection of dogwoods), reflecting Robin Compton's interest in plant collecting and in the conservation of garden plants, there is always an acute sense of the appropriateness of a particular plant in a particular place. Nor is this always a question of some great rarity set in a place of honour. Dramatic effects are repeatedly achieved with simple means – the striking pale bark of a birch against sombre yew, for example. The thickets of stooled *Amelanchier canadensis* which separate the Rose Garden and the Autumn Garden are another excellent example. Here, the trees were planted too close together and had become leggy. They were cut down to the ground and slender new stems shot up from the base. In spring they light up those parts of the garden with their profuse white flowers, followed by the pink-bronze new foliage. In the autumn they colour to a rich rust-red. When not performing in these dramatic ways they provide structural bastions that separate thematically different parts of the garden.

The Statue Walk has Irish yews marching down either side with a statue between each pair. At the feet of each statue the froth of *Cotoneaster horizontalis* simultaneously provides a green base for the figure and a firm horizontal counterpoint to the vertical emphasis of the yews and the statues, and makes weed-suppressing ground cover. The south side of the Statue Walk has a background of copper-leaved *Prunus cerasifera* 'Pissardii' which forms a curtain of contrasting leaf-colour especially attractive in the spring before the foliage has taken its full sombre colouring. These bold effects are especially valuable in a large garden, but the rules that underlie them are of universal value.

Although there is very little planting in the garden that dates back before Mr and Mrs Compton's time and much of the present layout is also theirs, there is none the less a feeling of permanence derived from the garden's ancient bones, here and there still visible. This pattern, honoured and indeed enhanced by the present owners, provides the essential background against which the Comptons have executed their bold new schemes. It emphasizes the importance of retaining what is valuable in an old garden but ruthlessly removing the second-rate.

MOUNT STEWART

THE Mount Stewart estate is east of Belfast, on the north-eastern shore of Strangford Lough between Newtownards and Greyabbey. To an exceptional degree the site and its privileged microclimate has had a determining influence on the garden, which is on gently sloping land that runs down to the shores of the lough. It lies on a curving peninsula with Belfast Lough to the north and the Irish Sea to the east. The climate is affected by the Gulf Stream drift and, although it has much sunshine, there is a relatively high rainfall of 875mm/35in. Winters are exceptionally mild with an average January temperature of 7°C/45°F.

The estate was acquired by the Stewart family in 1744 but the history of the garden

Above: The Mairi Garden has a soothing colour scheme of blue and white. Opposite: In the Spanish garden an arcade of Leyland cypress (× Cupressocyparis leylandii) – like a Spanish glorieta – gives formal contrast to exotic planting.

starts with Robert Stewart, 1st Marquess of Londonderry, who built the west end of the present house in 1804-5 to the designs of George Dance. The 1st Marquess also commissioned from James 'Athenian' Stuart in 1782 'The Temple of the Winds', on a wooded eminence east of the present gardens. The 3rd Marquess described this as 'a Temple built for Mirth & Jollity . . . a Junketting Retreat in the Grounds'. 'Athenian' Stuart had already built a less sophisticated version of the same garden temple in the landscape park at Shugborough in Staffordshire. Little is known about the garden at this early date but there is no

evidence that the Temple was part of any landscape scheme. It commands grand views south over Strangford Lough and it seems that it was built as a viewing place and, of course, for 'Junketting'.

The garden today was made almost entirely in the twentieth century and is the creation of Edith, Marchioness of Londonderry. Her husband became the 7th Marquess in 1915 and they moved to Mount Stewart in 1921. Of her first visit to the house she wrote, 'I thought the house and surroundings were the dampest, darkest and saddest place I had ever stayed in. Large Ilex trees almost

1. Mairi Garden 2. Dodo Terrace 3. Italian Garden 4. Spanish Garden
5. Sunk Garden 6. Shamrock Garden 7. Tir nan Og 8. Rhododendron
Wood 9. South Front of the House

touched the house in places, and sundry other big trees blocked out all light and air.' It was Lady Londonderry who first realized the unique potential of the site – as she wrote later on, 'The really exciting and important thing about Mount Stewart was discovering the climate and this I think I may claim to have done; making the gardens round the house was the second step.' Here it was possible to experiment with an immense range of unfamiliar plants which elsewhere in Britain would be on the perilous borderline of hardiness.

The garden was transferred to the National Trust in 1955, by which time Lady Londonderry was elderly and frail. When she died in 1959 the garden had not benefited from her detailed attention for many years. When Graham Stuart Thomas, as Gardens Adviser to the National Trust, came to supervise the restoration, he had several advantages. He had first seen the garden in 1949, at the peak of its perfection, and had been round it with Lady Londonderry. Furthermore, Lady Londonderry had kept detailed garden notebooks which survive at the house and proved a valuable guide to her gardening ideas – especially her colour schemes. In 1977, after he had been working on the garden for some years, Graham Stuart Thomas wrote, 'Lady Londonderry's creative genius becomes more revealed as restoration proceeds.'

After the demobilization at the end of World War I, with the threat of appalling unemployment, landlords in Ulster were urged to take on as many extra workers as possible. The Londonderrys employed the men to make the elaborate new garden. In the immediate surroundings of the house Lady Londonderry made formal gardens, clearing the trees that threatened to engulf the house. To the north, the entrance side of the house, a spacious gravel forecourt is separated from parkland by stone balustrades. There is no planting here except for a stately parade of giant bay trees, clipped into columns and mushroom shapes, that runs along the north wall. These topiary specimens were brought, at a cost of £99 18s. 9d., ready shaped from a nursery in Belgium in 1923 when some of

them were already fifty years old. There survives an almost surrealistic photograph of them cosily wrapped in hessian, setting off for England from the nursery in horse-drawn carts.

To the west of the house, the Sunk Garden was one of the first parts of the formal gardens to be made. Gertrude Jekyll was commissioned in 1920 to prepare designs for it. These were adopted but it appears that her planting schemes were not used in their entirety – although some distinctly Jekyllesque plants survive, including *Leucothoë fontanesiana* and *Sarcococca humilis*. A deep paved terrace runs along the west side of the garden with clipped sweet bays. When the National Trust took over, the four triangular beds in this part of the garden were infested with perennial weeds – especially the unholy trinity of ground elder, bindweed and couch grass. The only certain way of dealing with this was to clear the beds entirely, preserving any good plants by removing them to a nursery bed or replanting immediately elsewhere in the garden. The latter is a tricky proposition as any of these perennial weeds may linger in the roots of the plants. The beds were cleared in the winter and left fallow for a whole year. In the summer the top-growth of the weeds was sprayed twice with amitrole, dug over in the autumn, and replanting took place in the following winter and spring. Lady Londonderry's original colour scheme of blue, yellow and orange has been followed but incorporating a far greater number of herbaceous perennials. In her original planting much of the summer colour had come from labour-intensive annuals – snapdragons, lobelia and African marigolds. These have been replaced with orange and yellow lilies, blue delphiniums, the yellow-flowered *Euphorbia palustris* and blue *Baptisia australis* with clumps of yellow kniphofia in late summer. These beds are edged in clipped sweet bay (at the front) and heather (*Erica erigena* 'W.T.Rackcliff') at the back, 450mm/18in high. At each corner of the lower level of the Sunk Garden is a copper-leaved Norway maple (*Acer platanoides* 'Crimson King') in a stone surround. These were planted in 1972 as a 'temporary measure' to replace the clipped *Magnolia grandiflora*, which invariably failed to flourish.

From the lawns surrounding these herbaceous beds the steps leading up to a surrounding terrace are guarded with tall billowing bushes of the tree heath *Erica arborea alpina*, whose fresh green foliage is especially valuable in winter. Its flowers, a dull putty colour, give a lively scent of honey in the early spring. Planted all round this lower terrace are informal hedges of *Azalea* 'Coccineum Speciosum' which has vivid orange-red flowers making a dazzling display in spring. Further steps lead up to a paved terrace and a pergola of stone columns and oak beams, backed by a hedge of Leyland cypress (× *Cupressocyparis leylandii*) which encloses the garden on three sides. This hedge was originally planted in Monterey cypress (*Cupressus macrocarpa*), which was used as hedging and topiary in several parts of the formal gardens. This tree is perfectly hardy in many parts of Britain – indeed it grows more vigorously here than it does in its native California. It was very fashionable as a hedging material between the wars and was widely planted. Although it is a handsome, swift-growing plant, it has two substantial disadvantages. It is prone to losing its lower branches, which gives an unsightly ragged edge to the bottom of a hedge, and the juvenile growth

prompted by repeated clipping is much less resistant to low temperatures than mature growth. During World War II the macrocarpa hedges were not clipped regularly, and after the war they needed drastic treatment from which they never fully recovered; by the 1960s all the hedging needed replacing and an alternative was sought. It was decided to use Leyland cypress, which is a hybrid between the Monterey and Nootka cypresses. Its very vigorous growth, 600–900mm/2–3ft a year, was considered an important factor in this prominent part of the garden in which the hedges are a vital ingredient.

The new Leyland cypress hedging is clipped flush with the uprights of the pergola and level with their tops. This has enabled the uprights on the hedge side to be planted with decorative climbers, and the pergola is richly festooned with honeysuckles, vines, clematis and roses which have been chosen to fit in with the blue, yellow and orange colour scheme of the beds. There are also many much more unusual, and often tender, plants such as *Dendromecon rigida*, a Douglas introduction from California, the Chilean evergreen *Mutisia oligodon* and, also from Chile, *Lardizabala biternata* which bears curious brown flowers in the winter, followed in the spring by a crop of purple fruit.

On the west side of the Sunk Garden giant Irish yews (*Taxus baccata* 'Fastigiata') mark the entrance to the Shamrock Garden. The original Irish yew, incidentally, was discovered in Northern Ireland at Enniskillen in County Fermanagh. Towards the end of the eighteenth century a Mr Willis noticed two wild yew seedlings with strikingly upright growth. One of them was planted in the Earl of Enniskillen's garden at Florence Court, where it still survives, and from this single plant every existing Irish yew is descended. The Shamrock Garden is partly enclosed with yew hedges planted in the shape of a three-leaved shamrock. Originally planted in 1924, these were shortly after replaced with Monterey cypress which, once again, failed and had to be replanted with yew. In Lady Londonderry's time the crest of the hedge was ornamented with topiary

*In the Sunk Garden clipped domes of purple Norway maple (*Acer platanoides* 'Crimson King') and bay laurel (*Laurus nobilis*) give structural character.*

figures depicting a hunting scene copied from miniatures in Mary Tudor's psalter. Now that the yew is again growing vigorously it would be quite straightforward to allow a few leaders to remain unclipped at appropriate places on the top of the hedge and to train them round the original wire frames which have been carefully preserved.

A further problem in the Shamrock Garden was the worn state of the concrete paving, which was replaced with gravel. This, together with less complicated planting round the edge, the removal of many troughs and planters, and the slightly lower hedges without topiary, has meant that the shamrock-shape of the garden – its whole point – is much more visible. In the centre of this area is a bed in the shape of the Red Hand of Ulster, part of the royal arms of Ulster. In 1926 this was planted up with 600 crimson 'Hawlmark' roses; today there are two seasonal plantings – double red daisies (*Bellis perennis* cultivars) in the spring and begonias ('Crimson Devil') in the summer.

Otherwise much of the original planting survives, including some magnificent mahonias – *M. acanthifolia* and *M. lomariifolia* – which have grown to great size. Also dating from this time is a handsome *Acer palmatum* 'Senkaki' with striking pinkish-red stems which marks a way out of the Shamrock Garden. It stands out finely against a screen of *Mahonia × media* 'Charity' which, in turn, is backed by a low hedge of yew.

*On the shores of the lake Japanese maples (*Acer palmatum*) are underplanted with wild bluebells.*

To the south of the house is Lady Londonderry's magnificently theatrical Italian Garden in which she borrowed from the memories of her visits to Italian gardens and of her childhood home, Dunrobin Castle on the north-east coast of Scotland. Her mother was a daughter of the 3rd Duke of Sutherland and at Dunrobin there are Victorian parterres, one of which has an identical plan to these in the Italian Garden at Mount Stewart. Two parterres, separated by an avenue of cabbage trees (*Cordyline australis*), lie below a deep paved and balustraded terrace. Although there was much restoration to be done here, the problem of weeds was not so acute and only a few of the beds required the same treatment as those in the Sunk Garden.

The colour schemes of the two parterres are carefully contrasted. The East Parterre is of chiefly warm colours – yellow, scarlet and purple. The component beds of the parterres were originally outlined in clipped white heather but in the restoration unfamiliar new hedging materials have been used, appropriate to the colour schemes. In the East Parterre are the rich purple-leaved *Berberis thunbergii* 'Atropurpurea Nana', a golden-leaved dwarf *Thuja occidentalis* and *Erica erigena* 'W.T.Rackcliff'. This last plant, formerly known as Mediterranean heather, is an Irish native, found in Galway and Mayo in the west of Ireland. The cultivar 'W.T.Rackliff' has large white, richly scented flowers which emerge in February at Mount

In the Italian Garden the parterres are boldly edged with contrasting yellow (a golden-leaved form of Thuja occidentalis*) and deep purple* (Berberis thunbergii *'Atropurpurea Nana').*

Stewart. The hedges are clipped in May after their long period of flowering. Almost all the planting in these beds is herbaceous, although there are repeated structural plantings of standard-trained *Wisteria sinensis* and bushes of purple-leaved *Cotinus coggygria* 'Royal Purple'. In summer there is an explosion of colour – many penstemons, the perennial lobelia 'Scarlet Cardinal', phlox, purple delphiniums, crocosmias of yellow and carmine, the yellow form of Cape fig-wort (*Phygelius aequalis*) – all keeping strictly to the hot, rich colour plan.

The West Parterre, in the shade of the great specimens of *Eucalyptus globulus* planted in the 1890s, is a much cooler affair. Here the colour scheme is of blue, white, grey and occasional touches of magenta. The hedging, again, is an essential part of the overall colour scheme. There is the glaucous-leaved *Hebe albicans*, Jackman's rue (*Ruta graveolens* 'Jackman's Blue') and, making a link with the East Parterre, *Erica erigena* 'W.T.Rackcliff'. Within the beds, once again chiefly herbaceous, there is much grey or glaucous foliage – the herbaceous *Artemisia ludoviciana, Romneya coulteri* and the tender *Olearia moschata*. Appropriate anemones, geraniums, dicentra, border phlox, bergamot and irises provide colour.

The two parterres are linked together by repeated colours or plantings on either side. The same standard wisterias and purple-leaved cotinus appear in the same relative positions. In the centre of each parterre there is a circular pool with a fountain which is fringed with a bold edging of *Hosta plantaginea* 'Grandiflora' and *Iris laevigata* 'Rose Queen'. Some older plants, not necessarily fitting in with this scheme, but so good as to demand preservation, have been kept. For example, in the West Parterre there is a magnificent old *Sophora tetraptera* which soars over the flower beds.

One of the great delights of the Italian Garden and Dodo Terrace that lies on its eastern side are the decorative urns on pillars and a varied menagerie of animals. These were modelled to Lady Londonderry's design in cement strengthened with iron armatures by a local craftsman of

genius, Thomas Beattie. Running along the south side of the Italian Garden are tall pillars surmounted by distinctly cheeky-looking monkeys bearing urns on their heads. These were inspired by the similar, sixteenth-century marble urn-bearing figures (known as *canephori*) in the Renaissance Villa Farnese at Caprarola, which must have been known to Lady Londonderry. The dodos and the other extinct animals that guard the Dodo Terrace seem to have sprung from Lady Londonderry's own rich imagination and some of them commemorate members of the Ark Club which she founded. Over the years these figures have deteriorated, the iron within them has rusted and expanded, splitting the cement, and the occasional really cold winter has accelerated the process. A programme of restoration has involved recasting some of the sculptures (with stainless steel armatures) and patching up others. All have been treated with a carbon silicate wash which effectively makes them impermeable to water and they are now protected in the winter. Although in themselves distinctly whimsical, these animals are used in a formal way which prevents their seeming arbitrary.

Immediately to the south of the Italian Garden is the formal Spanish Garden which has an oval pool fed by narrow rills of water, and beyond the pool an open garden

From the Dodo Terrace (where the animals are made of modelled cement) a curving path leads through the woods to the Mairi Garden.

house roofed with glaucous-green pantiles. The colour of these tiles determines the overall colour scheme of this area, in which there are also many plants with strikingly architectural foliage. On either side are substantial clumps of *Hosta sieboldiana elegans* and *Kirengeshoma palmata* which are followed in late summer by sweeps of the glaucous-leaved pink-flowered *Kniphofia caulescens*. Several terracotta pots are planted with the salmon-pink pelargonium 'The Boar'.

On either side of the Spanish Garden are tall topiary arcades of Leylandii cypress which, once again, were originally of Monterey cypress. They resemble the *glorietas* of gardens in the south of Spain which are usually of clipped Italian cypress (*Cupressus sempervirens*) and often enclose cool, shady sitting places. Here they make soaring windows which frame the jungle-like planting on either side – the dun-coloured flaking bark of 100-year-old *Eucalyptus globulus*, vast Irish yews and many *Cordyline australis* among which are rarer treasures like *Cupressus cashmeriana*, a spectacular waterfall of glaucous foliage.

A path leads through from the Dodo Terrace to the Mairi Garden, the small garden named after Lady Londonderry's daughter who, as a baby, was put in a pram here. This is a complete contrast to other planting in the garden, an intimate cottage garden of soothing atmosphere. A bronze figure in a pool is at the centre of beds arranged in a rose pattern and about the pool is an inscription with the words of the nursery rhyme 'Mary, Mary, quite contrary'. The beds in this garden have needed to be completely replanted, but once again Lady Londonderry's colour scheme has been followed and the planting is almost entirely herbaceous in colours of blue and white. Here are many campanulas, taking up the theme of 'silver bells' from the nursery rhyme, *Anemone nemorosa*, scillas, chionodoxas, pinks, agapanthus and *Galtonia candicans*. A few shrubs continue the colour scheme – rose 'Boule de Neige', Russian sage (*Perovskia atriplicifolia*), *Ceratostigma willmottianum* and the grey-leaved *Buddleja fallowiana alba*.

Away from the flower gardens, in the parkland and

surrounding the lake to the north of the house, there has been much replanting and refining of the landscape. The lake itself, of five-and-a-half acres, was made by the 3rd Marquess in 1846-8 and is surrounded by woodland with

many trees from that time. Some of these, particularly firs, were reaching the end of their life and were felled. Some very large Douglas firs (*Pseudotsuga menziesii*), a fashionable Victorian tree that was introduced from north-west America in 1827, must have been planted by the 3rd Marquess. In addition there was much clearing of enormously overgrown clumps of *Rhododendron ponticum* and parts of the wilder areas were choked with brambles, elders and

A symmetrical layout in the Spanish garden, with waves of Wisteria floribunda *'Macrobotrys' in spring contrasting with the glaucous foliage of* Kniphofia caulescens.

lake, has red- and orange-flowered rhododendrons, scarlet maples and the purple-leaved hazel-nut *Corylus maxima* 'Purpurea'. Another glade is planted in blue and lavender, with forms and hybrids of *Rhododendron campanulatum*. About the lake rhododendrons provide vivid colour in the spring and there has been a policy of planting large areas of herbaceous plants to give colour later in the year – *Iris laevigata*, crocosmias and kniphofias.

A stream flows into the lake from the east and this area has been cleared and replanted. Here are many primulas – *PP. pulverulenta, denticulata* and *florindae* – against a background of ferns which include *Onoclea sensibilis*, the shuttlecock fern (*Matteuccia struthiopteris*) and the tender *Woodwardia radicans*. Later in the year there are bold plantings of *Euphorbia griffithii* 'Fireglow', *Iris ensata* (syn. *I. kaempferi*) and several astilbes. All these arrangements continue the Mount Stewart tradition of plantsmanship in an appropriate setting.

North of the lake, at the highest point of the garden, are the buildings of Tir Nan Og, the Londonderry family burial ground. Old plantings have been cleared which formerly obscured these buildings and they are now visible across the lake, making a decorative eye-catcher. Grassy walks were made leading up to the buildings and there has been much new planting on the sloping ground immediately south of them. This, protected to the north by oaks and beeches, facing south and sharply drained, is the best site in the garden for tender plants. Here many new Australasian plants – callistemons, leptospermums, hakeas and banksias and the sweetly scented *Jasminum simplicifolium suavissimum* – have been added to the metrosideros planted by Lady Londonderry.

THE ESSENCE OF MOUNT STEWART

Other gardens combine formality and informality – parterres and landscapes – but there is something swashbuckling about the way Mount Stewart has been created. The effects are bold and full of aristocratic panache, and

sycamore seedlings. The lake itself was in many places concealed by an impenetrable curtain of foliage and there were huge clumps of rushes which hid the foreshore. Thus the views across the lake were blocked, interrupting the reflections of trees in the water which are one of the great beauties of a landscape park.

The restoration of the area about the lake involved, first of all, a reduction of the heavy overplanting. Subsequently glades were opened with grassy walks leading down to the shore line. The lake is encircled with meandering paths which run quite close to the water, and enticing openings were cleared in the surrounding woodland revealing glades with fine specimen trees. These clearings serve two purposes. They add to the atmosphere of relaxation, giving points to pause and turn away from the dictatorial circuit path. They also provide sheltered positions for new plantings of particularly tender trees and shrubs, many of which are of great rarity in British gardens – for example the beautiful *Weinmannia trichosperma* on the west shore of the lake. This elegant evergreen tree from Chile produces insignificant but richly fragrant white flowers in summer. Some of these glades have a specific colour theme, continuing Lady Londonderry's ideas in the formal gardens. The Red Glade, to the east of the

*E*ast of the lake the banks of a stream are planted with
Euphorbia griffithii *'Fireglow' and wild bluebells*
*(*Scilla non-scripta*)*.

sometimes downright risky: it is not a garden ruled by the bland consensus of 'good taste'. How many gardeners would attempt anything as seductively dotty as the Shamrock Garden, full of nationalist symbolism, where the Red Hand of Ulster, slapped down on grey gravel, is planted in violent *Begonia* 'Crimson Devil' and a topiary harp beside it is forever silent? The sculptures in the garden, the mysterious monkeys perched on columns in the Italian Garden or the zoo of creatures in the Dodo Terrace might seem wilfully eccentric were they not subservient to the design of those parts of the garden. All this is attractive but, in the end, what is deeply memorable is the quality of the plants and planting.

The conditions make familiar plants grow rapidly and luxuriantly and allow tender plants – some of which may merely survive in colder parts of Britain – to flourish in unfamiliar abundance, giving the garden an atmosphere of jungle-like wildness only just kept in check. *Hebe albicans* used as hedging in the Italian Garden, and topiary of sweet bay throughout the garden, show lively decorative possibilities which less benign climates would forbid.

The vivid use of colour, and the understanding of each plant's particular virtues, are both distinctive. In the Sunk Garden the Australian *Billardiera longiflora* drapes a column of the pergola with greenish-yellow hanging flowers in July, to be followed in September by swathes of intensely blue berries, glistening like brilliant jewels among the slender leaves. In spring the Sunk Garden is ablaze with the orange flowers of *Azalea* 'Coccineum Speciosum' with at each corner, like the cherry on top of a knickerbocker glory, the emerging foliage of the clipped dome of *Acer platanoides* 'Crimson King'. To the east of the lake a sweep of blood-red fuchsia (which here grows to great heights) provides a dramatic foil for a grove of the elegant silver-leaved willow *Salix alba sericea* (*S. a.* 'Splendens'). On the very shores of the lake, yellow crocosmia, relishing the damp conditions, gives a sprightly accent to the landscape scene. On the hill rising to Tir Nan Og the path is fringed by a generous swathe of *Kniphofia caulescens*

whose fine evergreen foliage is a beautiful glaucous grey. In September the flowers appear, waves of coral-pink fading to a creamy-white. There seem no prejudices about what is a garden plant and what is appropriate for the naturalistic landscape. South of the Spanish Garden a procession of the New Zealand cabbage tree marches exotically into the woodland among the native beech and oak. An Elysian view south across the lake from a carefully placed bench is spiced by a foreground of bold yuccas. Mount Stewart boldly challenges preconceptions about what a garden should be like and how plants may be used.

In the Shamrock Garden a topiary harp of yew stands in a silver bed of Lamium maculatum. *Following page: Naturalized daffodils in the Alpine Meadow at Gravetye Manor are the epitome of Robinsonian wild gardening.*

UK Ornaments and Furniture

Antique garden ornaments and furniture are now very sought after and becoming extremely expensive. However, many of the modern versions of period ornaments made of reconstituted stone or cast lead are very finely made. Exact copies of benches designed by Sir Edwin Lutyens, beautifully made of hardwood, or modern mouldings of Coalbrookdale benches and ornaments, are in no way inferior to the originals. It should also be remembered that in the past furniture and ornaments were often produced in large quantities. Coade stone garden ornaments, for example, made at the end of the 18th and the beginning of the 19th centuries, were mass produced using a secret recipe for fired reconstituted stone. Thus, the modern reproductions of such firms as Haddonstone and Chilstone should not be dismissed. At first they may look rather too bright and new but they quickly achieve a patina of age. Many of them are exactly copied from dated originals and thus may be especially valuable for an authentic period setting. The attractive growth of lichens, incidentally, may be promoted by painting new reconstituted statues or ornaments with sour milk or yoghurt.

Antiques

Architectural Heritage Ltd, Taddington Manor, Taddington, Cutsdean, Cheltenham, Gloucestershire GL54 5RY (Telephone 0386 73414). Antique garden statuary, urns and furniture.

Christie's, 85 Old Brompton Road, London SW7 3LD (Telephone 071-581 7611). Occasional auction sales of garden statuary and architectural fittings.

Crowther of Syon Lodge, Busch Corner, London Road, Isleworth, Middlesex TW7 5BH (Telephone 081-560 7978). Antique garden statuary, ornaments, furniture, temples, arbours.

T. Crowther & Son Ltd, 282 North End Road, London SW6 (Telephone 071-385 1375). Antique garden statuary and ornaments.

Gaspar, New Place, Rowley, Westbury, Shropshire SY5 9RY. Antique garden furniture and ornaments.

Seago, 22 Pimlico Road, London SW1 (Telephone 071-730 7502). Antique garden ornaments and statuary.

Sotheby's, Summers Place, Billingshurst, West Sussex RH14 9AD (Telephone 040381 3933). Occasional auction sales of period garden statuary and architectural items.

Reproductions

Barnsley House Gardens and Decorative Furnishings, Barnsley House, Barnsley, Cirencester, Gloucestershire GL7 5EE (Telephone 0285 74561). Fine wooden and metal period garden furniture.

Bath Metal Design, 61 Walcot Street, Bath, Avon (Telephone 0225 446107). Reproduction period metal furniture.

The Cast Iron Workshop Ltd, Units 2, 3 and 4, Ings Mill Complex, Sale Street, Ossett, West Yorkshire, WF5 9HQ (Telephone 0924 280110). Restoring and making of cast-iron garden buildings, gates, railings and canopies.

Chilstone Architectural Ornaments, Sprivers, Horsmonden, Tonbridge, Kent TN12 8DR (Telephone 089 272 3553). Well-made reconstituted stone ornaments and garden buildings often in authentic period style.

Andrew Crace Designs, Bourne Lane, Much Hadham, Hertfordshire SG10 6ER (Telephone 027 984 2685). Garden furniture, gazebos and period-style shaped metal garden labels.

The David Sharp Studio, 14a Collinson Street, Nottingham NG7 5AS (Telephone 0602 422786). Reconstituted stone statuary and ornaments.

Finer Designs, 33 Main Street, Kibworth Harcourt, Leicestershire LE8 0NR (Telephone 0533 792532). Victorian gazebos.

Garden Crafts, 158 New Kings Road, London SW6 4LZ (Telephone 071-736 1615). Reproduction period ornaments and furniture.

Haddonstone, The Forge House, East Haddon, Northampton NN6 8DB. Garden ornaments, columns and balustrading well made from reconstituted stone.

J.F.B. Ornamental Ironwork, Talbot Works, Talbot Street, Brierley Hill, West Midlands (Telephone 0384 73823). Makers of wrought-iron period gates and railings.

Marston & Langinger Ltd, George Edwards Road, Fakenham, Norfolk NR21 8NL (Telephone 0328 4933). Makers of conservatories with authentic 19th-century period detail.

Minsterstone Ltd, Station Road, Ilminster, Somerset TA19 9AS (Telephone 04605 2277). Ornaments, balustrading and paving in reconstituted stone.

Peachstone, 1 Somers Way, Bushey, Hertfordshire WD2 3HR (Telephone 081-950 9488). Makers of fine stone ornaments.

The Pottery, Crossleaze Farm Woolley, Bath, Avon BA1 8AU. Handthrown frostproof terracotta pots in traditional designs.

Renaissance Bronzes, 107A Pimlico Road, London SW1 (Telephone 071-823 5149). Bronze statuary and fountains in period style.

Renaissance Casting, 19 Cranford Road, Coventry, CV5 8JF (Telephone 0203 227275). Lead statuary, fountains and ornaments in period style.

The Renaissance Restoration Co., Manor Farm, Offchurch, nr Leamington Spa, Warwickshire CV33 9AG (Telephone 0926 450430). Reproduction and original lead garden statuary. Restoration of period garden ornaments.

Whichford Pottery, Whichford, Shipston-on-Stour, Warwickshire CV36 5PG (Telephone 0608 84416). Fine hand-thrown frostproof terracotta pots and troughs.

Ascot Designs, 334 Boylston Street, Boston, MA 02116, (617) 536-9083, Hubert Moloney. Sole American representative, Minsterstone of England; variety of English styles, custom work, broad selection of furniture and ornaments.

Antique Cast Iron Restoration, RD 1, Box 187R, Cherry Valley, NY 13320, (607) 264-3607, Rocco V. DeAngelo. Restoration of antique cast and wrought iron, primarily Victorian; works on furniture and ornaments; restores antiques of other metals.

Bowhouse, Inc., P.O. Box 900, Bolton, MA 01740, (508) 779-6464, Jack Rogers. Colonial influenced bridges, gazebos, arbours, pagodas, pavilions; Greek temples.

Charleston Battery Bench, Inc., 191 King Street, Charleston, SC 29401, (803) 722-3842. Reproductions of the 1865 cast-iron bench, different sizes on request.

The Collector's Garden, Garden Antiques and Appointments, 229 Prince George Street, Annapolis, MD 21401, (301) 268-0662, Marianne Graham. American, French, English antiques, from the 19th century on; furniture and ornaments; some cast-iron pieces.

The English Garden, Inc. from Machin, 74 Sport Hill Road, Redding, CT 06896, (203) 938-3148, David Kettlewell. Sole American distributor, Machin of England. Period reproductions including Gothic, Roman, Versailles, and standard; covered seats, pavilions, gazebos, trellises, arbours.

Florentine Craftsmen, Inc., 46-24 28th Street, Long Island City, NY 11101, (718) 937-7632. Italian and English styles from Renaissance on; large selection of custom and reproduction furniture and ornaments in metal and stone; imports from Garden Ornament Stone in Italy; antiques.

Garden Accents, c/o Elizabeth Schumacher, 947 Longview Road, Gulph Mills, PA 19406, (215) 525-3287. Selection of antique and reproduction furniture and ornaments, including Victorian iron, English 18th-century lead, and Italian Renaissance and Chinese Ch'ing and M'ing Dynasty pieces.

Garden Concepts, Inc., 6621 Poplar Woods Circle South, Suite 6, Germantown, TN 38138, (901) 756-1649, John B. Painter. Turn-of-the-century English designs and custom work; manufactures furniture, planters, trellises, gates and fences, exterior accessories in iroko, teak, redwood, mahogany.

Garden Magic, 2001 1/2 Fairview Road, Raleigh, NC 27608, (919) 833-7315, Darlene Welcker. Broad selection of reproduction furniture and ornaments in traditional English styles; imports from England, Italy, Far East.

Allen Haskell Nurseries, 787 Shawmut Avenue, New Bedford, MA 02746, (508) 993-9047, Allen Haskell. Fountains, animals, statuary, pottery in lead and terracotta; diverse periods, English and American styles; reproductions, some antiques.

Heller-Washam Antiques, 1235 Congress Street, Portland, ME 04102, (207) 773-8288. 19th-century American antiques; furniture, architectural pieces, ornaments; cast and wrought iron, stone, wire.

Irving & Jones, Fine Garden Furnishings, Village Center, Colebrook, CT 06021, (203) 379-9219. Regency

In the Knot Garden spread out below Hatfield Old Palace, a potto clasps a fish from which water gushes.

wrought-iron furniture, some Gothic-influenced; sole American representative of Bath Iron Works of England; tables, chairs, benches, and rose arches; some custom work.

Barbara F. Israel Enterprises, 296 Mt. Holly Rd., Katonah, NY 10536, (914) 232-4271. 19th-century American antiques in wrought iron, cast iron, terracotta and stone, also some English; decorative garden accessories including gates and gateposts.

Kenneth Lynch & Sons, Inc., 84 Danbury Road, Wilton, CT 06897, (203) 762-8363, The Lynch Family. Variety of periods and styles; reproduction cast stone and lead ornaments.

Kesden International, Inc., P.O. Box 3573, Winchester, VA 22601, (703) 722-9783, Richard Kemp. Sole American distributor for The Regency Range of England; reproduction seats, planters, balustrading, ornaments, etc., all in natural English stone; styles from Victorian to contemporary; customizing.

Gary Marks Antiques, 1528 N. Milwaukee Avenue, Chicago, IL 60622, (312) 342-7990, Gary Marks. Victorian antiques: cast iron, wrought iron, and wire furniture, architectural accents, and ornaments.

New England Garden Ornaments, 38 East Brookfield Road, North Brookfield, MA 01535, (508) 867-4474, Nancy Grimes and Humphrey Sutton. Imports from two English companies: Chilstone and Stuart Garden Architecture; reproduction, antique, and customized work in a variety of styles; fountains, cisterns, balustrading, statuary, sundials, furniture, trellises, etc., in Chilstone, iroko, lead, bronze, terracotta, wrought iron, cast iron, granite; annual garden ornament auction in June.

Pompeian Studios, 90 Rockledge Road, Bronxville, NY 10708, (914) 337-5595, Pamela Humbert. Custom work, done in Italy, in bronze, marble, and limestone, also mosaic and wrought iron; objects, styles, and periods to order.

Robinson Iron, P.O. Drawer 1119, Robinson Road, Alexander City, AL 35010, (205) 329-8486. Ornaments and furniture in diverse styles, in cast iron or, on request, poured aluminium; imports from Salin of England; some custom work and restoration.

Rooms and Gardens, 1631 Wisconsin Avenue NW, Washington, DC 20007, (202) 965-3820, Margaret Rubino. Specializes in 19th-century French antiques, French Country style; imports furniture, ornaments, and architectural pieces from overseas.

Seahorse Trading Company, Inc., P.O. Box 677, Berryville, VA 22611, (703) 955-1677. On the West Coast: Eclectic Import-Export, P.O. Box 15313, San Francisco, CA 94115, (415) 483-9120. Sole importers for Haddonstone and R. & A. Rayment Wireworks, both of England; 18th and 19th century and medieval periods, English, French, Italian and Middle Eastern styles; reproduction furniture, ornaments, and architectural pieces; customizing through Haddonstone and Rayment.

Sotheby's, 1334 York Avenue, New York, NY 10021, (212) 606-7000. Held its first auction of antique garden ornaments 9 June, 1990; a second such auction is planned for 1991.

Southern Statuary, Inc., 901 33rd Street North, Birmingham, AL 35222, (205) 322-0379. Classical style ornaments – fountains, planters, urns, plaques, finials, animals, pedestals – in concrete, plaster, aluminum, and lead.

Speake Garden Furnishings, 351 Peachtree Hills Avenue NE #506, Atlanta, GA 30305, (404) 231-4808. Reproduction furniture and ornaments from a variety of periods; English and contemporary French styles; materials include teak, lead, cast and wrought iron, and limestone; can arrange custom work.

Stickney's Garden Houses and Follies, One Thompson Square, P.O. Box 34, Boston, MA 02129, (617) 242-1711, Arthur Stickney. Primarily Federal and Georgian wooden garden houses and follies; also covered seats, entranceways, arbours.

At Hatfield, seventeenth-century Italian sculptures are shown to advantage against a background of yew.

Plants

Anyone facing the restoration of a garden will want to know either what repertory of plants was available by a given period, or what was the date of introduction of a given plant. It should be remembered that the date of introduction means precisely that and it would be unwise to assume that the plant in question was generally available in gardens until about ten years after that date. Some standard reference works give dates of introduction. W. J. Bean's *Trees and Shrubs in the British Isles* (John Murray, 8th Edition, four volumes 1970-80 and Supplement, 1988) is very helpful and so, for non-hardy, herbaceous and bulbous plants, is the *RHS Dictionary of Gardening* (Oxford University Press, four volumes, 1956 and Supplement, 1969).

There are many aids to discovering which plants were available to gardeners at fairly precisely any time from the later Tudor period onwards. For the earlier period, John Harvey's *Mediaeval Gardens* (1981, Batsford) prints an ingenious list compiled by the author showing plants in use in gardens at various periods between 380 and 1538. The range of plants in this period was extremely limited – there is a total of 250 species listed of which about 150 are British natives. William Turner's *New Herball* (1551-68) and Gerard's *Herball* (1597) give much valuable detail about plants grown in the second half of the 16th century.

It is not until the later 16th century that there is any very significant increase in plant introductions. John Tradescant the elder (*c.*1570-1638) and his son, John the younger (1608-62) were responsible for introducing many new plants to England. The best source for their activities is *The John Tradescants* by Prudence Leith-Ross (1984, Peter Owen). The Tradescants travelled very widely in Europe, North Africa and America bringing back plants, bulbs and seeds. This book includes a transcription of the Tradescant plant list of 1634 and the list of the *Musaeum Tradescantium* (1656) both annotated with modern botanical names. John Parkinson's very attractively written *Paradisi in Sole Paradisus Terrestris* (1629) describes with great learning 1,000 plants in cultivation at that time.

John Harvey's *Early Gardening Catalogues* (1972, Phillimore) and *Early Nurserymen* (1974, Phillimore) contain a wealth of first-hand documentation of plants available commercially at different periods. The same author's *The Availability of Hardy Plants of the Late Eighteenth Century* (1988, Garden History Society) is very valuable. It collates the names of plants taken from the lists of various 18th-century nurseries, gives their 18th-century common name and modern scientific name and indicates their commercial availability today. As it also gives the date of introduction for each plant it is also useful for earlier periods. For the earlier period of the 18th century Philip Miller's *The Gardener's Dictionary* (1731) is a very valuable source. Miller was curator of the Physic garden in Chelsea and his *Dictionary* gives a great deal of practical information, including the history of many garden plants. Bernard McMahon's *The American Gardener's Calender* (1806) prints as an appendix a vast list of plants but it should not necessarily be assumed that all were in cultivation in America at that time; many could well have been remembered from his native Ireland.

By 1839 J. C. Loudon listed 18,000 species of plants cultivated in Britain. Loudon was a very great figure in the history of gardening literature, an encyclopaedist of genius. His *Encyclopaedia of Gardening* (1822) holds an immense amount of information about all aspects of gardening. Large numbers of plants are described, both ornamental and those for the kitchen (including, for example, a list of 65 different varieties of peaches 'commonly propagated in British nurseries') with much information about them. His magisterial eight-volume *Arboretum et fruticetum Britannicum* (1838) deals with trees and shrubs (hardy and half-hardy) in fascinating and valuable detail and gives an authoritative account of the plants available at that time. Andrew Jackson Downing's *Fruits and Fruit Trees of North America* (1845) and Fearing Burr Jnr's *The Field and Garden Vegetables of America* (1863) are both essential for the early American kitchen garden and orchard.

UK Sources for Historic Plants

For the current commercial availability of specific garden plants *The Plant Finder* by Chris Philip (regularly updated and published by Headmain Ltd for the Hardy Plant Society) is unique and indispensable. It lists 40,000 garden plants (hardy and not hardy) available in nurseries in Great Britain. It provides, incidentally, probably the best guide available to the latest position on the nomenclature of garden plants.

US Sources for Historic Plants

FLOWERS AND BULBS

Brand Peony Farm, P.O. Box 842, St. Cloud, MN 56302 (peonies), Gerald Lund, (612) 252-5234.

Canyon Creek Nursery, 3527 Dry Creek Road, Oroville, CA 95965 (perennials), John and Susan Whittlesey, (916) 533-2166.

The Fragrant Path, P.O. Box 328, Fort Calhoun, NE 68023 (flower seeds), E.R. Rasmussen.

J.L. Hudson, Seedsman, P.O. Box 1058, Redwood City, CA 94064 (seeds), J. L. Hudson.

Logee's Greenhouses, 141 North Street, Danielson, CT 06239 (indoor plants), Joy Logee Martin, (203) 774-8038.

Montrose Nursery, P.O. Box 957, Hillsborough, NC 27278 (cyclamen, perennials), Nancy Goodwin, (919) 732-7787.

Select Seeds, 180 Stickney Hill Road, Union, CT 06076 (flower seeds), Marilyn Barlow.

Anthony J. Skittone, 1415 Eucalyptus, San Francisco, CA 94123 (unusual bulbs), Anthony Skittone, (415) 753-3332.

TyTy Plantation Bulb Co., P.O. Box 159, TyTy, GA 31795 (bulbs), Patrick Malcolm, (912) 382-0404.

We-Du Nurseries, Route 5, Box 724, Marion, NC 28752 (perennials, esp. Chinese, Korean, Japanese & American wildflowers), Richard Weaver and Rene Duval, (704) 738-8300.

Woodlanders, Inc., 1128 Colleton Ave., Aiken, SC 29801 (perennials, vines, trees, shrubs), R. Mackintosh, R. McCartney & G. Mitchell, (803) 648-7522.

FRUITS AND NUTS

Bear Creek Nursery, P.O. Box 411, Bear Creek Road, Northport, WA 99157-0411, Donna and Hunter Carleton, (509) 732-6219.

Burford Brothers, Monroe, VA 24574 (apples), Tom and Russell Burford, (804) 929-4950.

Edible Landscaping, P.O. Box 77, Afton, VA 22920 (unusual fruits), Michael McConkey, (804) 361-9134.

Makielski Berry Farm & Nursery, 7130 Platt Road, Ypsilanti, MI 48197 (bush fruits), Edward and Diane Makielski, (313) 434-3673 or 572-0060.

Sonoma Antique Apple Nursery, 4395 Westside Road, Healdsburg, CA 95448 (apples, pears) Carolyn and Terry Harrison, (707) 433-6420.

Southmeadow Fruit Gardens, 15310 Red Arrow Highway, Lakeside, MI 49116 (fruit trees), Theo Grootendorst, (616) 469-2865.

OLD ROSES

Antique Rose Emporium, Route 5, Box 143, Brenham, TX 77833 (409) 836-9051.

Heritage Rose Gardens, 16831 Mitchell Creek Dr., Ft. Bragg, CA 95437, Virginia Hopper & Joyce Demits, (707) 984-6959 or 964-3748.

High Country Rosarium, 1717 Downing St., Denver, CO 80218, William Campbell, John Ray, (303) 832-4026.

Lowe's own-root Roses, 6 Sheffield Road, Nashua, NH 03062, Malcolm (Mike) Lowe, (603) 888-2214.

Pickering Nurseries, Inc., 670 Kingston Rd., Pickering, Ontario, Canada, L1V 1A6, Joseph G. Schraven, (416) 839-2111.

VEGETABLES AND HERBS

Good Seed Co., Star Route, Box 73A, Oroville, WA 98844, Harris Dunkelberger.

Heirloom Seeds, P.O. Box 245, West Elizabeth, PA 15088-0245 (vegetable seeds), Tom Hauch.

Johnny's Selected Seeds, 310 Foss Hill Road, Albion, ME 04910, Robert L. Johnston, Jr., (207) 437-9294, 437-4301.

D. Landreth Seed Company, P.O. Box 6426, 180 W. Ostend St., Baltimore, MD 21230 (301) 727-3922 or 727-3923.

Sandy Mush Herb Nursery, Route 2, Surrett Cove Road, Leicester, NC 28748 (herbs & flowers) Fairman & Kate Jayne, (704) 683-2014.

Seeds Blum, Idaho City Stage, Boise, ID 83706 (seeds), Jan Blum, (208) 342-0858.

Southern Exposure Seed Exchange, P.O. Box 158, North Garden, VA 22959 (heirloom vegetables), Jeff McCormack.

UK Organizations

Arcturus (12 Lyndhurst Road, Exeter, Devon EX2 4PA (Telephone 0392 412593) provides, for a fee, historical research and advice on interiors and gardens.

The Garden History Society (Membership Secretary: Mrs Anne Richards, 5 The Knoll, Hereford HR1 1RU) organizes visits to historic gardens and sites; conferences on garden history; and publishes an excellent Journal which is an invaluable source of scholarly information on garden history. The Society will advise on the restoration of period gardens.

Hortus (The Neuadd, Rhayader, Powys LD6 5HH, Wales) is a beautifully produced quarterly periodical which has articles on all sorts of gardening subjects including the history of gardens and garden plants.

Journal of Garden History (Taylor & Francis Ltd, 4 John Street, London WC1N 2ET) is a quarterly journal of garden history which frequently publishes original research of high quality.

The National Council for the Conservation of Plants and Gardens (NCCPG) will, through its local groups, give advice on historic gardens. Its headquarters are c/o R.H.S. Garden, Wisley, nr Woking, Surrey GU23 6QB (Telephone 0483 224234). There are regional groups throughout the country and a list of these may be obtained from the NCCPG headquarters.

The Royal Horticultural Society (80 Vincent Square, London SW1P 2PEO) issues a monthly journal, *The Garden*, which publishes much interesting material about the history of plants and gardens. The RHS also has an outstanding horticultural library (the Lindley Library at Vincent Square) with extremely helpful and knowledgeable staff. The library is open to the public as well as to members of the RHS.

US Organizations and other Contacts

Anderson Horticultural Library, 3675 Arboretum Drive, Chanhassen, MN 55317.

Abundant Life Seed Foundation, P.O. Box 772, 1029 Lawrence Street, Port Townsend, WA 98368.

Association for Living Historical Farms and Agricultural Museums, P.O. Box 52, Rushville, NY 14544.

Bailey Hortorium, Cornell University, Ithaca, NY 14850.

Foundation Plant Materials Service (grapes), University of California at Davis, Davis, CA 95616.

The Garden Conservancy, Box 219, Main Street, Cold Spring, NY 10516.

Hardy Plant Society, Mid-Atlantic Chapter, c/o Mrs Jean Schumacher, 49 Green Valley Road, Wallingford, PA 19086.

The Thomas Jefferson Center for Historic Plants, PO Box 316, Charlottesville, Virginia 22902.

Longwood Library, Longwood Gardens, Kennett Square, PA 19348.

Massachusetts Horticultural Library, 300 Massachusetts Avenue, Boston, MA 02115.

National Agricultural Center, Special Collections, 10301 Baltimore Boulevard, Beltsville, MD 20705.

National Clonal Germplasm Repository (berries, small fruits), 33447 Peoria Road, Corvallis, OR 97333.

National Colonial Farm, 3400 Bryan Point Road, Accokeek, MD 20607.

National Seed Storage Laboratory, United States Department of Agriculture, Colorado State University, Fort Collins, CO 80523.

National Trust for Historic Preservation, 1785 Massachusetts Avenue, N.W., Washington, DC 20036.

New York State Fruit Testing Cooperative Association, Inc., P.O. Box 462, Geneva, NY 14456.

North American Fruit Explorers, Route 1, Box 94, Chapin, IL 62628.

Pennsylvania Horticultural Library, 325 Walnut Street, Philadelphia, PA 19106.

Seed Savers Exchange, Rural Route 3, Box 239, Decorah, IA 52101.

Smithsonian Institution, Historic Research Division, Washington, DC 20560.

Society for the Preservation of New England Antiquities, 141 Cambridge Street, Boston, MA 02114.

Southern Garden History Association, Mrs Zachery T. Bynum, Old Salem, Inc., Drawer F, Salem Station, Winston-Salem, NC 27101.

Worcester County Horticultural Society (antique apple collection), 30 Tower Hill Road, Boylston, MA 01505.

The following is a list of selected British and American period gardens, open to the public, with characteristic examples of original, restored, or re-created features.

UK Gardens

THE MIDDLE AGES
Christ Church Cathedral, Oxford, Oxfordshire A re-created late medieval garden within the cloisters of the cathedral. Authentic planting and features taken from medieval sources.

Queen Eleanor's Garden, Winchester Castle, Winchester, Hampshire. A re-created 13th-century garden in an authentic medieval setting with correct period planting and features.

The Weald and Downland Open Air Museum, Singleton, nr Chichester, West Sussex. The Open Air museum has a collection of vernacular English buildings among which is the Bayleaf House, which has an imaginatively re-created 15th-century yeoman's garden, with vegetables and herbs, surrounded by a wattle fence.

THE TUDOR AGE
Hampton Court Palace, Hampton, East Molesey, Surrey. Parts of the Palace and its great garden both date from the early Tudor period. The Pond Garden has some of the original Tudor layout with inauthentic modern planting and the Knot Garden was replanted in 1934 to a late Tudor design.

Montacute House, Montacute, nr Yeovil, Somerset. A pair of beautiful late Elizabethan gazebos overlooks the garden in the East Court.

New Place, Stratford-on-Avon, Warwickshire. A re-created (1919-21)

Elizabethan knot garden with an arbour of carpenter's work, in the setting of an Elizabethan town house.

Tudor House Museum, Bugle Street, Southampton, Hampshire. A re-creation of a late Elizabethan garden with authentic planting and features giving a vivid idea of a garden of the period.

17TH CENTURY
Ham House, Petersham, Surrey. See pages 49-59.

Hatfield House, Hatfield, Hertfordshire. See pages 33-47.

Levens Hall, nr Kendal, Cumbria. A remarkable topiary garden of the 1690s laid out by the mysterious Monsieur Beaumont.

Little Moreton Hall, Congleton, Cheshire. A knot garden of box, yew and gravel, re-created by the National Trust in the shadow of the half-timbered old hall, is based on a design of 1670.

Moseley Old Hall, Fordhouses, nr Wolverhampton, Staffordshire. A re-creation of a 1640 knot garden of gravel, clipped box and an arbour of carpenter's work.

Pitmedden, Udny, Grampian, Scotland. See pages 61-71.

Powis Castle, Welshpool, Powys, Wales. A late 17th-century terraced garden with surviving yew hedges and distinguished 20th-century planting.

Westbury Court, Westbury, Gloucestershire. See pages 73-83.

18TH CENTURY
Claremont Landscape Garden, nr Esher, Surrey. See pages 101-111.

Crathes Castle, nr Banchory, Grampian, Scotland. A formal garden with yew hedges dating from 1702 and magnificent 20th-century borders.

Erddig, nr Wrexham, Clwyd, Wales. See pages 85-99.

Melbourne Hall, nr Derby, Derbyshire. Laid out from 1701 by George London and Henry Wise this is one of the few surviving gardens in England to show the influence of Andrêtre.

Painswick Rococo Garden, Painswick, nr Stroud, Gloucestershire. See pages 113-23.

Petworth House, Petworth, West Sussex. One of the best surviving landscape gardens designed by 'Capability' Brown and made in the 1750s.

Rousham, nr Steeple Aston, Oxfordshire. The most complete and beautiful surviving work by William Kent, a landscape garden in which statues and garden buildings direct the view over the river Cherwell and the countryside beyond.

Stourhead, Stourton, Wiltshire. An immensely influential landscape garden started by Henry Hoare in the 1740s comprising many outstanding garden buildings.

Studley Royal, nr Ripon, North Yorkshire. A very early landscape garden with formal features started in 1718 by John Aislabie and now undergoing careful restoration by the National Trust.

Wrest Park, Silsoe, nr Luton, Bedfordshire. Started in 1706 this formal garden has a great canal and woods crossed by *allées* in the French style. Undergoing restoration by English Heritage.

19TH CENTURY
Biddulph Grange, nr Stoke on Trent, Staffordshire. In the process of restoration by the National

Trust this garden was started in the 1840s and shows the exotic influences to which the Victorians looked – Chinese, Egyptian and so on – with characteristic Victorian plantings of recently introduced conifers.

Broughton Hall, Skipton, North Yorkshire. One of the few surviving gardens designed by W.A.Nesfield with a scrolled parterre designed in the 1850s.

Gravetye Manor, nr East Grinstead, East Sussex. See pages 143-55.

Oxburgh Hall, Swaffham, nr King's Lynn, Norfolk. A parterre made in 1845 copied from an early 18th-century design shows the typical historicism of Victorian gardening.

Sezincote, nr Moreton-in-Marsh, Gloucestershire. An exotic Indian-influenced garden made in the early years of the 19th century with some planting by Humphry Repton.

Tatton Park, Knutsford, Cheshire. In the 1840s Joseph Paxton added formal features – Italianate terraces, balustrades and a pair of parterres now beautifully restored by the National Trust. There is also a superb indoor fernery of 1859 and a very large Japanese garden of 1910.

20TH CENTURY

Buscot Park, nr Faringdon, Oxfordshire. Among many other ingredients Buscot Park has a superb stepped canal designed by Harold Peto after 1906.

East Lambrook Manor, South Petherton, Somerset. The apotheosis of the cottage garden made by Margery Fish from 1938 onwards, an informal plantsman's garden with Robinsonian undertones recently restored.

Hestercombe House, Cheddon Fitzpaine, nr Taunton, Somerset. See pages 157-71.

Hidcote Manor Garden, Hidcote Bartrim, nr Chipping Camden, Gloucestershire. Very influential garden made from 1907 onwards by Lawrence Johnston in which enclosed spaces are carefully articulated by paths, views and changing levels. Within these enclosures a very wide range of carefully chosen plants are grown.

Hill of Tarvit House, nr Cupar, Fife, Scotland. Formal garden in the spirit of the Arts and Crafts movement designed after 1906 by Sir Robert Lorimer.

Mellerstain House, nr Kelso, Borders, Scotland. Formal terraced garden designed in 1909 by Sir Reginald Blomfield in the architectural style of that period.

Mount Stewart, Newtownards, County Down, Northern Ireland. See pages 189-99.

Newby Hall, nr Ripon, North Yorkshire. See pages 173-87.

*T*he climbing rose 'Adelaide D' Orleans'
makes a scented canopy over a bench in
the walled garden at Westbury Court.

US Gardens section
US Gardens

17TH CENTURY

Magnolia Plantation and Gardens, Route 4, Highway 61, Charleston, SC 29407, (803) 571-1266. Blooms throughout the year; founded in 1680 and includes a small formal garden that remains from then; also fifty acres of informal gardens reflecting 19th-century style.

18TH CENTURY

John Bartram House and Garden, 54th Street and Lindbergh Boulevard, Philadelphia, PA 19143, (215) 729-5281. John Bartram's colonial estate, established mid 1700s, America's first botanic garden.

Middleton Place, Ashley River Road, Charleston, SC 29407, (803) 556-6020. The oldest landscaped garden in America, including terraces and butterfly lakes, begun by Henry Middleton in 1741, influenced by formal European styles.

Mount Vernon, Mount Vernon Ladies' Association, Mount Vernon, VA 22121, (703) 780-2000. Estate presented as it might have appeared in 1799, year of Washington's death; includes flower gardens, kitchen garden and orchards.

William Paca House and Garden, 1 Martin Street, Annapolis, MD 21401, (301) 267-6656. Complete restoration of house and garden built between 1765 and 1772, including formal parterres descending to the wilderness garden; outstanding example of Middle-Colony gardening.

John Whipple House, 53 South Main Street, Ipswich, MA 01938, (508) 356-2811. Re-created Colonial Revival interpretation of a 17th-century raised-bed herb garden, designed by Arthur

Shurcliff, all plants researched, documented, and planted by Ann Leighton (Isadore Smith); also an antique rose garden.

19TH CENTURY

Biltmore House and Gardens, c/o The Biltmore Co. Marketing Dept., 1 Biltmore Plaza, Asheville, NC 28802, (704) 274-1776. Former estate of George Vanderbilt, designed by Frederick Law Olmsted from 1889-96, formal gardens based on those of Vaux-le-Vicomte, entrance drive exemplifies Gardenesque.

Blithewold Gardens and Arboretum, Ferry Road, Bristol, RI 02809, (401) 253-2707. Designed in 1895, gardens typical of turn-of-the century summer residence, includes mature tree specimens and largest Sequoia in eastern North America.

Green Animals, c/o The Preservation Society of Newport County, 118 Mill Street, Newport, RI 02840, (401) 847-1000. Begun in 1880, Victorian with elements of Colonial Revival; fine examples of topiary; annuals, perennials, fruits and vegetables, and a herb garden.

Moffatt-Ladd House and Garden, 154 Market Street, Portsmouth, NH 03801, (603) 436-8221. House built in 1763, two plantings survive from the 18th century, present garden design from 1862.

Monticello, P.O. Box 316, Charlottesville, VA 22902, (804) 295-8181, (804) 295-2657. See pages 125-41.

Morris Arboretum of the University of Pennsylvania, 9414 Meadowbrook Avenue, Chestnut Hill, Philadelphia, PA 19118, (215) 247-5777. Begun in the late 1800s as the private estate of John and Lydia Morris; ninety acres open to the public, arranged into speciality gardens typical of the Victorian Age.

George Read House and Garden, 42 The Strand, New Castle, Delaware 19720, (302) 322-8411. Designed 1847-48 by Robert Buist in the style of Downing; retains much of its original shape, including formal parterre, park-like setting, orchard and vegetables.

Rockwood Museum and Garden, 610 Shipley Road, Wilmington, DE 19809, (302) 571-7776. House and grounds designed from 1851-57; house is Rural Gothic, grounds are excellent example of Gardenesque; no restoration, but many original elements still remain.

Rosedown Plantation and Gardens, P.O. Box 1816, St. Francisville, LA 70775, (504) 635-3332. The mansion and thirty-acre gardens date from 1835; many plantings from that period still survive, including formal gardens, roses, and oak trees nearing 200 years old.

20TH CENTURY

Blake Garden, 70 Rincon Road, Kensington, CA 94707, (415) 524-2449. Ten-acre garden designed in the early 1920s; includes Italianate formal garden and a number of rare plant varieties.

*Y*ellow heads of Achilleas in the East Garden of Hatfield House, with clipped holm oaks in the background.

Dumbarton Oaks, 1703 32nd Street NW, Washington, DC 20007, (202) 342-3200. Designed by Beatrix Farrand in 1922, ten-acre garden, incorporates elements of traditional French, English, and Italian gardens.

Filoli Center, Canada Road, Woodside, CA 94062, (415) 364-2880. Garden designed 1916-17 by Bruce Porter with Isabella Worn; sixteen-acre formal garden; combines formal design with natural surroundings.

Huntington Botanical Gardens, 1151 Oxford Road, San Marino, CA 91108, (818) 405-2100. Gardens begun in 1905 include over 15,000 different kinds of plants, many with historic value, and the Desert Garden, which has over 5,000 species.

Longue Vue House and Gardens, 7 Bamboo Road, New Orleans, LA 70124, (504) 488-5488. Built between 1939 and 1942, stylistically diverse gardens influenced by English and Spanish styles.

Naumkeag, The Choate Estate, Stockbridge, MA 01262, (413) 298-3239. House from 1886; gardens, designed in part by Fletcher Steele, from 1926 to 1958; gardens reflect several distinct 20th-century styles focusing more on landscape than on flowers.

Sonnenberg Gardens, 151 Charlotte St., Canandaigua, NY 14424, (716) 394-4922. Fifty-acre estate in the process of restoration to its original turn-of-the-century style; includes nine formal gardens.

Vizcaya Museum and Gardens, 3251 South Miami Avenue, Miami, FL 33129, (305) 579-2708. Gardens designed in 1916 and completed in 1921; Italian Renaissance style; formal garden with small speciality gardens including a secret garden and a theatre garden.

The following is a list of modern books which may be useful to anyone restoring a garden. It includes those current books described in more detail in the *Plants* section of this appendix.

General Reference

W. J. Bean *Trees and Shrubs Hardy in the British Isles* (John Murray, 8th edition, four volumes, 1970-80, Supplement 1988). The most valuable single reference book on woody plants. Contains much valuable information about the date of introduction of plants and background information about them.

Ray Desmond *Bibliography of British Gardens* (St Paul's Bibliographies, 1984). Contains references to writings on many hundreds of historic British gardens.

The Royal Horticultural Society Dictionary of Gardening (Oxford University Press, four volumes, 1956, Supplement 1969)

Graham Stuart Thomas *Perennial Garden Plants* (J. M. Dent, 1976. Published in the US by Sagapress). The best available reference book for herbaceous plants, with dates of introduction and much valuable background information.

History

Jane Brown *Gardens of a Golden Afternoon* (Allen Lane, 1982). A lively, profusely illustrated survey of the partnership of Edwin Lutyens and Gertrude Jekyll.

Brent Elliott *Victorian Gardens* (Batsford, 1986. Published in the US by Timber Press). A richly informative account of gardens and gardening in the period with many references to contemporary literature.

Miles Hadfield *A History of British Gardening* (Penguin, 1985). Attractively written, agreeably opinionated and deeply informative.

John Harris *The Artist and the Country House* (Sotherby Parke Bernet, 1979. Published in the US by Philip Wilson). An important collection of contemporary paintings with authentic detail of period gardens and very informative text.

John Harvey *Mediaeval Gardens* (Batsford, 1981. Published in the US by Timber Press). The most scholarly account of British and European gardens with valuable lists of medieval plants.

John Harvey *Restoring Period Gardens* (Shire, 1988). A wide-ranging survey of period gardens from the Middle Ages to Georgian times.

David Jacques *Georgian Gardens* (Batsford, 1983. Published in the US by Timber Press). Describes the landscape gardening revolution in England.

David Jacques and Arend Jan van der Horst *The Gardens of William and Mary* (Christopher Helm, 1988). Describes gardens and gardening in the Netherlands and in England with unusual illustrations and valuable information about planting.

Roy Strong *The Renaissance Garden in England* (Thames & Hudson, 1979). An original and scholarly history.

A. A. Tait *The Landscape Garden in Scotland 1735-1835* (Edinburgh University Press, 1980. Published in the US by Columbia University Press). A pioneer study with many unusual illustrations.

May Woods and Arete Warren *Glass Houses* (Aurum Press, 1988. Published in the US by Rizzoli). A deeply researched and finely illustrated account of conservatories and winter gardens, full of historic detail.

Plants

Christopher Brickell and Fay Sharman *The Vanishing Garden* (John Murray, 1986). A fascinating survey of threatened garden plants.

Ruth Duthie *Florists' Flowers and Societies* (Shire, 1988). Much information on the development of flowering plants.

John Harvey *Early Gardening Catalogues* (Phillimore, 1972). Covers the period from the 16th-19th century with detailed lists of plants grown.

John Harvey *Early Nurserymen* (Phillimore, 1974). Similar to the above but going back to the Middle Ages.

John Harvey *The Availability of Hardy Plants of the Late Eighteenth Century* (Garden History Society, 1988. Published in the US by Penguin). Garden plants of this time and their current availability.

David Stuart and James Sutherland *Plants from the Past* (Viking, 1987). A knowledgeable survey of old, chiefly herbaceous, forms of garden plants.

Practical

Geraldine Lacey *Creating Topiary* (Garden Art Press, 1988). Much practical detail on the making and maintenance of topiary.

Penelope Hobhouse *The Country Gardener* (Francis Lincoln, 1989. Published in the US by Little, Brown). An inspirational book that also contains much invaluable information on the practical problems of restoring the eight-acre garden at Hadspen in Somerset.

George Plumptre *Garden Ornament* (Thames & Hudson, 1989. Published in the US by Doubleday). A profusely illustrated guide to period garden ornament and furniture from the Renaissance onwards.

Index